AMERICAN OUTLAW

AMERICAN OUTLAW

JESSE JAMES

with Sam Benjamin

GALLERY BOOKS

New York · London · Toronto · Sydney

To Chandler, Jesse, Sunny, and my beloved Katherine

PROLOGUE

"Oh shit! It's *him*! Get ready, get ready!"

I walk out into the bright California daylight, a baseball cap pulled low over my eyes.

"Jesse! Yo! Jesse—look over here, man!"

"*Jesse James!* Hey, how's it going, asshole? Got time for a picture?"

Like most pack animals, paparazzi aren't nearly as charming when they've turned against you. In fact, Beverly Hills gossip photographers, seen up close, are snappingly vicious.

"Jess, you like *sluts,* right? Yo! Jesse!"

I clench my jaw and glance over at my sixteen-year-old daughter, Chandler, to check her reaction. She stares straight ahead numbly as we hurry toward our truck. It infuriates me that my children—Chandler, Jesse Jr., and my six-year-old, Sunny—have to deal with insults that should be for me alone.

But paparazzi never play by the rules. These guys make up their own moral code. And for the last week, they haven't hesitated to make my life hell.

"Come on," I order my kids, "let's hop to it. Let's go." Chandler quickly raises her science textbook to cover her face, so they can't get a shot of her. Smart.

"Jesse! Did you talk to Sandra?" cries a skinny, ragged-looking guy at the head of the pack. "Hey, did you talk to Sandra? Did you talk to Sandra?"

For paparazzi, peak performance hinges on volume and repetition. The loudest-crowing cock rules the roost. They hurl spiteful insults at the top of their lungs, their cracked lips hemmed in by patchy beards and wet mustaches.

"Jesse! Jesse! Are you a Nazi?"

Camera shutters click on full auto. I keep my head down: only a few more yards to the truck.

As we approach my vehicle, I open the doors remotely with a click of my key. Chandler helps Sunny into the backseat. Jesse Jr. hops up front like a champ.

Incredibly, the photographers continue to shoot. By now, each of them have likely taken several hundred pictures of me and my children just on the way to our truck, all interchangeable and nearly identical.

"You know what?" I say. "You guys got all the shots you need today. I'm trying to take my kids to school now, so just leave for a while. Let us have some space."

"Yeah, you heard the guy!" one guy says, laughing. "Back off! He needs his *space*!" Derisive laughter follows from the pack of sweaty, middle-aged men.

"Hey, *we* didn't screw up, Jesse," one of the men admonishes me. "*You* did, okay?"

Wow, I think. *Physical violence would feel* amazing *right now.* To just dole out a single blow to someone's greasy temple—or, even milder, to snatch a camera out of the nearest feeble grip and smash it on the curb, splintering it into black plastic glitter.

But I reproach myself. They *want* you to punch them. That's their wettest dream. A paparazzo punched in the solar plexus is a bottom-feeder who never has to work another day. No more endless late nights, coffee breath, melted candy bars on the passenger seat, weaving suicidally through Saturday-night Rodeo Drive traffic because the word is, *Chris Brown* just left Mr. Chow's . . .

I just grit my teeth, turn the key in the ignition, and pull away from the curb. I glance back at my three kids. Chandler and Jesse Jr. look pretty bummed out, but Sunny, mercifully, seems okay. For a second, nobody says anything.

"Want to listen to some music?" I ask, finally.

"Dad," says Chandler. "Will those guys be at school when we get there?"

I look in my rearview mirror. "Well, they're following us. So, yeah, I expect they will."

"Can't you lose them?" asks Jesse Jr.

"Not with you guys in the car."

"How long do you think they're going to keep following us to school?"

I glance at him through the rearview. "Don't know."

As I drive to the high school to drop off Chandler and Jesse, no fewer than thirty cars follow behind me closely. We arrive at the school, and I pull up to the side of the parking lot, as close to the doors as possible.

"Go ahead, hurry. Before too many of them can get out of their cars."

They gather their things hurriedly, Chandler clutching her books to her chest, and Jesse Jr. tossing his backpack over his shoulder.

"Hey," I warn. "If anybody at school gives you any crap, just don't listen to them. It's none of their business what goes on in our family."

"Dad, come on. We're not listening to anyone."

"All right," I say. "I love you guys. Go on. Hurry up. Get out of here."

They flee into the school without looking back. I turn to the backseat, to my daughter Sunny.

"You ready to go to school, Sun?"

She nods. "Daddy?"

"Yup?"

"Where's Sandy?"

I chew my lip as I consider my answer. *Well, sweetie, the truth is, I have no idea. Daddy fucked up, real, real bad, so your stepmommy decided to disappear for a few weeks.*

"She went away," I say finally, pulling out in traffic. Instinctively, the jackals fall into pursuit formation behind me. We set out down the street toward Cubberly Elementary.

"Is she ever coming back?"

"Are you wearing your seat belt? Put on your seat belt, sweetie."

"It's *on,*" says Sunny, impatiently.

"Just making sure."

We weave our way through the narrow streets of Long Beach, down Fourth, across Broadway, down to East Livingston. Everywhere I go, the swarm mirrors my movements. Cars swerve next to me, in front of me, buzzing me from all sides as their shutters click and their lenses refocus, retracting and extending, struggling to get a clear picture through my tinted windshield. Shooting digital is the cheapest part of the whole operation, so they roll endlessly, with infinite patience, waiting for something interesting to happen. Together, we crawl forward as a mass.

For a strange moment, I almost feel empowered by these idiots and the devotion they show for me. They're zealots. They would follow me to the ends of the earth. I could take us on the most boring of errands, and they would follow in rapture. Just as easily, I could lead them into the belly of the beast, South Central gang territory or a cartel-run border town in northern Mexico. Tempting as that is, my daughter is with me, so I remain calm.

We make our way into the parking lot of Sunny's school. I stop the truck and hop out of the cab, walking to the back door and opening it swiftly.

"Okay," I say, unstrapping her from the backseat. "We're here. Ready to be a good girl for Dad?"

"Yep. I'll be good," Sunny agrees.

"So what we're gonna do," I say, "we're gonna walk real, real fast, and I'm gonna kind of be a *shield* to you, okay? I'm gonna be super big, and you're going to be super small."

Sunny kind of looks at me askew.

"Just walk real fast, Bub."

We speed walk down the short patch of pavement that connects the parking lot to the kindergarten building. She takes small, bouncy steps, and I lumber after her, my coat stretched wide, trying to create a sort of no-camera zone around my small, towheaded daughter. We make it to the front doors in record time.

"Nice work," I say, dropping to her level for a good-bye kiss on Sunny's forehead. "Go on, get inside. I love you."

"I love you, Dad," Sunny says, as she glances over her shoulder and slips inside, giving me a quick wave.

I walk back to my car, furiously angry, my jaw clenching. My kids have become part of the hunt, and there's no one to blame but myself. This realization fills me with an intense rage that I need to vent. Clearly, the best target for my fury, at this moment, are the pale, flimsy cuttlefish with cameras fluttering before me.

I nod to them, hatefully.

Now it's on, motherfuckers.

Hopping into the cab of my truck, I take a moment to focus myself and crack my knuckles before driving in a slow and controlled way out of the elementary school parking lot. I lure them away from the school zone, across the winding, flat, black pavement of the industrial wasteland that is Long Beach, the proud biker armpit of Southern California. I have lived in Long Beach my whole life. It is my home, my haven. My den of pride. And they have followed me here, dead set on staking me out. They must pay somehow . . .

But no matter how much I'd like to, I can't just drag one of the sleazebags from his car, clutching his oily neck with my bare hands, shaking him until his consciousness dims. No, that would look pretty terrible.

"Okay then," I mutter, "let's go for a ride."

I know this city like the back of my hand. I know its ins and outs, its secret crannies—the pockets where the paved roads end and lead to stretches of dirty gravel and dust.

I drive just fast enough for them to think I'm trying to outrun them, but I'm not. I want them close. I dive under an overpass, finding an open spot where the pavement dips and then dies. I check the rearview: the shoal is going to follow.

We are off the map now, on the hardpack California dirt. I breathe in, relishing the small but undeniable freedom that washes over me. The large, thick wheels of my truck ramble over gravel and dry, broken road, onto the hard flatness of the Long Beach dust bowl. The flotilla of Kias, Sentras, and Subaru wagons gives chase.

Slowly, I begin to increase my speed. I watch as the speedometer climbs from forty to fifty. With barely a tremble, my heavy vehicle cruises to sixty, then seventy, then eighty miles per hour . . .

Behind me, the dust is rising in a plume of massive gray clouds. I know that visibility is gradually becoming more and more obscured for the photographers. A whiteout, a driver's ultimate nightmare, will be their reality in less than a minute. And what will they do then? Will they change course, or attempt to follow still?

A jagged rock flies up from underneath my back wheel. Spinning, it flies directly into the front windshield of the paparazzo following closest behind me. The windshield of his car shatters. I watch as he brakes hard, pitching jaggedly.

Satisfaction washes over me, intense and immediate. *One gone,* I think, smiling, *twenty-nine to go.*

I begin to drive more and more dangerously, careening from side to side without reason or warning, and more and more dust flies up in the air behind me, churned up by my massive wheels. A chorus of tinny horns heralds general panic and mayhem among the paparazzi. Their plaintive war cry doesn't inspire any fear in me, though: I increase my speed to ninety, then a hundred miles an hour.

Behind me, I hear the dull smash of metal on metal, followed by a furious volley of frightened horn blasts. Some men have damaged their flimsy cars beyond repair. Perhaps they will leave them to bake in the pitiless desert. Or maybe the collision is only incidental, a mere fender bender that won't shake even one of them off my tail, and instead will only inspire them to more relentless pursuit. I don't know.

And suddenly, my satisfaction from winning a temporary, meaningless battle against a couple of bottom-feeding photographers turns sour in my throat. *What's the point?* I think bitterly. *None of this will stop the real story: my front-page failure.*

I crush the gas pedal to the floor, flying through the envelope of rising earth, as if maybe, if I go fast enough, drive recklessly enough, I can disappear through the cloud, into a place where my mistakes never existed, where I had never betrayed myself so infinitely in the first place.

Go.

1

---◆◆◆---

I've had a violent life.

When I was six, my parents split up after a crazy screaming fight in their bedroom that ended with my dad punching something and breaking his hand. When I was seven, I took my first ride on a chopper, courtesy of my mom's drunk boyfriend. I got trashed for the first time when I was ten, on California Coolers. Pretty standard blue-collar upbringing, I suppose.

By the time I was fourteen, I'd grown into a huge, strong, confused, zit-faced punk. My main purpose in life seemed to be stealing shit from the Riverside mall, alongside my best friend, Bobby, a beefy guy with long hair and a mess of scars on his forehead, just like a WWF wrestler.

Bobby was a fearless, relentless, and almost absurdly enthusiastic thief. Not a week went by without him honing his skills.

"Let's take us a little walk, Jesse. What do you say?"

"Aw, man," I groaned. "Really?"

I was tired, and I was hot. It was the summer of 1983, and Riverside, California, was in the midst of yet another sticky, smoggy heat wave.

"You heard me, man! You haven't been stealing SHIT lately. You're getting soft. Worse than that, you're getting *lazy*. Come on. Get up off your ass. We're going to the mall. Let's steal shit."

Bobby led the way, strutting through the heat of the Riverside afternoon, wearing a three-quarter-length-sleeve Ozzy Osbourne *Howl at the Moon* baseball shirt. I followed him dutifully, dragging my large feet, squinting in the bright sunlight as I eyed the industrial crap that dotted our landscape: the brake shops, the strip-mall vet clinics, a batting range. Finally we made it down to the Tyler Mall, where we headed toward our favorite target—the RadioShack.

"Watch the master work," I announced, as we stepped through the doors.

"Sure, fucker," Bobby said. "Go ahead."

As I took a slow lap around the store to divert the salesman, I checked out the merch, casually.

"Poor bastard," I whispered to Bobby when I reached him again. "Doesn't suspect a thing."

"Wow," he said, totally unimpressed. "You're a real operator, James. I'm just *so* proud to know you."

"Quiet, buddy. Watch and learn. Watch and—" I cut myself off midsentence. The clerk had turned momentarily to assist a customer, leaving his back to us. I reached out and swiped a Sony Walkman, stuffed it under my shirt and under the waistband of my jeans. I hopped out of the store in a quick beat.

My heart was amped. I racewalked to the other end of the mall. Every so often, I glanced back over my shoulder: no one was following. I was safe.

Twenty minutes had elapsed before I dared to come back to the RadioShack side of the mall. As I approached, I saw Bobby's hulking figure appear on my horizon. In his thick arms, he appeared to be cradling an entire home stereo system.

"You still here, asshole?" He hefted a receiver, amp, and two speakers.

I stared at him, confused. "How did you . . . get that?"

"Nothing to it." He stared right back at me. "Should we head home?"

"Bobby, man," I said, laughing. "How'd you just walk out of RadioShack *with a full system?*"

He shook his head at me sadly, like I was slow. "You dumbass, I just stared the clerk dead in the eyes and walked out with it. I mad-dogged him." Bobby grinned at me, proudly. "I got real big balls on me, James."

Stereos were all fine and well, I guess, but I felt more badass when we were stealing cars. Second- and third-generation Camaros were ideal, because they were easy to chop up and sell. It wasn't that big a deal to steal a new Camaro back then: the 1980s muscle cars still had 1950s technology inside the door.

There was a flat steel rod in the door, and you could take a screwdriver with a rubber mallet and bam, pound it right underneath the lock. You'd hit the rod and pry it open, and it would unlock the door. Then there'd be a cast-aluminum tilt column behind the steering; you could hit that with a hammer and it would crack open like a nut. Then you just put anything in the ignition, and *WHOOM!* Good to go. A real operator could pull it off, from start to finish, in thirty seconds.

We could only drive around in a stolen car for about a day. That's all it was safe to do, and we weren't quite stupid enough to go longer. Then our aim would be to rip out the motor and the wheels, and try to sell them. We'd cut the rest of the car up with an acetylene blowtorch and toss the wrecked parts into a Dumpster.

I split time between my parents' houses growing up. My mom had stayed in Long Beach after the divorce, while my dad had moved to neighboring Riverside, only a short drive away. Neither of them tried too hard to keep a close eye on their unruly, pissed-off son, though, and mostly, I was left to my own devices.

And that meant plenty of time with Bobby. Once, I remember going over to his house, and finding him up on the roof, shooting up his next-door neighbor's yard.

"Hey, Bobby," I said.

"What's up, fuck face?" Bobby said politely. He didn't look up at me: instead, he continued to stare through the range finder of his .22.

I watched him for a moment. "What's all this?" I said.

"What's it look like?" He pulled the trigger on the gun once: *whoop.* "I'm shooting shit."

"You're shooting dirt," I observed.

"Yes," Bobby agreed. He pulled the trigger again: *whoop.*

"Did your neighbor's yard do something to you?" I asked.

Bobby looked up at me curiously for a moment. "Nothing in particular. Why?" He turned back to his gun and squeezed off another few rounds. *Whoop, whoop, whoop.* Clods of dirt and grass flew up from the perfect green turf of his next-door neighbor's lawn.

"Hey, you got a silencer on there, huh?"

"Mm-hmm," Bobby said. "Made it myself out of a plastic two-liter."

Just as Bobby took aim at the next clod of dirt, the neighbor's dog bounded out to investigate the odd, silent disturbance that was causing his yard to erupt magically from within.

Whoop.

Bobby's rifle jerked up as the Labrador fell to the ground, dead.

"Holy shit!" Bobby croaked.

"You fucking asshole!" I shouted. "Goddamn you! You sick fuck!"

"Geez, James, don't get so excited," Bobby said, shaking a little and laughing nervously.

"Man, I should kill *your* dog, and see how you feel about it!"

"Chrissakes," Bobby said. He removed the silencer from his gun. "Calm down. You're acting like it was your girlfriend."

Bobby handed me his rifle. Slowly, he climbed down from the roof. I watched as he walked into his neighbor's yard and examined the dog, turning its head back and forth in his hands a few times, until he determined it was indeed dead. Then he lifted up the dog's body, hefting up the deadweight in his arms. He carried the carcass over to an open trash can and threw it in.

"There," he offered. "Feel better?"

———

One night, we were watching TV in Bobby's dim house, and he was flipping channels. For the second in between each station, the house would go almost completely dark. Bobby's house was always about three lamps short of being able to see.

"Jesse, you know George's?"

"Sure. Up there on Magnolia and Riverside. Best cheeseburgers around."

"Exactly. BUT, did you *also* know that Allan's dating a chick who works there?"

Allan was Bobby's older brother. To no one's surprise, he was just as mental as Bobby. He was a dangerous fuck, actually. He would beat the shit out of Bobby and anyone else for the flimsiest of excuses.

"Didn't know that." I shrugged.

"I go there sometimes when she's working—she lets me go behind the counter and stuff. Eat all the fries I want."

"She cute?"

"She's okay," Bobby said shortly. "What I'm trying to tell you, Jesse, is that there's a *safe* there." He smiled broadly. "And I know the combination."

"How'd you get it?"

"You don't need to know. All I'm saying is . . . well, I think you see what I'm getting at." He smirked. "That money could be *ours*."

We waited a few days, and then, one night, after making sure his brother's girlfriend wasn't working, we pulled up behind the store in a boosted Ford Pinto. Not the best choice, but it was all we had been able to swipe at the last minute. It was just before closing time. Bobby killed the engine.

"Look, Bobby," I said. "I don't know about this."

Bobby looked at me calmly. "You got that little gun with you, right?"

"Yeah, sure, I have the gun, of course," I said, "but, Christ, I mean . . ."

"*Fuck. You.*" Bobby smiled. "Let me see it."

I showed him the gun. It was a Ruger .357, a Security Six. The gun was my dad's—I had lifted it out of his drawer that afternoon.

"Let me hold it."

"I'm taking it in. It's my gun."

"Well, all right," Bobby said, looking pleased. "Finally. You grew some balls, James. Tiny hairless ones, no doubt, but I'm proud of you just the same." He took his backpack from beneath the front seat. "Got a little present for you."

Bobby reached into the flimsy nylon sack, retrieving two worn blue ski masks. He handed one to me. "Put it on."

Bobby and I both pulled on the masks. We checked ourselves out in the rearview for a second, impressed by what we saw. Over the course of just a few moments, we'd transformed from punk kids into badass monsters capable of fucking shit up on a major level. We huddled close together, a pair of teenaged shitheads wearing scratchy blue masks, breathing hard in Riverside, California, in a busted Pinto. The gun felt sweaty in my palm.

"Let's go get some fucking money," I whispered.

We strutted into the store, knocking over dishes and a trash can.

"Nobody fucking do *anything*!" Bobby yelled. "The first person who moves a single inch, my friend is gonna blow a hole in him!"

Only two customers were in the store: an old man reading a crumpled paper and a middle-aged guy with a lonely-looking burger in front of him. Both of them looked up, mild alarm registering.

Bobby walked up to the guy working the counter. "Don't do anything stupid." He motioned toward me and my gun. I nodded, not really sure what to do.

"Nobody fucking . . . move," I ventured, lamely. I waved the gun.

Bobby laughed at me. "Now, I'm gonna go back and clean out the safe," he explained to the clerk. "And if you so much as look at me, I'm gonna make sure you die tonight, understood?" He glanced toward me for emphasis.

Bobby slipped to the back and worked on the safe. "Fuck, I thought I knew this," he muttered.

"You don't remember the combination?" I hissed. I kept the gun trained on the customers and the clerk. They didn't look very inclined to make sudden movements, but still. "You don't *remember* it?"

"He doesn't remember the combination," the old man repeated.

"Shut up," I snapped. "I heard him, okay?"

"I swear, man, I knew it yesterday," said Bobby. He stood up and thought hard. "I probably should have written it down."

"Let's just go, man!"

"No way." He looked at the clerk. "Hey, fuckhead, give me a hint. Is the first number twenty-one? Just tell me that."

The clerk remained motionless for a second. I shook the gun in his face. "Tell him, asshole!"

He nodded nervously.

"It's twenty-one!" I shouted.

"I *knew* it!"

"Let's *go*," I pleaded. *"Goddammit!"*

The safe clicked open. "There we go," he crowed. He reached into the safe. His hands emerged holding an enormous stack of bills. Bobby turned toward me. "Do you understand why we didn't bail out, buddy? God, there must be more than a thousand bucks here . . ."

"Can we fucking GO now?" I cried, the tension in my arms and neck unbearable. "Fucking *please*?"

"Of course, don't have a nervous *breakdown* over it. We're leaving right this very minute. You can put the piece away." He motioned to my gun. I lowered it, trembling.

We stumbled out of the place, Bobby holding the money, rifling through it excitedly. When we stepped through the door, both of us broke out running, and as we exited, Bobby waved through the plate-glass window to our little audience of three.

———

Back in those days, my stepmom was a young chick named Joanna who couldn't have been more than twenty-one or twenty-two years old. I can still see her now: a rosy-cheeked, naïve blonde with a bubble butt and a Little Orphan Annie perm that circled her head like a curly yellow halo.

She wasn't a bad lady, but she wasn't equipped to deal with an irate fucker like me.

"Jesse, it's dinnertime. Come to the table."

"What'd you make this time?"

"Meat loaf!" She beamed. "Where's your dad?"

"He's probably doing shit," I mumbled. "Making money . . . so he can *support you*."

Joanna smiled cheerily at me, like she hadn't heard a word. In fact, she probably hadn't. I don't remember her being the most attentive person I'd ever met. She never heard half the stuff I said to her, probably for the best.

"How was school, Jesse?"

"It's still summer vacation." I stared at her like she was stupid. "Are you serious?"

"Did you learn anything new?"

"Goddamn, I said," my voice rising, "it's *summer,* you friggin' idiot. Are you simple?"

"Hey," my dad said, emerging from the garage. "None of that crap in the house." He looked tired, like he was working on some big issue. My dad was a big guy who refurbished antiques and sold junk for a living. He cut an imposing figure. He was bald on top, but he had a full beard and long hair in back. "What's for chow?"

I pointed at the pan. "This shit."

"Don't say *shit,*" my dad said, frowning. "Your stepmom just worked for a long time to make that for you."

"All I'm saying is, why does this meat loaf have hunks of Wonder Bread in it?" I asked. "I'm just interested."

"That's enough," my dad warned.

"Bread meat loaf, with a side of ketchup," I said. "Great combination there, Joanna."

"Shut your mouth, Jess." My dad glared at me. "Let's eat in peace."

My dad worked long hours. He was always wheeling and dealing—buying up auction lots, fixing up the crap he found, turning it into salable items. He was money hungry and talented at what he did; subsequently, his life was his business. He didn't really have interests outside of it, as far as I could tell.

"I need you to come to the swap meet with me this weekend, Jesse." My dad helped himself to a huge serving of Joanna's meat loaf. "Help me unload the truck. I got a good feeling about this weekend. Gonna make a shit-ton of money if everything goes right."

"Sure," I said. I liked working for my dad. He paid plenty of attention to me, as long as I was laboring for him. "But hey, Dad, if I do it, can you spare a couple of bucks for school clothes? School's gonna start up in a couple of weeks and—"

"Jesse, you know how tight things are right now." He frowned. "I can hardly keep a roof over our heads." He motioned to Joanna.

"Now, look at your stepmom. She doesn't bother me all the time for a bunch of new shit, does she?"

"No," Joanna agreed. "I'm happy with the way things are."

"But I don't have any clothes for *school,* Dad."

"I said no," my dad snapped.

I huffed angrily. "But that's not fair—I mean, I work for you and—"

My dad slammed his fist on the table. The plates jumped. "Shut the fuck up." He turned to look at me with deep, angry eyes. "And quit fucking asking."

"And eat your meat loaf," Joanna added, quietly.

———

By now, you might be wondering why I'm not in prison or dead. The answer is simple: football. If I didn't have football, I would have never made it. I am one hundred percent sure of this fact.

Ever since I started playing, I loved football more than anything else in my life. I was just primed for it: all the hurt and anger I felt growing up pulled me to the game, like a gravitational force. I was always a big kid—other kids' parents used to complain about me when I was eleven or twelve, because I had a goatee. More than once, I had to bring my birth certificate to prove my age.

Once, an opposing coach demanded, "Let me see those gloves!"

"Huh? Why?" I had been hitting kids so hard, they fell back, unable to breathe.

"Because I got a pretty good feeling they're filled with *sand.*"

He proceeded to produce a pocketknife and slash both of my gloves open—there was no sand, of course. All they contained was an oversized, angry fucker.

Football attracts all the crazies, for some reason. Gil Lake, my coach when I was kid, was absolutely out of his tree. He was the guy who taught me how to be mean.

Gil's specialty was a drill called the Gauntlet, where all the kids on the team would line up about ten yards apart, and one by one, they'd run in and give one kid a hit. You always give the guy taking the hits a few moments between each knock, so he can recover—that's just the way you do the drill. But when I would get up there, it was different.

"GO, GO, GO, GO, GO, GO!" Gil screamed. He was bombarding me with all the kids, not allowing them to give me a second between hits, even if they wanted to. It was like this crazy mosh pit, but with everyone in the pit trying to slam just one dude. He kept it going until I was on the ground. When one of the kids hesitated, Gil went nuts. "WHAT THE FUCK ARE YOU DOING? YOU FUCKING HIT HIM ANYWAY!!!" So the rest of the kids proceeded to run up and hit me after I was on the ground.

Pretty soon, that kind of treatment made me tough. That guy made me into a monster. Soon enough, during hitting drills, I began to notice kids changing places in line, so they didn't have to face me. That was when I knew I was good—when I realized people were scared of me.

Day of the big game. Gil went up to the other kids, all solemn and quiet and respectful. "I want you to have a good game, son, I need you to play tough for me . . ." You could see the encouraging effect of his voice. But then he came to me, last in line. He got up in my face, *grabbed* me. "YOU *MOTHERFUCKER*!" he growled. I looked up at him, terrified. His fingers dug into my shoulders. "YOU *MOTHERFUCKER*! YOU GET THE FUCK OUT THERE AND I WANT YOU TO KILL SOMEONE ON EVERY PLAY! WHAT DID I JUST SAY TO YOU?!"

"Kill someone!"

"THAT'S RIGHT!! IF YOU DON'T KILL SOMEONE ON EVERY PLAY, I'M GONNA FUCKING KILL *YOU*!! WHAT DO YOU THINK ABOUT *THAT*??"

"I'LL KILL THEM!!"

"WELL GODDAMMIT THEN, FUCKER—LET ME HEAR YOU *ROAR*!!!"

"*RAAAAAAAARRRR!*" I roared like a fucking beast. I get

goose bumps just remembering it, because he totally got inside my head. I was so malleable, I really would have killed for him.

———

When high school started, I was sent to La Sierra, the crappiest public school in Riverside. The city had three nice schools, but those were not for me. I had grown even more over the summer, and although my face was still covered in acne, I was feeling less awkward in my own frame. I was still pretty shy and nervous when I wasn't on the football field, but Bobby was right there by my side.

"James, we really hit the big time now. These high school girls are gonna shit when they see us."

"Yeah, right," I said. First days were the worst, when you walked through unfamiliar hallways, not knowing anyone.

"I'm dead serious, Jess. God, I look so damn handsome, I'm gonna get laid a *ton* this year. That's all I'm saying. Tell you what, after I take the virginity of a few chicks, I'll pass 'em right over to you. How does that sound?"

I sighed. "I heard some guys on the football team want to kick our asses."

That whole summer, there had been some chatter about how me and Bobby thought we were too tough for our own good, how we were going to get taught a lesson once we got to school. No one wants a freshman stealing his thunder, so I could see why the guys on the team might not have dug us all that much.

"So?" Bobby asked. He seemed genuinely confused as to why I would give it a second thought. A cute girl in tight jeans walked by, and Bobby's eyes followed her down the hall hungrily.

"So, those guys want to kill us."

"Fuck 'em," Bobby said, tearing his gaze away from the girl's perfect ass for the briefest second. "It's not happening."

Bobby's attitude toward life was simple: *fuck you*. He was a tough kid who'd never been given anything by anyone. And you know, that's how I wanted to feel, too. But in my head, things were always much more tangled up . . .

The bell rang.

"Class."

"You go ahead," he said. "I have pressing business to attend to." He strode off in pursuit of that ass.

I walked down the hall slowly, watching the crowd part in front of me: permed-out cheerleaders and red-eyed stoners, math nerds and Mexicans, Dungeons-and-Dragons freaks in tight corduroys pressed up against gym rats walking the steroid swagger, Zeppelin dorks eyeing hair-metal chicks with horny hostility. And then I saw Tom Dixon, the captain of the varsity football team, coming toward me.

Dixon was an eighties jock dickhead straight out of Central Casting: a chick magnet with tight, white pegged pants, who must have owned the best Conair blow-dryer money could buy. He used it skillfully, creating a blond feathered 'do that winged out majestically. Tom stood in front of me, blocking my way.

"Hey, fag," he said pleasantly, "I know who you are. You're that Jesse James kid."

I didn't say anything.

"Didn't you *hear* me?" Tom's smile curled into a sneer. He looked at me and kind of snorted. "So, what's that you're wearing, kid?"

I looked down at the used button-down shirt I'd bought for school, with my own money. The collar was frayed.

"Don't you have any fucking pride, kid? I mean, I wouldn't come to school wearing a piece of shit like that if you *paid* me." He laughed again. The two kids who flanked him, his football flunkies, laughed, too.

"Goddamn, kid, aren't you gonna say anything back to me?" His voice lowered menacingly. "I mean, I'm *talking* to you. Are you deaf, faggot?"

Suddenly, *BOOM!* He sucker-punched me in the stomach as hard as he could. It knocked all the breath out of me. I struggled for a second, but I didn't fall. We stared at each other for a long second, motionless. A small crowd of kids had gathered around us, and they watched us now, breathing quietly.

We both stood there for a minute, eyefucking each other.

Then I pushed past him and kept walking.

"Exactly, dick!" called one of Dixon's flunkies, laughing. "Go cry to your mommy! And don't even *think* about coming to tryouts unless you want some more."

I stomped off to class. I was never too great in school in the first place—composition I was okay at, and metal shop was my specialty, but beyond that, I just never tried. Shop was a good opportunity to laugh at all the stoners in there, who all seemed to be making either bongs or silencers. I remember the day one kid got his long hair caught in a drill press. It was real high-speed shit: didn't even move his head, just scalped him. It was all bloody.

That afternoon, Bobby and I walked down to the football field together.

"So, we gonna rock this shit, James?"

"Of course," I answered. Inside, I wasn't so sure.

Uniforms were doled out. The returning varsity got theirs first, of course. They all seemed to know one another: cool kids with big muscles and giant shoulders, making jokes and cracking wise. From a short distance, I saw Tom pointing over at me. He said something to one of his flunkies, and the whole group of them laughed.

"Hey," Bobby said, curious, "did that fucker just point you out?"

"Nah. Don't think so."

"He just fucking *pointed* at you, man! Why are all of them laughing?"

"It's nothing," I said. "He just punched me in the stomach today, that's all."

"You're kidding, right?" Bobby said, aghast. "That kid *punched* you? What are you going to do?"

"Nothing. I'm gonna play football."

"Jesse James, I swear." Bobby's face grew dark. "If you go pussy on me, I will personally kick your ass myself."

"All right, jerkoffs!" a coach called out. "Enough yapping! Come and get your rags." The JV kids swarmed around the coaches, trying to get uniforms. We were an ugly little crew. Tiny runts, fatsos with man-tits, white trash, mean losers, and punks with messed-up lives. As a whole, we were one big zit cluster, a dog pile of teenaged assholes hoping against hope to make the big squad. But even we knew that most of us didn't have a fucking chance.

Another coach blew his whistle. "*Gentlemen!* Line up! Let's toss, sweep, block!"

Slowly, the varsity center, along with his quarterback, fullback, and tailback, all strutted up to the line together—they'd done this drill before. Tom, of course, was the quarterback. Big, imposing linebackers came to stand on either side of the formation.

"Oh, hey, it's the faggot, with the gay clothes," Tom called to me. "I thought I told you not to come down here today, didn't I?"

I said nothing.

"Let's get a defensive line!" the coach called, motioning over to the crew of JV kids. None of us moved. "Guys! Let's not be shy. I don't have all day."

I walked up to the outside linebacker position. Bobby came out and stood beside me. Another tenth grader, a chubby kid named Mike, walked up and joined us. Slowly, the defensive line filled.

The coach tossed the ball to the center. "All right, boys. Let's see what you got."

"Hut, hut!" Tom shouted. He looked both ways, put his hands down underneath his center's thighs, got ready to receive the ball. I stared at him, dead-eyed.

"Hut, hut, HIKE!"

As soon as the ball was snapped, I tore off the line, heading straight at him. Dixon looked to his left—no one there. He drifted back, looking for his tailback. I snuck around the end. The fullback tried to chop at my legs, but I straight-armed him and pushed him down.

Dixon looked to his right—drifting back again. His tailback approached, and he was just about to sweep, when I arrived.

I tackled the fucker hard, right around his ribs, and brought him down to the field violently. The ball flew loose, and all the air expelled from Tom Dixon's mighty lungs with a clumsy *"OOOF!"*

"Nice *hit,* Jess," Bobby hooted. "Show 'em how we do it!"

Tom Dixon squirmed under me uncomfortably. He looked dazed. "Get off, kid!"

He lay there, trapped under my knees.

"Nah, I don't think so," I whispered.

I wrenched his helmet off his blow-dried head and smashed him in the face with my fist. I hit him as hard as I could, my knuckles hammering the bone of his cheek, driving his head into the ground. I pulled him up by the collar of his jersey, punched him in the temple again, then socked him below his eye. I hit him in the face again and again, over and over, until blood was gushing.

"He's crazy!" Dixon's buddy cried. "Get him off! Fuck, this kid needs to be put in jail!"

They tried to rip me away, but I was locked on like a pit bull. I bashed his skull against the ground over and over again, filled with rage. Finally, Tom Dixon made a terrible, high-pitched squeal: an inhuman, pig-shriek sound. The sound of complete defeat. As soon as I heard that, I smiled and loosened my grip. I let the rest of the team peel me off him.

I staggered back over to Bobby and the JV kids, on shaky legs, feeling like I had to vomit.

"Fuck, James, that was *awesome,*" Bobby said, collapsing with laughter. He clapped me on the back. "You see that fucker's face? Man, I had no idea you even had that *in* you!"

I was still shaking. I hadn't come close to depleting my rage. I wouldn't for a long, long time.

2

———◆◆◆———

"You gotta grow up," our head coach advised me, shaking his head. "You know, I think a year on the JV squad might be just the ticket for you."

I guess it was meant to be a lesson: you know, don't pulverize the quarterback, kid—can't do that and expect to advance in life . . .

But I was real butt-hurt about being put on JV. To be sent down to the little-kid squad? Man, I couldn't even sleep, I was so pissed off. *I'm bigger and meaner and faster than* any *of those varsity motherfuckers!* I'd never felt so desperate or cheated.

So when I suited up for that first JV game, I had a chip on my shoulder.

"You look a little crazy, Jess," Bobby said. "What's going on in that sweet li'l head of yours?"

"Shut up, motherfucker."

They blew the whistle, and I just went completely haywire. I knocked out two of the opposing team's quarterbacks in the first quarter. One of them I laid out flat-cold with a hit, and the other one, I fucking broke his leg or something. After that, the ref called a quick meeting with my coach.

"Look, you gotta get the nut job out of there," the ref said. "He shouldn't be playing with the tadpoles."

So they moved me to the varsity after that. Finally, I felt happy—vindicated, I guess. I was an outside linebacker, which meant my job was basically to kill the quarterback. And that's just what I did, over and over again. I was quicker and crazier than any of the kids out there, and I was out for blood. By my sophomore year of high school, I was six foot three, weighed 220 pounds, and could run a forty-yard dash in 4.7 seconds. I was just a horrible person to have gunning for you.

Due to the fact that I could play ball, I was given an identity at school: jock. I guess I looked the part, due to my build, and the fact that I was sporting a flattop back then. Not too many kids wore flattops in the mid-eighties in Southern California. It was more of a long-hair period. Inside, though, I didn't feel much like a jock. I loved football and lived for being on the field, but I didn't really *like* other jocks. I wasn't going to jock parties or drinking jock beer. A glorious secret remained hidden in the sinew of my fifteen-year-old body: deep down inside, where no one could see it, I was a *punk*.

"Are *you* back again?"

"Sure am, back again," I mumbled to the clerk at Zed's, the best record store in Long Beach.

"Gonna *buy* anything this time?"

"Maybe," I said, rifling through the tapes as fast as I could. "You guys have that new Misfits album?"

"Nah," the clerk sighed. "Try me later this week. Maybe you can shoplift it then."

So they were on to me. I didn't really care. I loved the music. I was going to get it any way I could. Suicidal Tendencies, D.O.A., Circle Jerks, Black Flag—it was all just full-on aggression and rage and manic energy, channeled into thrash. To people who hated the sound, I know it probably sounded like a bunch of screaming. But to those of us who loved it, it was powerful. It was a way to say that something rotten and fake and wrong was going on in the world. Punk said we'd evaluated the situation, and weren't going to nod along.

Punk was sort of the *opposite* of jock in that way, actually.

If I was going to listen to Social Distortion, then I needed punk *style*. No punk would be caught dead with long hair, let alone Tom-Dixon-blow-dried-jock hair. I longed to shave my head, like a true hard-core, but I couldn't, because my dad wouldn't let me. I shaved my head exactly one time, and afterward, he wouldn't talk to me for a couple of weeks. He was just a dick like that.

So I settled on the flattop as a compromise. My barber was a retired military dude who'd cut hundreds of heads every week for twenty-five years running. He slapped apple pectin on my scalp, so the bristly blond strands stood straight up, looking tough.

Of the flattop, my dad approved. But it remained clear that no matter what, I'd be fending for myself when it came to school clothes. Exasperated, I decided to take matters into my own hands. Hidden under my mattress, I still had most of the cash that I'd gotten from the burger stand robbery. Gingerly, I removed the giant wad of money and flipped it through my hands carefully. Even after all this time, the faintest whiff of French-fry grease still clung to it.

The preppiest store in the Tyler Mall was GHQ. All the rich kids shopped there; the shirts in the windows at GHQ were precisely the same ones that the preps would be wearing in the halls on Monday mornings. Publicly, I scoffed at the fuckers, but secretly, I wished I could show up to school just once looking store-bought. I'd never had the money for it before. Looking at my wad, I knew it was time.

The heat felt stifling as I stepped out of my house. I had no wheels, so I had to hoof it over to the mall. Only a few determined strides into my journey, I was sweating hard. By the time I got to the store, my ratty shirt was soaked all the way through.

"Man," I muttered, disgusted, trying to peel my shirt off my chest. The Tyler Mall felt freezing. Blasts of air-conditioning made the wet fabric next to my skin feel like a cold blanket. I felt ridiculous, and for a moment, I considered turning back—but that would be like admitting defeat. I'd come this far. So, ducking my chin into my chest, I stumbled my way into GHQ.

"Can I help you?" A very pretty girl who appeared to be several years older than me, maybe a college freshman, was working the counter. She stood there, looking tan and cool, like she'd never sweated in her entire life.

I was still out of breath from my walk. "Yeah," I huffed, then paused to compose myself. I never quite knew what to say to really pretty girls. "I need to get some . . . shirts."

She smiled warmly. "We have lots of those. Do you know what kind of shirts you're looking for?"

I blushed, momentarily at a loss. "Something . . . with a collar?" I mumbled.

"Something . . . with a *collar*," she said teasingly. "Hmm . . . wait, what about this?" She moved to the nearest rack and pointed her elegant hand at a long-sleeved button-down Madras shirt.

"Yeah," I said. "That looks good."

"You know, we also have that shirt in red."

"Okay."

"Okay . . . to which shirt?" She smiled and leaned over the counter. The tiniest fraction of her bra could be seen down the front of her blouse. My pulse quickened.

"Both," I said, woozy. "In fact," I said, clearing my throat, "I'll take every color you have in that size."

"Every single color?"

"Every color," I repeated, fingering my wad of stolen money. I looked up and met her gaze fully for the first time. "And then I'd like to look at some pants."

She smiled at me. "Let's get you all set up, hon."

I walked out of GHQ half an hour later, my hands full of bags and boxes. I'd bought all the shirts they had in my size, plus about six pairs of nice pants, and a pair of slip-on boots with a black sole. Yeah, I was feeling like the preppiest punk in Riverside, indeed.

I threw on my new threads as soon as I got home. Primping in front of the mirror in my bathroom, I couldn't believe what I saw reflected back at me. For the first time outside of the football field, I liked the way I looked. Repeatedly, I sniffed at my shirt, savoring its aroma: brand new.

Grinning, I waltzed into the living room, clad in new pants, new shirt, and new boots. I hung out there, watching TV, feeling pretty damn good. Then my dad came home from work. He took one look at me and frowned.

"Jesse."

"What's that?" I was watching the screen and didn't look directly at him.

"I'm gonna need you to go change."

"What are you talking about?"

He pointed at my shirt and my pants. "Go change out of that costume."

"What are you talking about?" I was confused. "Why?"

"Doesn't look right," he said.

"Huh?"

"You look like a *faggot* in that!"

I stared at him, stunned.

"Go change."

And he left the room.

I sat there for a few minutes, stung. Soon Joanna hovered over me, her arms crossed. "You heard your father. Hurry up and change into your regular clothes."

"Beat it," I muttered.

She took a deep breath. "Jesse, I don't want to have to tell you again."

I stomped out, slamming the door behind me. I knew what my dad was so pissed off about. It wasn't that he knew I'd stolen money—he wouldn't have cared about that. Rather, he'd realized I could survive without his help. I didn't have to go through him anymore.

I set off down the road to Bobby's. His house was only about ten minutes away from mine—we lived in the same shitty part of Riverside. I was still fuming when I got to his house.

"Jesse James, fuck me, you've gone fashion model!" He cackled, taking in my tacky new duds. "So, sexy, what's happening?"

"Cut it out," I said. "My dad's already been giving me hell."

"Sensitive," Bobby observed.

"My stepmom is even worse," I complained. "I hate that little bitch."

"No way, James," Bobby disagreed. "That stepmom of yours is *cute*, man."

I groaned. "Come on, Bobby."

"What are you talking about?"

"That's disgusting."

"*Disgusting?*" Bobby asked. "I don't think so, my friend. That blond hair? So darn *cute*. I'd do her in a heartbeat. You would, too, if you had the chance."

"You're sick."

"Were you born without a penis?" Bobby said seriously. "It's okay if you were. I swear I won't tell anyone."

"Dude, come on."

"Man, that is *tough*. But I promise, I'll never tell a soul." He kept up his serious face for about five seconds, then fell over laughing.

"You're an idiot."

Bobby cackled. No one could crack up Bobby like Bobby himself. "Now look, man, *cheer the fuck up*. That's an order."

"I am cheered up," I grumbled. "You've made a big difference."

"Finally," Bobby sighed. "Jesus. Can we go steal shit, now?"

I wasn't going to tell him the truth, of course: that in part, Joanna freaked me out because I had come across a stash of naked pictures of her when I was twelve.

I was all alone in the garage after school one day, picking through the thousand or so magazines that my dad had collected across the years at flea markets and swap meets. He'd bought up stacks and stacks of old *McCall's* and *Life* magazines and *Saturday Evening Posts* and *National Geographics* on the cheap; some were valuable collector's items, others were just discolored garbage that he hadn't gotten around to throwing out. From time to time, I leafed through them idly, just for something to do.

I was methodically making my way through a stack of *Posts* when I came upon a small box with a canvas cover on it. Just for the hell of it, I decided to open it. When I did, I found a black-and-white photograph of Joanna wearing a thin, lacy teddy. She was contorted in an awkward position that showed off most of her skinny little body.

"What the hell . . . ?" I muttered.

I peeled the picture back, revealing another. There was a whole avalanche of them. In some, my stepmother's lips were puckered up dreamily. In others, she offered up a teasing pose. With equal parts dread and curiosity, I slowly examined each photo in the stack. A blank expression often played upon Joanna's face, as if she was receiving direction she didn't quite understand. In most, a freckled hand was atop her bare hip, awkwardly.

Joanna was small and pasty, with blunted breasts and an epic bush. This was the woman behind my nightly meat loaf. I felt confused, and somehow tricked. You don't want to see your stepmom naked. At least, I didn't.

I shoved the photos back underneath the stack of *McCall's* and left the garage, face burning.

———

Joanna left awhile after that. It had nothing to do with my discovery.

"Dad?" I asked.

"Huh?"

"Where's your wife?" About a week had passed with no trace of my stepmom. We had eaten dinner alone together for several nights running, mostly in silence.

He took a long, slow look at me. "Joanna doesn't live here anymore."

"Uh . . . where does she live?"

"Don't know," my dad admitted. After a second, he laughed shortly. "Try asking the guy she ran away with."

I didn't quite get it, but later I concocted a theory that Joanna and my dad had been "swingers." It was the right era, and that would explain the racy pics. My dad was always a real ladies' man, with a silver-tongued kind of charm. Maybe the photographs were meant to be sent off to swingers' magazines, so on weekends they could ride out to Bakersfield or San Bernardino, taking part in wacky wife-swaps and oiled-up orgies. Of course, I had no evidence of this, but hey—I was in high school and I had a vivid imagination.

He'd posed her like a plastic love doll, but never in his wildest dreams could my father have predicted that his obedient and sedate wife of four years would suddenly spring to life, bouncing off over the Fresno horizon with another guy. *Who the hell understood women, anyway?* And so, just a few years after she'd entered my life, Joanna was gone.

So began a brief, cautiously happy era. It was just me and my dad at home together, like a couple of bachelors. I would cook or he would. I'd watch TV and he wouldn't care what it was. I was staying up late and he didn't seem to mind. Dishes got done haphazardly. But peace reigned in the James household.

"Jess!"

"Yeah, Dad?"

"Need you to work tomorrow for me."

"I have school, Dad. Tomorrow's Friday, remember?"

"Then you're just gonna have to be sick. I'm going to Pasadena for a big job, and I need you to help me out." He grinned at me. "Your old dad's getting feeble. He needs the young blood to step up and do its part."

I flushed with pride. "Hell yeah." It didn't matter to me that I had a test the next day in algebra.

The next day we both woke up at six and ate breakfast together. "You want coffee, Jess?"

"No, thanks."

He laughed. "Come on, kid. Live a little. Try coffee the way I do it: plenty of sugar and plenty of cream. A coffee made the right way can be a whole meal. Give you vitamins you need for the rest of the day!"

I grinned. "Okay. Just a little bit."

"That's what I'm talking about!" my dad bellowed. He reached out and pounded me in the chest twice. "My son is a walking beast, goddammit!"

In his better moments, my dad seemed to me like the perfect combination of Redd Foxx and George Carlin. He could make me laugh without even trying. I remember literally crying, tears running down my face, listening to swap-meet stories of his that I'd heard a million times before.

I loaded up his trucks like a madman. I tossed mattresses every which way, stacking boxes of books and antique tables next to refrigerators next to dinettes next to racks of chairs.

"Careful, careful!" my dad warned. "You're wasting room, Jess! No, no fucking way! Let's start this over. Don't half-ass it. Unpack the whole thing. Start over from scratch."

Turning around on a dime, I started unloading the truck. Just like on the football field, I attacked any physical task with enthusiasm and a kind of animal rage. I was going to be the *best in the world* at packing up junk trucks. No one would do it faster or better or meaner than me.

My dad just watched, a bemused look on his face.

"*Much* better. Fuck, kid," he said, laughing, "I should keep you out of school every day. My life just got ten times easier."

The swap meets became my home away from home, and molded me into an even weirder teenager than I already was. Besides Bobby, I just didn't have that many friends my own age. My peer group wasn't really kids, they were my dad's friends, Rick and Joey and Paul and Ronnie, sleazy pimplike dudes who were constantly running game, smoking cigarettes, and cutting deals, wearing three-quarter-length leather trench coats with floppy denim hats and loving every minute of it.

"Look at the *milkers* on that one," Joey would say, motioning toward a young blond California mom pushing a stroller.

"Watch the mouth, Joe," Rick would go, laughing and motioning to me. "The kid isn't used to that kind of language."

"Hell he isn't! He's seen a pair of tits before. You know what a good rack looks like, dontcha, Jess?"

"Sure do," I bluffed, puffed up with my own newfound machismo.

"Yeah, but do you know what to *do* with 'em? Jesse, tell you what, how about you go over there and put those in your mouth, huh, kid?" He made a sucking sound with his lips and teeth. "*Milk* 'em, is what I say!"

They were good-time guys, the original dirty rotten scoundrels. Fun for them was breaking a jar of mayonnaise on the supermarket floor. One well-timed slip-and-fall later, and they were suing the store for negligence. They fascinated me and made me feel sick to my stomach at the same time. I remember going out to find Joey in the parking lot one time, because he had an interested buyer for a lamp of his. He hadn't been near his booth for about half an hour.

I craned my neck, looking for his green Thunderbird in the vast parking lot.

"Hey, Joey! Where you at?" I stretched my neck in vain. "Joey!"

Finally I located his car. I saw him sitting behind the driver's seat and ran up to the window, knocking on it with my knuckles.

"Hey, Joey, someone's looking . . . oh, sorry!"

A woman's blond head was moving over his lap with a rhythmic tempo.

He glanced up and gave me a triumphant grin. "Little busy right now, kid." His right palm rested lazily atop her crown of mussed golden hair. "Gimme five minutes."

They were shitheads, creeps; I knew that. But they were my dad's world, and I'd been given a ticket to the main show. As long as I pulled my weight, worked hard, and made sure everyone liked me, I'd be allowed to stay. That's what mattered to me.

The year I spent alone with my father was unlike any other part of my childhood. It was exciting and gratifying. The most compelling moments came when my dad would take odd, brief fits of interest in me. One night over dinner, as he sipped from his Coca-Cola, he regarded me with a curious kind of look.

"Do you even *like* girls?"

"What . . . what do you mean?" I said, blushing.

"I mean just what I say, kid. Do you like girls, or what?" He chuckled. "Not that complicated."

"Sure, I like girls," I said defensively. "Of course I do."

"Ya ever DONE anything with one, though?" he said, picking up a thigh from the take-out box of fried chicken that lay there between us. He gazed at me with a kind of intensity.

"I mean . . . there's a girl at school who I kind of like." That was true. Her name was Rhonda. She was the prettiest girl in the whole high school, as far as I could tell.

"You *like* her, huh?" My dad had an evil grin on his face.

"Yes," I said protectively. I didn't like the way he was smiling.

"Why don't I ever see her over here, then?"

"Because, well . . . we're not even together or anything. She doesn't even really know I like her, in fact."

My dad sighed. "Say no more," he said, holding up his hand. "I get it."

"What do you get?" I said angrily.

"You're a goddamn virgin," he said.

"Whatever." I reached for some potatoes, awkwardly scooped a huge portion onto my plate.

My dad continued watching me for a second.

"Hey, it's fine. You're just a kid. No hurry." Then he frowned, adding, "Christ, you eat like an ox, kid. Did you realize that? Leave some for your old man. You'll eat both of us right into the poorhouse."

I didn't think much of our conversation until about a week later. It was late afternoon. I carried my book bag over my shoulder. There'd been no one to pick me up from school, so it had been the bus for me. Another long ride.

I opened up my front door and let myself into my house. The house was quiet, as usual. I dropped my bag and went into the kitchen, where I opened up the refrigerator and poured myself a glass of juice.

"Mind if I have some?"

I jumped, startled.

"Who are you?"

A girl extended her hand to me. "My name's Tracy." She was about nineteen or twenty, and pretty. She was slim with a fair complexion.

"Oh," I said, not sure of what to say next. "I'm . . . um . . . Jesse."

"Hi, *Jesse*." She smiled widely. "It's so nice to meet you."

"Did you . . . did you want some juice?" I asked.

"I'd love some."

Carefully, I opened up a kitchen cabinet and searched for a clean glass for her. My dad had all kinds of vintage glassware, but like I said, we weren't the best housekeepers, so it took a moment. Finally I found a passable tumbler. I reached into the freezer, unstuck a few cubes of ice, and plopped them in the glass. Then I poured some from-concentrate orange juice into the glass and handed it to the strange girl who was in my kitchen.

"Thank you," she said pleasantly. She sipped from the glass and smiled at me again. "Yum."

I shifted uneasily. "Uh . . ."

"Yes?"

"Who are you?"

"I told you. I'm *Tracy.*" She giggled. "I'm a friend of your dad's." She spooled some of her pretty hair around her fingers and played with it coquettishly.

"Is he home?" I asked.

"Nope." She giggled again. "*You* are, though."

I couldn't think of anything to say to that, so I just stared at my feet. Tracy sipped at her juice, looking at the framed posters my dad had put up on the walls as she walked around my kitchen. Then, decisively, she strode toward the living room. I followed. She plopped down on our couch and motioned to me.

"Come sit down, Jesse."

I did what she said.

"So, how old are you?" Tracy asked. She appeared to be poring over me in a way I couldn't quite interpret.

"Fifteen."

"Wow." She laughed. "You look *way* older than that." She reached over and stroked my arm gently. "You're pretty strong, huh?"

"Yeah," I said softly. I didn't know where to look.

"Do you have a girlfriend or anything?"

"No," I mumbled. "I'm too busy . . . football."

"Oh, that's *crazy.* A boy as cute as you should have a girlfriend. I mean, that's really crazy."

"Well," I said, awkwardly. "Thanks."

"Jesse?" she said. "I just had an awesome idea. Do you want a massage?"

"Uh . . ."

"It'll feel great, I *promise*! I'm super good at massage."

"I guess so," I said.

"Come here." She reached for my shoulders and started to rub them very gently. I was still sitting bolt upright.

"How does that feel?" she asked.

"Nice."

"You could give me a massage next, if you want." She giggled. "I bet you're really good at it."

I didn't say anything.

"I *really* like your body," the girl whispered. I could feel her hot breath on my neck. Her hands strayed from my shoulders. They grazed my sides and came to rest on my thighs.

I didn't say anything. My whole body tensed.

"What do you think of my body?" she whispered. "Do you want to see more of it?" Her lips came so close to my ear that I could feel how wet they were. "Do you want to see me . . . naked?"

Abruptly, I stood up. "I gotta go."

Tracy looked at me, startled.

"Where are you going?"

"I'm sorry. I just—I really, really gotta go." I raced up the stairs to my bedroom and slammed the door behind me.

A couple of minutes later, I heard the front door open, then close. Tracy, who I guessed was a teenaged hooker my dad had hired to deflower me, had left the building.

———

"I would give my left *nut* for that girl," Bobby moaned.

"You'd give your nut for any girl," I said.

"Yeah. But I'd give my *left* for Rhonda Clark, and my left is my *special* nut." He stared at me. "It's the low hanger."

Rhonda Clark was tan and dark. She was so gorgeous that everyone always seemed to be staring at her. But she wasn't the kind of girl who went out of her way to talk to everybody.

"Bobby, just to let you know," I said, "you might have some competition there."

"You got your eye on Rhonda?"

"She's amazing," I admitted.

"You gotta be kidding me."

"Sorry," I said.

Bobby snorted. "Well, good *luck,* is all I can say, James. I mean, come on, man—that girl is *far* too fine for you."

"What are you talking about?"

"Frankly, a girl like Rhonda would be a lot more comfortable on the arm of someone with a touch of *class.*" Bobby looked at me pityingly. "Which would be me, naturally."

I patted Bobby gently on the back. "Let's not fight over someone who probably doesn't even know either of us exist."

"Get your hand off of me," Bobby said. "Whoa. Don't seduce me, James, you sick freak."

I never expected even to talk to her. So I couldn't even believe it when Rhonda started looking back at me when I shyly stared at her in the halls. She smiled right at me.

"Hey, come over here," she commanded one afternoon.

"Who, me?"

She giggled. "Yes, *you.*" Rhonda crossed her arms over the books she was carrying. "You keep *looking* at me. What's your name?"

"I'm . . . uh . . . Jesse," I said, finally.

"Don't you play football or something?"

I nodded. "Yes."

"I heard you were pretty good," she said.

"I'm okay," I said.

"No, I heard you were *really* good." Rhonda smiled. "Is there anything else you're good at?"

I thought for a second. "Swap meets?"

She looked unimpressed, and I hated myself for being so lame. I racked my mind to think what was *cool* about me: What could I boast about to impress this pretty girl who, against all odds, was talking to me in the La Sierra hallway?

"Well, I know a little bit about cars," I said, finally.

"Oh my God!" Rhonda squealed. "You know how to *fix* cars?"

"Sure," I said, delighted I'd stumbled on to something that this girl actually cared about. "I mean, it depends. But I can fix a lot of stuff."

"My mom's Chevy has been broken for *three* weeks!" She shifted the books in her arms, displaying casually a little bit of her rockin' bod. "I don't suppose you would want to take a look at it for me?"

"Shit," I said, "I'd love to. I mean . . . sorry. I didn't mean to say—"

"What?" Rhonda giggled. "Look, Jesse, if you fix my mom's car, then you can say 'shit' all day and all night."

"That's not what I want," I said.

"Oh, really?"

"Yeah," I said. I looked at her. "If I fix your mom's car, then I want you to go out to the movies with me."

"Oh really? What movie?"

"I . . . really don't care," I said honestly. The whole school throbbed and moved around us in the halls. I ignored everyone. It was just me and her, locked in a gaze. And it felt like the best thing ever.

She stared at me for a really long time, then finally broke out into the most gorgeous smile I'd ever seen. "Yeah," she said. "That sounds good."

Please note: I fixed the living *shit* out of that car.

———

Soon Rhonda and I were an item. Her perfect teenaged scent pervaded every aspect of my being. It was all roses and hair spray and cheerleader pom-poms and white cotton panties twisted up in a ball on the floor of my car.

Not to be outdone, my father embarked upon a romance of his own. Nina was a cocktail waitress at a bar in Long Beach. She boasted stringy hair that hung down from her forehead, moplike.

"*So* pleased ta meet you," she sneered, the first time she came over to the house. The way Nina talked, it was like there was an invisible cigarette hanging from her bottom lip. I could almost see the butt moving up and down.

My dad was never one to beat around the bush, so before long, they'd gotten hitched, and I had a new stepmom. One day, she arrived at my house smacking gum like it was her job, her skinny, weather-beaten hands on her hips, and a household of possessions thrown haphazardly into a dented Ryder truck behind her. Two kids stood by her side, staring at me hostilely.

"Jesse," came my dad's voice, "unload the truck for Nina."

I knew this action would officially end my time alone with my dad, and the realization put me momentarily beyond words. Had anybody thought to ask me if three new people could move into my house? Would they really be allowed to invade the first taste of happiness that I'd been trying to cultivate for my whole life?

"Well?" Nina said. She jerked her chin. "You gonna do what your dad said?"

With no other choice, I put my head down and walked slowly toward the truck.

"Don't *break* anything," Nina snapped.

Nina was a better homemaker than Joanna: she could actually cook a little bit. But she was not what you would call a stellar conversationalist.

"Hey," I said. "I think your kids stole some money out of my desk."

No response.

"Excuse me," I repeated. "Did you hear what I said? I had ten bucks in my desk. Now it's gone, and I think one of your kids *stole* it."

Nina looked at me, as if just discovering I was there. "My kids don't steal," she grunted, moving hair out of her face. She stirred the soup she was making for dinner, sucked on the oversized spoon. "Weren't raised that way."

"Yeah, well, look, I hate to tell you," I said, my voice rising, "some money is gone, and I sure as hell didn't spend it. My dad didn't take it, and I guess that leaves you and your kids." I folded my arms and stared her down. "So what are we gonna do about it?"

Nina stirred, her concentration intense. She peered into the oven, attending to her casserole. The contents of the Pyrex captivated her attention entirely.

"Hey!" I said. "Hello?"

Nina looked back up at me and squinted, as if meeting me for the first time. "I *told* you, my family don't steal shit." Her jaw worked up and down.

Defeated, I stomped out of the kitchen. The next day, I visited a hardware store and bought a dead bolt for my room. Without it, I was convinced my stepbrother and stepsister would take everything that wasn't nailed down. I thought this, because that's what I would have done. They didn't want to live with me any more than I wanted to live with them. Yet now that they were here, they would do their best to exploit the situation.

We coexisted uneasily for several months. Nina and I grew no closer. However, I grew to tolerate my stepsister and stepbrother, and then to like them. The unshakable force of the dead bolt imposed a kind of boundary, and they learned to act right. We were pillars of decency in an otherwise shitty adult world: one riddled with deception, neglect, and high-sodium food products. Incredibly, despite the chaos that it grew out of, our friendship exists to this day.

Maybe it would have been an okay family to ride out my high school years with. Nina could never have been a mom to me, but on the plus side, I probably wasn't going to happen upon a box of nudie pictures of her. No magazine in the world would publish one of those.

But it all turned out to be moot, when the house burned down.

It was a Sunday afternoon, and I was down the street at a neighbor's house, drinking beer with Bobby.

Bobby was getting a pretty good buzz on. He could always drink, and when he was in the company of a woman, as he was now, with my neighbor Kelly, he tipped them back at double speed.

"We're about to be the kings of the school," he babbled. "State champs, probably, and then of course, the NFL is my personal plan . . ."

Suddenly I smelled something.

"What *is* that?"

"What are you babbling about, Jesse?"

"Yeah," Kelly said, giggling. "Are you getting *weird,* Jesse?"

"Jesse's always weird," Bobby announced. "Ain't you," he said, slurping.

"Yeah," I said quietly, helping myself to another drink. It wasn't exactly my style to drink in the middle of the afternoon, but hell, it was Sunday. My dad and Nina and her kids were up in the Bay Area, attending one of his auctions; I had the town all to myself. Something felt pretty good about the way these cold, watery beers were going down, too. "I just thought something smelled off."

"Pardon him, please, he's retarded," Bobby apologized for me. He tried to slip an arm around Kelly's shoulders. She slipped out from underneath his grasp, giggling. "I'll be happy to ask him to leave, if you like."

We continued partying, working on a collective buzz, listening to music.

"You guys like Bon Jovi?" Kelly asked. "Their lead singer is such a *doll.*"

Bobby laughed. "I dig their bass player." He screwed up his face, then belched violently. "Giant teenage crush."

I laughed, not really listening. "Seriously, you guys don't smell that?"

"I don't know what you're *talking* about," Bobby said.

"Hold on," Kelly said, seriously. "I smell something, too. Doesn't it smell like something's—"

"Burning," I finished for her, my insides flushing with ice water, and we jumped to our feet and ran out the door.

Outside, half a block down, my house was ablaze.

As I watched, shocked, the house started igniting seemingly of its own accord. Loud, crazy explosions rocked the frame.

"What is *that*?" Bobby asked, awed for maybe the first time in his life.

"It's my fireworks," I said. A sinking, helpless feeling was building in the pit of my stomach.

I'd been storing fireworks—black powder, bottle rockets, and bricks of M-15s—in the garage for years, for so long I'd forgotten they were even there. In terrible bursts, they began exploding violently. I had ammo in there, too, bullets and shells. It sounded like a war. Flames began to lick at the windows, at the walls, at the roof.

Soon a siren's wail could be heard. The fire engines were coming.

Scared out of our minds, Bobby, Kelly, and I watched from the sidelines as a team of firefighters jumped down from the truck. They chopped down my door with axes and began to douse my whole house in water and chemicals.

"This your house, son?" a fireman asked me gruffly.

I nodded.

"Where are your folks?"

"They're not here," I said, watching over his shoulder as more and more water streamed into my garage. Everything in there that wasn't melted in the fire would be ruined by water damage. "My dad and his wife are up in San Francisco."

"You better notify him," the fireman said. "He'll want to know."

So I walked back to Kelly's and called him. I was half-drunk and totally in shock. He told me he would leave his auction immediately and come down to assess the damage. I sat down on the stoop to wait.

All night, I waited for him to arrive. The firefighters kept working at the house, and within a few hours they had extinguished the worst of the blaze. The foundation remained intact, but the roof had completely burned off. The walls of the dining room and the living room were black and wet, with burn marks over every inch. Worst of all, the garage was gone. I'd lost everything I cared about, including a motorcycle I was working on, my first bike ever. The roll-around toolbox containing all my tools was completely melted. I felt like dying.

Finally, at dawn, my dad and Nina showed up. None of us had slept. A small squad of firefighters was still there, dousing out hot spots.

"Goddamn," my dad cried, getting out of his car. He walked up to me and stood over me. "How'd this happen, Jess?"

I didn't say anything. There was nothing to say. I shrugged.

"The place is *fucked*," he said. The tone of his voice was dangerously hoarse.

I remained silent, scared of the anger that I knew was building.

"No one can live here anymore," he said. He nodded slowly, as if taking in his own comment. "We don't have a house anymore."

"I'm . . . I'm sorry, Dad. I didn't mean to."

"Yeah, he didn't mean to," Nina said sarcastically. "He just *loves* that house."

I whirled to face her. "What are you talking about? Why would I burn the house down on purpose?"

She shook her head at me. "How'm I supposed to know what goes on in that head? All I see is my house burned down."

"Your house?" I cried. "You've only lived here for six months!"

My dad looked at me. "You burned this down on purpose?"

"I *didn't* burn it down!" I shouted. "I was down the street and I came out and *it was on fire.*"

"Yeah, and it just caught on fire by itself?" Nina taunted.

"What is wrong with you, Jesse?" my dad asked. "After all I've given you, you go and burn my fucking *house*?"

"*I didn't burn it!*" I yelled. "How many times do I have to say I didn't *do* it?"

"All I'm seeing," my dad said, with blood in his eyes, his jaw clenched, "is a rotten, useless, burned-up building!" He pushed me aside. "It was your fireworks in the garage! And you have the goddamn *gall* to stand right in front of me and tell me you had nothing to do with it?"

"Fuck you," I whispered. It was the first time I had ever said that to my dad in my whole life.

My father reared back and punched me in the face. His fist hit me with all the force of a grown man's hate, and he broke my nose for me. Blood everywhere.

In disbelief, I touched my nose and watched the blood begin to drip down all over my hand and arm.

Years of frustration and rage coursed through me in one furious instant. I put my head down and tackled him, pinning his aging body to the floor, and with my fists and legs, I tried to kill him.

"Get off me!" my dad cried, but I was bigger than him now, and stronger.

We rolled over each other with our bodies, tangled in a death grip. We crashed through the living room wall, the sick smell of burned drywall and reclaimed water enveloping us.

I hated him so much. I tried to crush him with my hands. If the firefighters hadn't been there, I would have killed him. I remember their slick raincoats against my skin, their hats falling off their heads, as two of them tried to pull me off my father, and a third joined to help them.

"Son!" they cried. "That's enough! Let go! Let go of him."

They ripped us apart and threw me into the corner, where I lay sobbing for what seemed like a long time. My dad lay on the ground, too, ten yards away from me. He didn't make a sound.

Slowly, I rose to my feet, walked out of the blackened shell of the house, and got into my car. I drove away without looking back.

3

I was alone and homeless. So I went to Rhonda. I felt like I had no other options left.

"Can I . . . can I stay with you for a while?" I asked.

"I don't know, Jesse," Rhonda said. "My mom might not like it."

But her mother, Linda, surprised us both. She looked at me real hard when I told her what had happened, listening to every word. Then she informed me that, if I agreed to a few conditions, I was welcome to stay.

"First things first, Jesse," her mom said. "There's not going to be any *bullshit* going on with my daughter under this roof."

I blushed. "No."

"I mean it. We have a spare bedroom, and that's where you'll stay. You're not to sleep in Rhonda's room." Rhonda's mom was pretty, just like her daughter, and when she smiled you could see how they were related. However, she wasn't smiling now. Not even a little bit. "Not on special occasions, not when I'm not around—*you don't do it*. Is that understood?"

I nodded. "Yes."

"I want you to have a job. I know a couple of people who could probably use a strong kid like you to help make deliveries. How does that sound to you?"

"It sounds good," I said.

"You're to go to school," she continued. "*Every* day. I mean, if you're not trying, then I don't see any reason I should let you live with me and my daughter. Do you?"

"No," I agreed.

"Good." Now she smiled. "And hell, if you have the energy, help me out a little around here. I *hate* doing the damn dishes. So far, Rhonda's hopeless. How are you at doing dishes, kiddo?"

I laughed, relieved. Rhonda gave me a hug. "I'm super good," I said, too choked up to add more. My arms remained braided around her daughter's waist. "I'm the best dishwasher in the whole world."

So I moved into their spare bedroom, and for the first time in my life, I was part of a family. We ate meals together every night. It was what I had dreamed of. Linda was such a great person to me—she made a point of checking in to see whether I was doing my schoolwork and whether I was actually going to my job, which turned out to be working at a furniture store. She didn't pretend to like my dad, either. That made me appreciate her even more.

Rhonda and I were totally in love. By necessity, we were pretty chaste, but that didn't keep me from being one hundred percent sprung over her. She was going to turn sixteen soon, and I wanted to blow her mind with a great surprise.

"What do you want for your birthday?" I whispered to her one night when we were cuddling together, outside the house.

"Oh, I don't know," Rhonda said. "Whatever you get me will be great, I just know it." She smiled at me.

"I'm gonna totally bowl you over," I boasted. "I'm gonna blow your mind."

"Sure, Jesse." She laughed. "Blow it!"

I'm sure she was expecting me to spend twenty dollars at the mall jewelry store. Maybe show up with a gold-leaf necklace, one of those babies that turn your neck spinach green in two days. Instead, the day of her birthday, there appeared in her driveway a 1961 seafoam green Volkswagen Beetle.

"Jesse!" she exclaimed. "What . . . is this?"

"It's your car," I said.

"Oh my God!" She was so excited, she was literally dancing from foot to foot. "What?"

"It's your car," I repeated, proudly. I held out a key ring to her—a single key dangled from it. "Here. Take it for a ride, if you want."

I still haven't forgotten the way Rhonda's face looked when she took that key. She was totally intoxicated on surprise and hyperexcitement. But I saw that she also looked proud. Of me, for having gotten this done for her.

"Oh, Jesse," Rhonda said. "You are so sweet. You are *so* good to me." She gazed up at me lovingly. "How in the world did you do all this?"

I grinned. "Don't worry about that."

I hadn't bought the car outright, of course. I was way too broke for that. I'd gotten a working engine from one guy, and a Volkswagen shell from another. The wheels and fenders came in from yet another source. Truthfully, there were a few stolen parts on it—Linda hadn't reformed me completely. But I'd painted it myself, and done lots of body work to the car, removing every dent I could find. It looked cherry.

"What can I do for you in return?" she said, smiling.

"You could drive me to football practice," I answered truthfully. "If I'm much later, coach'll freaking kill me."

That year, my junior year, was when I really became a star. The coaches realized they could play me on offense and defense, as well as the special teams, and I would never ask for a breather. The whole season, I never came off the field—much to the dismay of my backup, a good-natured roly-poly kid named Mike.

Mike had the kind of fat girth you could get away with on a football field: his shapeless bulk packed tight around an oblong skeleton. His bright red hair was complemented by freckles and a hapless expression on his doughy face.

"Jesse," Mike whined, "why don't you ever get hurt, man?"

"Built way too tough," I explained. "Bones made of titanium, Mike."

"I'll shoot him for you, Mike," Bobby volunteered. "For the right price, he's a dead man."

Tom Dixon and his gang of seniors had graduated. That meant that it was pretty much Bobby's and my team, even though we were only juniors. We kind of battled with each other for authority. I preferred to lead by example; Bobby, by the force of psychotic bluster.

"No FUCKING *UP* tonight!" he'd scream in the locker room before our games. "NO PUSSIES, NO CRYING!"

"Let's play smart and hard," I announced firmly.

"TAKE 'EM OUT AT THE KNEES AND GOUGE THEIR *EYEBALLS*!!" Bobby boomed.

The kids on the team looked vaguely confused, not to mention mildly frightened by the spastic giant screaming in front of them. "It's all about protecting the football," I explained.

"TAKE 'EM HARD, CUZ THEY DESERVE TO *DIE*!"

"Let's get out there and win," I added.

It was interesting, because I was such an angry, sick fuck on the field, but in the locker room, I was your average kid. Maybe even a little bit quieter than the rest of them. Yet under the lights, it was like a switch would turn over in me, and I was out for blood.

Our first game that year was with Notre Dame, our rival high school. There had been several articles about me in the paper, referencing the good year I was coming off of. Well, the other teams didn't like that at all. So right away, the first play of the game, Notre Dame decided to try to get into my head. Their tight end was a big white guy with an even bigger mouth.

"Yo, Jesse James," he yelled. "I heard your mom's a whore! Actually, I *know* she is, because I put my *balls* in your whore mom's mouth just last night! Hey, are you deaf, Jesse James?"

I didn't say anything. I was letting the hate build up in me, letting it heat my blood.

He kept going. "You know what? Fuck you, faggot! And your whore mom, too." His voice was harsh and loud, and he was so relentless, people up in the stands could probably hear him. "She didn't lick my balls right! Can you finish the job?"

No response. I just stared into the top of his skull, at the stripes that bisected his helmet, willing them to become the entire universe for me.

"Aren't you gonna say SHIT?" he said, just as his center hiked the ball.

I flew off the line and punched him. It was maybe the best uppercut of my life. I punched him so hard, and in precisely the right place, that my knuckles punched up *behind* his sternum, and my hand disappeared beneath his rib cage.

He gasped awfully. He dropped to the ground, and I ran over him and sacked the quarterback. As I was lying there, on top of the QB, savoring the moment, the foulmouthed kid stumbled to his feet, then jumped on my back. He wailed away at me with harmless, puny blows. "You DIRTY SON OF A BITCH!"

I just covered up and laughed, letting him work my back. Eventually, my teammates pulled him off me and beat him down into the ground some more. Their team came to his rescue, and soon a whole bunch of heads were getting knocked, just like they should in high school games.

"Nice punch, James," Bobby whispered to me, out of breath, as we lined up again.

"Maybe I should get into boxing," I said, laughing.

"Both of us should. There's good money in it."

I wasn't all that surprised when my dad started coming to games. I was getting press in the local papers and stuff, slowly becoming a star player. So sure enough, that's when he started showing up. He would sit up in the stands all alone, high up, in a section all by himself, so I could be sure to see him.

"That your pops, James?"

I frowned. "Yeah, that's him."

"I thought you and him didn't talk anymore."

"We don't."

"So why's he here?"

"Beats me," I muttered. "Maybe the man just loves a good game of football."

I didn't know what my dad wanted me to think. Was it a white flag, his fucked-up way of saying sorry, since he sure wouldn't say it out loud to me? It wasn't really his style to be remorseful, though, not even in silence. After a while, I kind of figured he was sending a different kind of message: by sitting there, he was telling my coaches and my community that he had some part in my success. That I never could have gotten this way all by myself.

"What's wrong, Jesse?" Linda asked me one night, when we were eating dinner together.

"Nothing," I said. I never wanted to unload myself onto Linda. I felt guilty enough just sleeping under her roof and eating her food.

"Uh-huh," she said slowly, looking at me unbelievingly. She was a smart lady, way too smart to fall for my act.

"It's nothing," I said. I nodded at her and Rhonda. "Promise."

"You know," said Linda, in the tone of someone who knows she's got your number, but is too kind to put it in a mean way, "I happened to see your dad up in the stands the other night."

"Well, yeah," I said, after a while. "He comes to the games nowadays."

"Does he ever try to talk to you? Talk about what happened?"

I shook my head. "No. We haven't discussed it."

Linda was silent. She looked across the table at her own daughter.

"Did your folks move to another house?" Linda asked.

"They didn't have to," I said. "The insurance paid for them to fix it up. There's a new roof on the house. They still live there."

Linda looked at me real straight for a second. "Jesse, I want you to listen to me."

I looked at her.

"Your dad doesn't know what he's missing."

I just looked at my plate and shrugged.

"You hear me, son?" Linda snapped. "Do you even *get* what I'm trying to say?"

I looked at her. I had never seen her worked up like that.

She shook her head, then closed her eyes, massaging her forehead. "You are always welcome in this house, Jesse. Please, please know that."

Gradually my dad started driving by Rhonda's house after work. It would always be in the early evenings—he'd cruise by real slow in his work truck loaded high with tons of junk. I figured he was showing me how much work he had to do without me.

When both of us had watched him come by for the third time in as many days, Rhonda asked me, "What are you going to do, Jesse?"

I shrugged. "Nothing, I guess."

Seeing him ate me up inside. Was he really in trouble? If I turned my back on my own dad, then I wasn't much better than he was. But I just couldn't tell him I was sorry. I needed to hear it from him first. *He* had started it. He chose to believe that I could have burned down his home on purpose.

So I didn't contact him, and I didn't show my face at the swap meets. My weekends were free to work a real job, the one that Linda had gotten me, delivering furniture from a store in town. I became a dedicated worker ant for them, happily getting lost in the physical labor of it—the driving, the lifting, the sweating. The money wasn't too hot, but secretly it felt kind of gratifying to be earning some legit cash for once.

I was at the store one Saturday afternoon when my boss told me that Linda herself had bought something.

"It's that big armoire in the back, kid. Can you get this one yourself, or you need some help on it?"

I eyed the armoire she had purchased. It didn't appear to be too unmanageable. "No problem. I can take this one myself. Be back in an hour."

"Don't get lost over there, kid!" my boss called after me. "I know your girlfriend lives there!"

Happily, I drove the big furniture truck to Linda and Rhonda's house. It was my house, too, now. It felt good to realize that.

I parked the truck in their driveway and unloaded the armoire from the back of the truck. Though it was big, it was a light piece, and I carried it easily to their front door, where I set it down. I had my own key, so I unlocked the front door and stepped inside.

"Jesse!" Rhonda yelped.

She was tangled up on the couch, her shirt halfway off, and there was another guy there with her.

"What . . . what are you doing here?" she asked.

My mouth hung open and I pointed dumbly to the armoire that was still in her driveway. I was too stunned to even comment on the scene I saw before me. "Your mom . . . bought something."

As I stood there, staring soundlessly, I recognized the kid on the couch with her. He was a quarterback on an opposing high school's team. John something-or-other, from Ramona High. *I guess I'm supposed to kill this kid,* I thought.

But there was no power in my arms or legs. John gave me a *so what?* look, a tough guy thing, I guess. But I didn't move an inch toward him. I wasn't feeling rage or vengeance. I just stared sadly at my girlfriend for a second, who was tucking her shirt back into her pants. Smoothing her hair.

"Jesse . . ." she started, with a pained look, but I cut her off and walked out of her house. I left the armoire standing there in the driveway.

I got back in the truck and started up the engine. For a second, I just sat there, letting the truck idle. Then, slowly, I reversed out of their driveway, and made my way back to the office. There was hardly any traffic on the street; I made every single light.

"That was quick," my boss remarked. "No lunchtime nookie, huh?"

"No," I shook my head dully, "not for me."

—

That evening, I walked over to my dad's house. I hadn't been back in almost a year. I stood outside in the street for a while, scrutinizing it carefully.

The house looked surprisingly good. It had a new paint job and a new garage had been tacked on to it. The roof was brand new, covered in red asphalt shingles. From the outside, it almost looked as if nothing was wrong at all.

I stood there in the dark for a long time, shifting from foot to foot. Once in a while, a car would drive by and its headlights would illuminate me. Then they'd be gone.

I screwed up all the courage I had and walked up to the door and rang the bell.

Footsteps came. Nina opened up the door. She surveyed me warily. "What do you want?"

I cleared my throat. "I want to talk to my dad."

She shrugged at me. "What if he don't want to talk to you?"

"Just get him," I told her.

She scowled, then disappeared. After a while, I heard the heavy footsteps that I knew to be my father's. He appeared in the doorway and loomed down at me. He wasn't smiling. But then, he didn't look mad, either. He just kind of stared at me in the face, as if curious to see me standing there, this person who happened to be his son.

"Yeah?"

"I . . ." I felt at a loss for words. "I don't have anywhere to sleep tonight."

He nodded, considering. "You want to come on in?"

"You got room for me?" I mumbled.

My dad remained silent for a second, then he spoke. "Why not?"

I stood there on the front mat, my arms folded in front of me. Neither of us looked at each other.

"Well, come on in, already," he said.

Essentially, I struck a deal with my dad. He and I rarely talked to each other, and we never discussed our fight. But I started getting up early and helping him out. As long as I pulled my weight, helping him load up that truck, he was okay with me staying there.

School was uncomfortable. I'd see Rhonda in the hallways, and now we'd just look through each other. She'd been my roommate, my love. Now we were just strangers again. She never really tried to explain herself to me, and I was grateful for that. I missed her in a huge way, and I missed her mom, too. But it felt like a chapter had ended, so I let it close.

I had to quit over at the furniture store. The place held bad associations for me, but I would have had to quit regardless. My dad needed me all day on weekends. Hello, swap meet city. Felt like I'd never left.

"What's up, Jess, how you been?" Joey called to me. "Christ, you're a *monster*!"

"Heard you been killin' 'em, Jess!" Ricky yelled. "Hey, big favor, you big fucker, move this crate of Slim Jims for me, would you? I got an interested buyer!"

Soon after I started living with my dad again, football season tapered off. I got several awards, and we made it to the third round of the playoffs before being eliminated. I was all-conference in defense, and the coaches gave me this little plaque at our banquet. We were just a great team.

But my punk sensibilities dictated that when I was off the field, I was *really* off the field. Within a week of our season's end, I was just a shithead again. It was like I'd executed this really abrupt about-face: I had been disciplined for such a long period, kind of like a teenaged warrior. Now it was time for me to let off some steam.

The first thing I needed to do, I decided, was get back at the kid from Ramona High School who Rhonda had cheated on me with: *John.*

"Whatcha gonna do, James?" asked Bobby. He rubbed his hands together evilly. I knew he was itching to spill some blood.

"None of that, man," I said, smiling. "I'm going to try a more peaceful route."

That Friday evening, Bobby and I boosted a car, and we drove around until we found the Ramona party we were looking for. There were all kinds of Beemers and Jags and XKEs outside; Ramona was a much nicer high school than ours. It was where the rich kids went. As I slipped into the living room and made anonymous, Bobby went on a reconnaissance mission to find John. He located him in the kitchen, and immediately latched on.

"Lord almighty, did we fucking *spank* you guys this year!" Bobby sighed, snagging a Coors Light breezily from the twelve-pack that John was carrying. He cracked it open and began pouring it down his fat face.

"Hey, what's the idea, pal?"

"Suck it, chump," Bobby said, staring him down. "Ain't that right, John? Didn't we crush you? Didn't you guys bow down to the sanctity of our scrotal sacks?"

"Shit," John growled. "The game was close. Next year, we'll

be right up there with you. Our offensive line has some incoming *beasts.*"

They talked pigskin, but meanwhile, in the living room, I was inching up closer to John's girlfriend, Patty, a super-hot chick who was so cute that kids from other high schools all around Riverside knew who she was. She was a stunner, all right: a dark-haired girl with eyes that said she was smarter than your average cheerleader and an ass that told you she was going to be one, anyway.

"Hi," I said to her. I nodded. "Nice party."

She grinned at me. "Who are you?"

"Oh, I'm Jesse James," I said. "I'm a good friend of your boyfriend's."

"A good friend, huh?" She smiled at me mischievously. She was sipping some light-colored booze from a plastic wineglass. "How come I never heard of you before, then?"

"Well, listen, I'll tell you a secret," I said, putting my head down close to hers. "We aren't really friends," I whispered. "It's more like, we share similar interests."

"Interests?"

"Yeah," I said. "Of course, it's highly confidential stuff."

"I want to know," she begged, laughing. "Please?"

"Well, okay, since you asked so nicely," I said, shifting my body even closer to hers. "Me and John, we're both very interested in beautiful girls. That's our *thing.*"

"Beautiful girls, huh?" said Patty, laughing. "I guess that's a good enough way to spend your time."

"The best," I said, bullshitting freely. I guess I had a little swap meet in me after all. Gently, I put my hand on the small of her back and tried to guide her over to a more private spot.

"What's going on here?" she asked, still in her bemused tone.

"I'd like to speak with you about something in private," I said. I guided her to the small bedroom where everybody had been tossing their coats.

Patty looked at me with a spark in her deep brown eyes. "I'll give you sixty seconds, Mr. James." She handed me her drink as we stepped into the room. "Hold this for me?"

"My pleasure," I said, closing the door behind us.

We necked passionately, laughing, rolling around on the bed of coats beneath us.

"Hey," said Patty, after a couple of minutes. "I better get back out there before my boyfriend misses me."

"Wait," I said. "Give me your phone number."

"Who do you think you are?" Patty asked, smiling.

I shrugged, and after a moment, Patty found a pen. Shaking her head, she proceeded to scribble out her digits on a ripped piece of paper, then handed it to me.

———

Gradually, I started stealing again. I shifted over to the Bobby school of theft, which is to say, based less on deception and more around the fact that I figured no one would fuck with a beast like me. The way I saw it, I was huge and mean-looking, so why not capitalize? Food was by far my favorite thing to pilfer. I was always hungry. I would go into supermarkets and just pick up an apple, a banana, and a cake and walk out, eating them. No one ever said boo.

One day, during lunch period, I found myself in the Circle K. It was only a couple of blocks away from school. Often I'd go there during a free period to leaf through the bike magazines or the new *Penthouse.* On this particular afternoon, I felt hungry, so without even thinking about it, I reached out and jammed a Butterfinger in my pants. I didn't even consider what I was doing. I just kept reading the magazine casually.

"Hold it right there," came a voice from behind me. "You're stealing!"

A big, bald guy grabbed my shoulder. He was wearing the orange uniform of the K, and he was glowering at me.

"What are you talking about?"

"This," he roared, and triumphantly he seized the Butterfinger out of my right front pocket. "I'm calling the *cops,* fucko."

"Hell you are," I said. "I was going to pay for that. You just didn't give me enough time."

"Come on, you're coming with me." He took my collar roughly and tugged at me.

"Dude," I said. "It's a fucking *candy bar,* man."

He only yanked harder. He tugged at my collar with as much power as he had in his big arms. "Let's go, now."

Without even thinking about it, I decked him in the face. He dropped like a load of scrap, directly to the floor, screaming in agony. "Here's your Butterfinger," I said casually, as I threw the candy bar and it bounced off his head. "See ya later."

Moronically, I thought that was it: I figured, hey, situation taken care of. Apparently, I was very wrong. Half an hour later, in my algebra class, cops came and knocked on the door. They held a quick conference with my teacher, pointed at me, and hitched up their police belts.

"Mr. James? We'd like you to come with us."

I was hauled into juvenile custody. The Circle K guy had easily figured out who I was—that was the downside of being one of the biggest kids at the school, I guess. He wanted me charged with assault, which is what happened. I got the kids' version of aggravated assault, and they threatened to send me to the California Youth Authority for a thirty-day period.

"So why don't you?" I asked, pissed.

"We know you've done well for yourself in football. We think you can help this community. So we're going to give you probation instead."

I was introduced to my probation officer then, a fairly attractive older woman who wore a gold crucifix around her neck.

"I'm Ms. Torres, Jesse," she said sternly. "I'd like you to explain to me what happened."

"Sure," I said. "A guy grabbed me. So I hit the fucker in his face."

"He grabbed you without provocation?" Torres said dubiously, glancing down at her paperwork.

"Yes," I insisted. "In fact, I'd like to request that he be charged for assault. Can we do that here?"

"The gentleman in question says that you were shoplifting from him, Jesse," she remarked.

"Sure," I said. "Stands to reason he'd say that. It shifts the blame from the real guilty party: him."

Ms. Torres folded her arms and stared at me. "Why don't I believe you, Jesse?"

"I can't control what you believe, Ms. Torres. I can only speak the truth." I nodded toward her crucifix. "We'll have to leave it to the big guy upstairs to decide, right?"

Torres frowned. "Jesus has more pressing matters to attend to, Mr. James, than your tall tales. For now," she said, "you are under my supervision. Is that understood? Keep out of trouble. No more altercations."

Whatever. I figured it was all bullshit. It was more fun being a knucklehead. Bobby and I roamed around, sizing up burger stands and electronics stores, fantasizing that we were going to knock off another one when the mood seized us.

"Wouldn't you love to get a taste of that, James?" Bobby said, leering at a Burger King shutting down for the night.

"You bet," I agreed. "A nice big score, set us straight for the rest of the year."

We had plenty of company in asshole-dom. Teenaged Riverside thieves gathered around Bobby like he was king shitpile. There was one kid who fairly idolized him. He was an auto thief who collected Clubs—as in "The Club"—just to be a massive dick about it. The crowning achievement of his life was the double closet in his bedroom that, no bullshit, contained a six-foot-high mountain of Clubs.

He was so proud of that mountain. He'd slim jim his way into a car, take a pair of bolt cutters, and snip through the steering wheel, which is just wire underneath the padding, and slide the Club off. Sure, the steering would go all wobbly after he did that, but hey, that wasn't his problem, right? He wasn't going to be driving that car for very long, anyway.

We pinched cars and cut them up. We sold them to various scumbags for next to nothing, or ripped them apart and tried to deal the parts. On weekends, I was chained to the swap meet for my dad. But on weeknights, I'd drive into L.A. and hang out at Golden Apple Comics, with my cousin Dave and his girlfriend. She had a Silver Surfer tattoo on her forearm, which was pretty hard-core for the eighties. Golden Apple was down on Melrose, and they stayed open pretty late. We'd geek out on comics for hours at a time.

After a couple of months of hanging out there, the owner of the store started looking at me all funny.

"Hey, kid. Come over here."

I looked at him suspiciously. "I haven't stolen anything, if that's what you're worried about."

"No, it's not that," he said. "Listen, I need a big kid like you to work security for me. We got an event coming up tomorrow night, and my regular guy's busy. You ever work security before?"

I shook my head. "What do I have to do?"

"You just make sure no one gets in without paying. And once they're in, you gotta see to it that no one stuffs anything in their pants. Not rocket science."

"What do you pay?"

"Fifty bucks a night, plus you get to listen to everything, front row. How's that for a deal, kid?"

I agreed for the pure hell of it. I thought it was very funny: me of all people making sure no one pilfered anything. But then I decided to take the job seriously. Golden Apple had a lot of great readings in those days. Charles Bukowski came around two different times when I was working. The second time he was there, he brought me several signed first editions of his books. I really had no idea who he was until years later. I just liked him because he was the crusty, angry type of fucker I'd gotten used to at the swaps.

The days passed, and soon I missed having a girlfriend. Before long I got it into my head that I'd like to try making Patty into Rhonda's replacement. Beyond the fact of knowing it would piss off that John kid no end, she was just really adorable. I called her up a couple of weeks after the party to see what the deal was.

"So, I was just thinking about you," I said.

"I was thinking about you, too," she confessed.

"That's great," I said. "Well . . . are we gonna get together sometime?"

"Sure," Patty said. "You can take me out to the movies this Friday, if you want."

"No way!" I said, unable to believe my luck. "I mean, yes. Yes, I want."

"Great, smooth talker," she said, laughing. "Come over around seven. You can meet my dad and my stepmom then."

So I got all excited. That Friday, I showered up and dressed to the preppy nines: Chess King shirt, flared jeans, the whole thing.

Patty lived on the other side of Riverside, in an upper-class neighborhood with big, quiet houses and sports cars in the driveways. Her front yard was well manicured. No misfit washing machines rusting in the front yard; clearly, this was not my 'hood.

I rang the doorbell and a familiar face answered. A gold crucifix glinted in my face, and to my utter dismay, I realized I was looking at Ms. Torres, my probation officer.

I watched her face turn from puzzled, to disgusted, to plain frightened, as she remembered me. Finally, she muttered, "Please, come in."

"Jesse!" Patty sang, coming down the stairs as I entered. "I see you've met my stepmom."

"Patty," Ms. Torres said drily. She folded her arms and looked at Patty pointedly. "You and I need to have a little talk in the kitchen."

That was the sum total of my first—and last—date with Patty.

Still, life went on. I got up early every Saturday morning to work the swaps. Gradually, I learned how to read customers, sell them on whatever crap my dad had found at auction: a bundle of rags, ten boxes of Tupperware, didn't matter. If we acquired it, I could sell it. Nights, I'd play tough guy at Golden Apple. A hesitant Southern California winter shuffled in for a visit. Six weeks later, it was gone.

Home was home. I didn't much want to be there. Despite the renovations, the house still smelled like the fire. It may have had a new roof and new carpets, but the walls had a faint stench of black smoke that you couldn't ever get rid of. Bad memories came flooding back every time I walked down the hall.

My dad and I spoke to each other only when we had to—by this time, I was old enough to understand that I no longer respected him. Yet there was literally no other place I could go.

Except, of course, jail. And that's where I was headed next.

4

Looking back, I'm tempted to blame it all on Bobby. Of course, I won't. Still, the appeal is there.

"We're gonna hit Rybeck's Saturday night," he confided to me. It was late afternoon, just before our senior year was going to begin. We were lounging on his roof. You could see the whole shitty neighborhood from where we were. Kings of all we surveyed. "And we need you."

I frowned. Rybeck's Cameras was the biggest photo store in Riverside. "Who's we?"

"Me and Dave," Bobby whispered, naming one of his old friends. He looked over both shoulders, hamming it up. "We're going to go in after hours and clean up, man."

"That sounds perfect," I said. "For you."

"Noooooo," Bobby said, slowly wagging a finger. "For all of us."

I shook my head. "I can't do it, Bobby. This year's going to be big for me. I'm going to have scouts at the games this year. I gotta stay focused. It's my ticket out."

"James," Bobby said, "I'm very disappointed. How could *you*, of all people, leave me alone, when I got the heist of a lifetime all primed and ready?"

"I'm not leaving you alone," I pointed out. "You have Dave."

"Dave's no fun," Bobby protested. His shoulders slumped, and he looked like a giant, sad dog. "He's all business. He'll just want to get in and get out. Thanks a *bunch*."

"I'm sorry, man," I said, laughing. "Maybe some other time."

Football just felt too critical. It overshadowed even my desire to screw around. Over the summer, I'd attended an offense/defense camp at UC Riverside. Among my coaches were Ed "Too-Tall" Jones and Lester Hayes, both former stars in the NFL. Under their guidance, I'd won most valuable defensive player of the whole camp. I was going to be captain this year. I felt ready to take on the world.

High school football was a pretty big deal in Riverside in those days. People came to the games looking for entertainment and adrenaline. We held our games at Riverside Community College, instead of at the high school, because we'd draw such a huge crowd. Local rivalries were crucial and intense. Sometimes, looking out at the thousands of screaming fans in the stands, I'd realize with satisfaction that I wasn't the only fucker out for blood.

Our biggest rival was Notre Dame. My senior year, their quarterback was a heavily recruited kid named Tony Nordbeck. He was an excellent athlete and a talented passer, but a big crybaby, too. That combination always exasperated me.

I took Nordbeck down hard in the first quarter. "Good *hit*, James!" Bobby cried.

"Thanks," I grunted, lining up again.

"Listen, I gotta talk to you," he whispered. "It's about Rybeck's! Dude, we got an *unholy* load!"

"Not now, Bobby." I waved him off.

"Sure, you're right! Let's play football!"

I flew off the line, smashed through a double team block, and took Nordbeck out at the knees before he could get rid of the leather. Ten-yard loss. Third and twenty. No chance, Notre Dame.

We punished them that game. Thrashed them into the ground, embarrassed them, made them hate the sight of a football and everything it stood for. They had thousands of their own fans at the game, and the lewd chants and rowdy discontent between the opposite sides of the stadium increased palpably as the time ticked down on the clock. By late in the third quarter, the game had long since been decided, but we were still gutting hard, going for murderous hits on every play. You could feel the drunken hate of the crowd hovering in the fall air. It was special. It was why we played.

Our cornerback, Albert Cornejo, looked up at me and grinned. "Almost too easy, huh?"

"*Way* too easy," I yelled, loud enough for the other team to hear.

"You guys think you're funny, huh?" spat one of their linemen. His uniform was messy, ripped, dirt-smeared and grass-stained.

"We are pretty funny," Cornejo agreed. He pointed up to the scoreboard, which read 45–14. "But *that* shit . . . is *hilarious.*"

A play or so later, I faked a charge at Nordbeck, then immediately cut back to cover the short pass. The ball came spinning in the air only a few feet out of my reach. I jumped as high as I could, and managed to bat it lightly with my fingertips. The football played in the air for a moment, then descended straight into my hands. I pulled the ball to my chest and took off running down the field, uncontested.

Halfway to the end zone, I realized that no one on either squad had bothered to follow me. The entire Notre Dame football team, to a man, had executed a rotten sneak attack on Albert Cornejo. They were hell-bent on bludgeoning him to death with his own helmet.

Immediately, our squad retaliated with the deranged force of teenaged fury. Our littlest man, Paulie Thompson, jumped atop Notre Dame's giant center, clawing at his face, trying to force his mouth guard down his throat.

Both benches emptied. I dropped the football and fled back to the scene of the crime, screaming gleefully. Even our band rushed on the field, swinging their tubas and drum kits like barbarians.

"Save CORNEJO!"

Bobby was buried under a pile of Notre Dame assistant coaches who flailed about, determined to smother him and send the funeral bill to his mother.

"SAVE CORNEJO!"

The stands emptied and packs of psychotic parents jumped into the melee, swinging. Cops swarmed the field, and the rabid mob instantly seized their billy clubs.

The fighting and general mayhem raged on for what seemed like forty-five minutes. Finally, backup cops arrived and the crowd was subdued. The game was called: a double forfeit. I felt it was a pretty punk rock night of football.

"My jaw feels broken," Bobby groaned, when we were back in the locker room.

"I'm kind of torn up myself," I admitted, surveying the damage the mob had exacted upon me.

"I don't even really *like* Cornejo," Bobby confessed. "I was just there for the punching."

Gingerly, I pulled my sweaty uniform off me. "So . . . what was it you wanted to talk to me about before?"

"Oh yeah, the *store*!" Bobby said, instantly cheered. "The *haul*. Man, we got so much shit, we don't even know what to *do* with it."

"That easy, huh?"

"Goddamn, man, it was child's play." Bobby spat on the floor. "You'd think they'd have realized that people know how to disable a burglar alarm these days. I mean, they truly gave us no credit at all."

"That's . . . very rude of them," I said, gently.

"Eh," said Bobby, shaking it off. "Anyway, I can't keep all of it at my place. I literally don't have the closet space. What do you say you hold some pieces for me, until I can sell them off? I'll give you half the dough I make in exchange."

I considered. "Yeah, sure. Whatever I can fit in my room, how's that?"

"Perfect." Bobby looked relieved. "Look, I owe you one, okay?"

"Save Cornejo," I answered. We looked at each other, then busted out laughing.

—

As the season wore on, I began to realize that it could actually be really cool to bring up the kids who were struggling. When we ran our sprints at the end of practice, I'd generally be among the first guys to finish, but I'd push myself to continue running until the last guys were through.

"Come on!" I'd encourage them, doing my best to channel Gil Lake, my crazy first coach. "Let's get it, guys. Let's *go!*"

We didn't have any bullies on the team. I made sure of it. And we didn't follow a big-dick hierarchy, where the grunts carried all the equipment while the seniors sat back all rested and laughing. We were a tight unit. We watched one another's backs. I came from a fairly crazy one, so maybe I'm not the best judge, but it almost felt like a family to me.

"Dude, Jesse," moaned Mike, my backup on offense, "aren't you *ever* gonna let me get in, man? I haven't played a dang play the whole season."

"Mike, I'm sorry, man," I said. "I swear, I'm gonna take a quarter off one of these days. That sound good?"

"Sure," he said. His big freckled face looked glum, resigned to benchwarming. "Coach wouldn't let you come out of the game even if you begged him to."

"Hey," I said seriously. "We'll get you in a game before the season's over. I promise."

Mike looked at me. "Yeah, okay," he said, finally.

It seemed like my life was finally leveling out. Scouts had been coming to my games all season. Bit by bit, I'd begun to receive recruitment letters from a handful of Division One schools. In my dresser at home, all stacked up on top of one another, I had envelopes from Pitt, Hawaii, Iowa, and Colorado. At night, I'd take them out and read them over and over again. A hazy vision of the future was beginning to build in my mind, and it felt promising.

I was feeling so good, I guess I let my guard down. And that's when they got me.

I was reading a comic book in my bedroom one evening, dreaming about college cheerleaders and spacious, comfy dorms, when Nina came knocking at my door. Two uniformed Long Beach police officers stood behind her. "These men need to talk to you, Jesse," she said, with a smug tone in her voice.

"We just need a moment of your time, son," one of them said. Both of them walked into my room. Their eyes scanned every surface.

"Hey," I objected. "You don't have permission to come into my room. Where's your warrant?"

"We do have permission," he said, pointing to Nina. "You're still a minor. Aren't you, son?"

"Your dad said you were probably up to no good," said Nina. "He said he figured these gentlemen had plenty of reasons to see you."

The policeman smiled pleasantly. "Mind if we take a look around?" He didn't wait for an answer.

My room was tiny. It took them less than two minutes to discover the pile of Canon cameras and lenses that Bobby had unloaded on me.

"Funny," the first cop said, looking at the expensive equipment. "That's precisely what he said we'd find here."

"Who, my dad?" I fumed.

"No," the cop said. He checked a notebook. "I'm referring to . . . Robert Murphy."

"Bobby?"

"You're acquainted with Mr. Murphy, son, are you not?"

I shrugged. "Yeah, he's my friend. So what?"

The cop patted his notebook in a businesslike manner. "We found stolen goods at Mr. Murphy's house this afternoon, goods that appeared to match those taken from the burglary at Rybeck's Cameras on September sixteenth of this year."

It was a small town. It figured that even these idiots had been able to put two and two together. "Yeah, and?"

"Mr. Murphy has stated on record that he received these stolen goods from you." He smiled again, then shoved the knife in deeper. "He informed us that if we came to your house, we'd find the real stash. According to him, he was simply holding the cameras until you had time to sell them."

With his own ass on the line, Bobby had sold me down the river. For a minute, I didn't say anything. I shook my head, sadly.

"Yeah," I said dully, after a minute. "You got me. I did the break-in."

The cops looked at each other and shared a victorious grin. "We're going to need you to come with us, son."

"He's in trouble?" Nina asked.

"Oh yes, ma'am," the cop said, smiling. "This young man is in quite a *lot* of trouble."

———

I had an extensive record and a probation officer. I'd already used up all my chances. Now they were ready to do me in.

"Do you realize the severity of your crime, Jesse?" Ms. Torres asked. I suppose she felt kind of vindicated—I'd been proven to be a real-life criminal, after all.

"Yep," I said curtly.

"You can't just go around burglarizing places. Do you understand that?"

"Are you done yet?"

"You have absolutely no remorse, do you?" she snapped at me. "Well, listen to me, you better change that attitude before you see the judge. You are going to serve time for this, Jesse. Do you realize that?"

What she said scared me. But I was so furious, her words barely cut through. My father, Bobby, the cops: none of them gave a damn about me. Just like it had been for my entire life, the people closest to me had fucked me over the hardest. So the state wanted to send me to jail, huh? Well, then *great*. Maybe that was the best place for me.

At my hearing, several of my coaches showed up and spoke on my behalf. They said I was a good leader and a credit to our town. They pled with the judge to give me another chance, or, barring that, to reduce my sentence.

He frowned. "How much of the football season do you have left, gentlemen?"

"Two more weeks."

The judge looked me over sternly. "Given the gravity of your crime, Mr. James, and your past criminal record, I'm inclined not to hear any pleas on your behalf. But these men seem to believe in you."

I looked up at the judge, who held my future in his hands.

"I will reluctantly agree to suspend your sentence, Mr. James, until you have completed the final football game of this season. Immediately after, you will enter the California Youth Authority, where you will serve ninety days of rehabilitative therapy." He banged his gavel. "That is all."

I exhaled, relieved. I'd have a chance to finish out the season. But I'd miss the following three months of classes. If I wanted to graduate, I'd have to go to summer school for sure. Awesome. I was well on my way to being a loser.

"Hey, man, let me explain," Bobby said, when I saw him at practice the next day.

"No," I said coldly.

"Aw, James, you don't get it, man. If Dave got nabbed for this, he'd do real time. You're just going to juvie, man."

"Beat it," I snapped. "I don't want to talk to you."

He nodded. "I wouldn't talk to me either, James. I get it, man," he said. "I really do." And Bobby loped away.

I walked around for my last two weeks of freedom in a depressed stupor. The football field was my only refuge. More recruitment letters arrived at my house each day. Clemson, Michigan State, Wisconsin: everybody was talking scholarship. They all wanted to come down and meet my parents "when the time was right." I laughed drily, picturing Nina serving up a martini to a Big Ten coach, my dad trying to sell him a case of reclaimed tuna, found at auction.

Our last game was against Norte Vista. I played with a fury that surprised even me. I knew a few of the kids on the team personally, and I decided to go for each of them, one by one. I ignored the quarterback and the direction of the play, focusing instead on taking each opponent out at the knees for one last time, simply because it felt so good to smash them down to the ground.

We were down by three in the last quarter, and it looked like I might just lose the last game of my high school career. With three minutes remaining, we made our final drive down field. We drove the ball inside the twenty, and our quarterback grimaced in the huddle, trying to decide what the hell to do.

"What do you think, Jesse?" he finally said. He looked shaken.

I shrugged. "Let's run it," I said. "Come on, guys! This is it. Our last time. Let's make it count."

We ran a play for Bryson Young, our speedy halfback. The

quarterback shoved it into Bryson's chest, and he slipped around the end. Norte Vista's defensive back came rushing in to grab him, but I leveled him with a block that put both of us on our asses.

Bryson made it to the three. We were just a play away from a touchdown.

"*Aargh!*" I yelled. "I pulled something!"

I lay on the ground, grimacing in pain.

"I must have pulled a muscle in my groin, man," I told the offensive coach who ran onto the field. "You gotta get me out of here. I can't freaking move."

I limped off the field, my arm around my coach's shoulders.

"Mike!" Coach barked, when we reached the sideline. "Get in the fucking game!"

Mike's eyes were wide. He stared at me, unwilling to believe his eyes. "Jesse," he sputtered. "What happened?"

"*Mike!*" our coach screamed. "What are you waiting for, an engraved fucking invitation?"

"Pull on your helmet, Mike," I advised. I pointed to the field. "They need you out there."

With an expression of pure dread on his face, Mike jammed his helmet over his mop of red hair.

"Go on, Mike," I urged. "You can do it."

He gulped big. "All right, I guess I got no choice, now." Eyes blinking rapidly, he sped out to the line as fast as his fat haunches would carry him.

"How's that groin, James?" my coach asked.

"Ooh, yeah," I said, rubbing it. "Hurts bad."

I had never before witnessed a play of high school football from the bench. It was a strange vantage point. I stood next to my teammates on the sidelines, cheering loudly as the two teams lined up for the final play of the game.

The whistle blew. Our center fired the ball through his legs to the quarterback, who in turn deked, then handed off to Bryson Young.

I watched, flabbergasted, as none other than Mike threw a perfect block for him. Bryson clambered over Mike's broad back into the end zone and scored the winning touchdown.

Our bench cleared. We ran to mob the players. Mike was standing up, waving his arms excitedly.

"Fuck, man!" he yelled. "I did it!"

The look on his face was indescribable. I'd never seen anyone in my life that stoked or that amazed at what was going on. Then I happened to look into the stands. A huge man with a mop of red hair and a hefty frame was doing a wild dance of joy.

"Hey, Mike, is that your *dad*?"

He grinned. "Aw, yeah. That's him." He waved up to the stands. After a second, his crazed dad whooped it back.

"MIKEY! Way to DO IT, SON!"

It kind of gave me the shivers. I was real happy for the fucker. Yeah, sure I was.

———

The California Youth Authority was your standard concrete hellhole of a government facility. Razor-sharp barbed wire encircled the top of the aluminum fence that surrounded the unit, discouraging even the fantasy of making a run for it. Hostile guards and wary administrators patrolled the halls, looking dour and threatening. I was fingerprinted at intake, made to fill out a thick sheaf of forms, then issued a bunk in a giant room with seventeen other kids. I received two undershirts, four pairs of underwear, a tan uniform with a shirt that buttoned down the front, tan pants, and a tan jacket—a typical junior-jail outfit. I got the shoes, too, junior-jail slippers. We lacked many full-length mirrors in the facility, but if I'd been able to check out my reflection, I would have seen that I approximated the genuine article.

I was directed to a little dented locker, where I would be allowed to store any personal items I might accumulate. Then I received a half-sized green toothbrush, a travel tube of toothpaste, and a plastic yellow soap dish.

"Don't lose 'em," a sullen attendant warned me. "Replacements will not be furnished."

The California Youth Authority was a transitional zone. It was more serious than juvie and the sentences were generally longer, but it was still for minors, and that meant it was way less dangerous than real jail. If you fucked up after you got done here, however, then you were probably headed to the next level, meaning grown-up prison. There, you wouldn't be met with the same kind of mercy. Boneheads and punks roamed the hallways and the cafeteria of CYA, thinking they were tough, but I saw through that illusion pretty swiftly. The grand majority were just a bunch of confused stoners, trying not to get their heads lumped by the guards.

It was a depressing place, to be sure. The name of the game was rehabilitation, but it felt a lot more like "time-out." We'd all done something stupid; now an annoyed parent-type was going to make us see we'd been wrong. My probation officer and the judge had promised that the CYA was the place where I'd get my head screwed on straight, but I couldn't help but wonder, *by what?* All I saw around me were teenagers walking around like doped-up zombies in their prison-issued pajamas, getting yelled at every time they spoke louder than a whisper.

We had few outlets there. Sports, however, was one of them. By law they were required to exercise us, so we played touch football in the yard. No tackling allowed, which was probably for the best. Lining up, I couldn't help but laugh: I'd played on the best teams in Southern California for years. Now I found myself next to Stinky, the bad-check forger, and Danny, the blue-light bandit. It was kind of awesome.

"Go long, dirtbags," I called to them, inserting myself into the game as quarterback. I tossed the ball in a wobbly spiral toward Johnny Pinece, a tiny black-haired boy who'd been cordially invited to the CYA for trying to sell homemade amphetamine. His ill-considered brew, handcrafted in the privacy of his own bathtub, was remarkable for the simple fact that it contained only two ingredients: Sudafed and old bleach water.

The ball hit Johnny's spidery hands and bounced off like a brick.

"I was *that close*," Johnny swore as we lined up again.

"You were right with it," I said. "You absolutely were."

Kiddie jail wasn't all bad. At least I had the ball in my hand, reminding me of what I'd be doing when I got out of here. Two of my football coaches, Frank Stoudemire and Bill Pfieffer, had off-season positions in the Youth Authority as administrators, and although they never said as much, I could tell it kind of tickled them to see me playing touch ball with this gang of miscreants.

One fellow, however, didn't find the sight of me amusing in the slightest. His name was Troy Zuccolotto, and he worked at the CYA as a guard. Troy was an erect, veiny man, with gigantic muscles and skin as orange and leathery as a catcher's mitt. "Zuke" was a member in good standing of the International Federation of Body Builders; not only that, but he'd been crowned Mr. California or something, too, several years before. A fact his frosted hair would allude to.

We had only one weight machine in the CYA, a square, rudimentary Universal bench press with stack plates. We all fought among ourselves for the privilege of using it, but Troy used the petty power and candy-ass authority granted to him as a prison guard to skip the line and claim the machine as his own.

"What do you want it on, Zuke?" asked one of his little sycophants, readying to move the weight pin for the master.

"Whole stack," Troy said, grinning proudly. "This is Zuccolotto we're talking about."

I despised him—his ego and his strut. Even worse, he was a bully. Our football games were touch, but when Troy would participate, they magically became physical tests of endurance. He was brutal, crushing kids seven years his junior and a hundred pounds lighter.

Troy insisted on playing running back. Every play went through him. Stoner after stoner would come at the guard, and he would stiff-arm them in the face, or simply mow them over with the brute force of his testosterone-fueled rage.

"Chill out, dude," I finally told him, one day when we found ourselves on opposing squads.

"Yeah? Who the fuck do you think *you* are?" he spat. "Are you tough, is that it?"

"They're about ten times littler than you," I said quietly, "so why don't you just take it down a notch?"

Troy's huge jaw tensed and clenched. I could see the cords of his neck pumping a quick slug of extra blood to his reptilian brain. "Tell me again what to do, fucko."

I shrugged my shoulders.

"Ball," Troy ordered.

His hapless quarterback handed it to him.

Troy came running straight at me. Steam was coming out of his nostrils. I held my breath as the huge, tanned wildebeest swung the full weight of his perfectly sculpted deltoids and trapezius into my teenaged body.

I had no helmet on, of course. The only thing I could do was square up. I dipped my shoulders down, got low to him, and at the last possible moment, I extended straight into him, with my shoulder on his chin. The force of the impact lifted Troy Zuccolotto into the air and put him on his back. *GUUHH!*

Total silence fell over the yard for a good fifteen seconds, as Troy lay on the ground.

Finally, Johnny Pinece whispered, "Fuck."

All the stoner kids were stunned. No one had ever touched Troy, because he was a guard, and he was a bully, and he was huge.

Troy came to his feet slowly. He dusted himself off, and cradling the ball in his hands, he approached me. I was kind of laughing. I couldn't help it.

"You think that's funny, you punk asshole?"

I shrugged. "I don't know. Maybe."

From four feet away, he winged the football at my face. From the crunch it made as it bounced off my nose, I knew that he'd broken it. As I bent to staunch the flow of blood, he walked slowly toward me.

"Still funny, right?" Troy hissed. *"Still funny?"*

I reached out and grabbed a hank of his precious blond hair and wrenched it downward, so that his head bent toward me. His huge neck strained like a bull, reddened and possibly about to burst. Amid his confusion, I smashed the side of my elbow into his temple. He looked at me, dazed. A river of crimson blood dripped down the front of my tan uniform, soaking and ruining it.

The guards separated us. I got put in an isolation cell for a month, for striking a guard. No surprise. By now, I knew the drill.

———

There is nothing to do in the isolation tank: absolutely nothing. Still, I thought it would be more of a party than it was. No roomies to bother you, and sleeping in every day—cool, huh? But I did all my sleeping on the first two or three days. After that, my body just wouldn't sleep anymore. It was too rested. I just had the walls to stare at, and my hard iron bunk to lie on.

My immediate surroundings offered little in the way of distraction. My cell was tiny and cramped, its only outstanding feature a stainless-steel toilet with no lid.

So I would do Nothing. All day long. These days they would call it meditation, but for me, it was just survival. I had been hurt so badly for my entire life, and repeatedly so. But in isolation, I found a center of me that had never been touched. I don't know how to describe it: all I was doing was sitting and being silent. But somehow, I found a way to go inside myself.

And to my surprise, I found a calmness there, the peace that comes with inspecting yourself and knowing that although you might not be perfect, you've sort of done the best you could. Defying all reasonable expectations, I actually still kind of liked and respected myself.

Every other day, I would receive a break from my Zen-like routine of doing Nothing, and thinking of absolutely Nothing, when I'd get handcuffed and escorted sixty feet down the hall to take a shower. The guard who took me to my beauty appointment would never speak to me. He wouldn't even look at me.

"Doing good today?" I'd ask.

He'd respond with Nothing.

"Me? I'm terrific. Thanks for asking."

The shower for those on isolation was tiny. The tile was scummy and the water never got warm. Five minutes in there was your max. Then the guard would bang hard on the door and you had to dry yourself off fast.

"That was *fantastic*," I'd say, on the way back to my cell, my hands in cuffs, my face tingling from the cold water. "I feel utterly refreshed, thanks." Zero response.

The key to not going completely batshit crazy, I quickly learned, was to keep moving. If I stopped moving, time stopped moving with me. So I stretched. I did push-ups and sit-ups. I stood on my head in my little square cell. I tried to jump straight up and land flat on both feet with my knees bent. It was a kind of Yoga for Delinquents, and I practiced it like a freakish devotee.

But after a week alone, I started to lose my focus. There were no books in isolation for me to Malcolm X myself into a genius. This was the eighties, and all the California Youth Authority could spare was a couple of *Highlights* magazines.

Eventually, without my permission, my calm evaporated, and my mind began to show me pictures of my past. It spun rapidly, a laser-light show of all the things I'd rather be doing than sitting in a dank padded room wearing prison jammies. I dreamed of punk shows, crowd-surfing, and killing the world. I dreamed of Rhonda. I dreamed of my mother. I dreamed of touchdown after touchdown in front of screaming fans. I dreamed of lightning-quick motorcycles and stolen IROC-Zs with wobbling steering wheels and my friend grinning next to me. I dreamed of long stupid letters from an apologetic Bobby and swap meets with Johnny and Quick Rick laughing in their leather coats and day after day I was locked inside this fucker and please won't you let me out I mean *what exactly did I do?*

"Jesse," came a knock. "Hey. I'm coming in."

It was Coach Pfieffer. He had something behind his back.

"How you doing in here, kid?"

I shook my head, feeling a little dazed. "I don't know," I admitted. "It's pretty . . . weird."

He laughed shortly. "I figured as much. Here." He extended his compact little hand. "Brought you something."

It was a McDonald's Happy Meal.

"Jesus," I breathed gratefully.

"All yours," Pfieffer said. "I figured the food had to be killing you in here."

"It's awful," I said.

"Yeah," said Pfieffer. "I know. Eat up."

I wolfed down the hamburger and French fries, then ate the apple pie in two bites. I swear, it was the best-tasting food I'd ever had in my entire goddamn life.

"Thanks," I said, embarrassed, as I realized my coach had watched me tear into the food like a starving coyote.

"No problem," he said. "Hey, give me that box. Can't have people saying I give one of the football kids special treatment, you know."

I crumpled up the greasy paper, placed it carefully inside the box, and handed it to my coach. He accepted it and turned around to go, but stopped before his hand turned the knob.

"Listen," he said. "I've got something I need to tell you." He looked grim.

"What?" I said.

"Jesse, you made Parade."

"*Really?*" I felt myself break out into a real smile for the first time in over a month. "Coach, are you serious?"

"You're an All-American, Jess. It came out a couple of weeks ago. I just thought you'd like to know."

"Wow," I said. But there was something more. I could tell by the way he was staring at me. "That's great. Why are you looking so down?"

"They came, Jesse. They came and went."

"Who did?"

"The coaches," Pfieffer said slowly.

My lips tightened.

"When the season was over, they all were calling. We had requests from all over to see you. Stoudemire had OSU in his office. Kansas and Nebraska sent their people, too."

"What happened," I mumbled, already guessing the story.

"We had to tell them the truth, Jesse. There was no way around it." He shook his head. "I'm real sorry, son. I know you would have done a great job at any of those schools."

"They don't want me anymore?" I asked, unwilling to believe my own ears. "Just because I'm in here?"

Pfieffer looked pained. "They withdrew their scholarship offers."

I was stunned into silence.

He rotated the fast-food box in his hands, carefully. "We'll figure out something for you. Meanwhile, I want you to do the rest of your time like a man." He looked at me hard. "Do you hear me? No more fights. No more hardheaded shit."

I swallowed hard over the lump in my throat. "Sure thing, Coach. Thanks for the Happy Meal."

For the remainder of my time in isolation, I went over Pfieffer's words in my head a hundred times. Slowly it sunk in: I wasn't going to be playing big-time football, after all. I wasn't going to escape to another part of the country, to an Iowa cornfield or a rainy Pittsburgh steelyard, or any of that. It all had been just a fake little dream. I shook my head. I should have known better.

A six-week tail remained on my sentence after I got out of the tank, and there was little choice but to serve it. For the remainder of my time at the California Youth Authority, I composed myself to be a model inmate. I spoke rarely, and when I did, I didn't cause any trouble. When Zuccolotto made his rounds, I didn't give him any eye contact.

"James," Johnny Pinece whispered. "I hear Zuke wants another shot at you."

I shook my head. Just wasn't going to happen.

Christmas came when I was in there. I remember lying in my bed during the day, feeling lonely and tired. A religious group came and handed out oversized candy bars. I chewed mine slowly, ruminating. Savoring every little piece of nougat.

I asked for more responsibility. I was given a job: floor polisher. Twice a day, I'd wheel the big silver machine into the middle of the mess hall by its plastic handlebars. Unwinding the long, blue electrical cord from around its base, I'd find an outlet in the wall. The plug was big and black and had dirt and gunk smeared onto its casing, the collected detritus of ten years of hard cleaning. But I'd jam it into the outlet enthusiastically, and then flip the switch, kick-starting the whirling machine to life.

I pushed the floor polisher for two hours every day, watching the bristles speeding in a ring-shaped orbit, until they blurred with their own purposeful velocity. Patiently, I worked every inch of grime off the cafeteria floor. I worked the machine for six weeks, every day, twice a day, until it felt like it was mine.

UNIVERSITY OF SOUTHERN CALIFORNIA
DEPARTMENT OF INTERCOLLEGIATE ATHLETICS · LOS ANGELES, CALIFORNIA 90089-0602   TELEPHONE: (213) 743-2751

FOOTBALL

May 5, 1986

Jesse James
c/o Head Football Coach
La Sierra HS
4145 La Sierra Avenue
Riverside, CA   92505

Dear Jesse:

You have been recommended to the University of
Southern California as an outstanding student athlete.
Congratulations on this accomplishment! I hope you will
consider becoming a Trojan. USC has a rich heritage of
excellence and we are recognized as a prominent leader in
both academic and athletic achievement.

I am enclosing a football questionnaire which I would
like you to complete and return to me as soon as possible.
This information will enable me to become more familiar
with you and your desire to become a USC Trojan. Also, you
should contact your school counselor and sign up for the
next available Scholastic Aptitude Test (SAT) or American
College Test (ACT). Please be sure to identify the
University of Southern California as one of the colleges
which should receive the test scores. These test scores
are required for the application process.

Thanks for taking time to fill out the questionnaire.
I am looking forward to hearing from you and learning more
about your interest in becoming a USC Trojan. I wish you
continued success in the future.

Sincerely,

Ted Tollner

Ted Tollner
Head Football Coach

Enclosure

5

When I finally got out of the California Youth Authority, I'd missed eighty-three days of class.

"Would you like to graduate, Mr. James?" my guidance counselor asked me wearily.

"You know what?" I said. "I would."

So it was off to summer school for me. They had some pretty cool classes in summer school in those days, gotta say. My favorite was High School Cafeteria. They tossed me an apron, jammed a white paper cap on my head, and taught me how to be a short-order cook. Not bad, not bad at all. A couple weeks in, I could flip a mean hamburger. Just add ketchup.

At nights, I was back at Golden Apple, either leafing through comics or working an event. One evening my boss motioned me to his side.

"You interested in more work, kid?"

"Always."

"A buddy of mine needs a security guy to work a volleyball tournament. He needs someone to supervise setup and breakdown—is it okay if I give him your number?"

"Absolutely," I answered.

"Lucky kid," he said, shaking his head. "Chicks on the beach. Man, I wish I was you!"

The tournament was put on by the AVP, the Association of Volleyball Professionals, but they were sponsored by Miller Lite, so there were all kinds of bikini girls there. One young woman in particular caught my eye. Her dark, bobbed hair and tight little body stood out against her red swimsuit.

"Need help with anything?" I asked her, hoping for a crumb of affection.

She just sort of looked me up and down.

"No," she said kindly, after a moment. "Thank you."

I shrugged, moved on. I don't know, maybe she smelled teenaged convict on me. Little did I suspect that *adding* to my bad-boy image would catch her eye later. Midway through the summer, I amassed enough cash to get myself a used motorcycle, a broken-down, turquoise 1976 Harley-Davidson. I know, turquoise Harley: sounds pretty wretched. But this was the eighties. It was my Duran Duran bike.

I loved that cycle dearly. It seemed so incredibly fast to me. And the sound! When I started her up, the straight pipes were like two cannons going off. *BAHPAHBAPABAH!!* I felt like I was going to bust windshields. It was pure bliss.

The following weekend, I had another volleyball tournament, and of course I rode my cycle all the way to Manhattan Beach. As it happened, the bikini model I had a crush on saw me getting off it.

"What's *this*?" she said, smiling.

"Just my Harley," I said casually. "It needs some work."

"Oh, wow, I love bikes!" she exclaimed, caressing the handlebars. "Do you think you might take me for a ride sometime?"

"Yeah, of course," I said, grinning, unable to believe my luck. "Anytime you want."

"Well, how about . . . tonight?" she said coyly. Her hand drifted from the bike to my forearm, as if it were an extension of the machine.

Nothing much ever came of us; I think she figured out pretty soon that I was fresh out of high school, and that kind of killed it. But damn, the motorcycle had sure opened the door for me. Of that, I took careful notice.

At the end of the summer, I received a battered cardboard package in the mail. I sat down on my front steps and ripped it open with my hands. It was my diploma. *Well, how about that?* I thought, laughing. They'd pushed me down, but they hadn't beaten me yet. Life could have been a lot worse.

After all, I could have been Bobby. He called me one night, out of his mind with worry.

"What should I do, man?" he asked, tense. "My girl . . . she's pregnant."

I shrugged. Bobby and I had never really been the same after the CYA. He'd apologized, of course, and I'd accepted it, but I was still pretty touchy about serving his sentence for him.

"That's up to you," I said finally. "I can't help you make that decision."

He sighed. "I have the strangest feeling that I'm about to do the honorable thing."

He did. At the age of eighteen, Bobby married his girlfriend. They found a place to live and set out to raise their child together. You had to respect him. He'd stepped up.

And me? Well, I was headed to community college. The Division One schools might have withdrawn their scholarship offers, but that sure as hell didn't mean I was never getting on a football field again.

"Jesse," Coach Pfieffer said, "you do a strong couple of seasons on one of these teams, and we'll have Kansas banging on the door again, I promise. And this time when they come, you'll be ready."

I nodded, not fully convinced. "I'll do my best."

Luckily for me, a strong junior college was right around the corner: Riverside Community College. Like all junior colleges, they were a bit more forgiving when it came to tolerating players' various idiosyncrasies, like having committed multiple burglaries. They needed a linebacker, and with Coach Pfieffer's help, a scholarship had been set aside with my name on it.

"I made my decision," I told my dad one afternoon, as he was restoring an oak dining set for the coming weekend's swap meet. "I'm heading to RCC."

My dad didn't look up from his lacquering. His small brush moved steadily and with confidence. "That's good."

I watched him work for a while, my hands stuffed into my pants pockets.

"So, I guess I won't be seeing you for a while."

Patiently, my father continued to apply lacquer to the chair's thin, ornate spindles.

"Any thoughts?" I asked impatiently.

"You got a place to live?" he said, finally.

"I'll be in the dorms."

"We can't afford that."

"You don't have to pay a dime," I said. "I'm on scholarship."

"Oh. Okay." My dad glanced up at me briefly, his paintbrush held between his index finger and thumb. He appeared lost in thought. "Well, stop by when you can."

"Right," I said. After a long silence, I added, "Thanks."

—

On our first day of football practice, our new team assembled in a small locker room, unconsciously segregating ourselves according to ethnicity. The black kids, most of whom came from Compton

High and South Central L.A., sat sullenly on one side of the room, staring down the beefy, working-class white knuckleheads who'd gathered together on the other side. In between us sat the Mexicans, the Samoans, and the Tongans in one big group. Instead of a football team, we looked like three gangs getting ready to rumble.

The assistant coach squinted at his clipboard, his chewed-up yellow pencil poised over the roster.

"Jackson, Anton?"

A thin, muscular black kid raised his hand. He wore cornrows and baggy jeans. His eyes emanated a quiet hate. I recognized him immediately from the California Youth Authority. He hadn't been a friend, exactly.

"James, Jesse?"

I raised my hand. "Right here."

Anton Jackson sneered. "I know you, motherfucker," he said softly, looking right at me.

I didn't smile.

Our team could not have differed more strikingly from my high school squad. Riverside Community College specialized in tough kids from rough neighborhoods, standout athletes with messed-up families and severe attitude problems whose extensive juvenile criminal records and inability to function inside a classroom had conspired to keep us out of real colleges and universities. We were hoods, every one of us. And we were none too happy to join forces.

"You thought you were the *baddest* dude at the Youth Authority, huh?" Jackson said, his voice low and soft.

"Was I wrong?" I said, disliking him more every second.

He nodded. "Real wrong."

A sick feeling filled my stomach as I studied my teammates. But my mood darkened further that evening, when I discovered that I had been assigned to live in the "football dorm."

"*BREWWWWW!*" Peter Ososoppo bellowed. The curly-haired,

three-hundred-pound Samoan was the cornerstone of our offensive line. "BREWWWW!"

"Line up, bitches," cried Kevin Ososoppo, Peter's fraternal twin. "Get your mouth open, it's chuggin' time!"

"Yo, Jesse, what the fuck!" Peter yelled happily. "Get *in* here, man. It's Miller time!"

"Hi," I said politely. "Look, I think I might try to get some sleep. Up early, you know?"

"Sleep? In *this* place?" Kevin shouted. "Good LUCK!"

As if to further convince me of the futility of ever closing my eyes again, Kevin wrenched the volume knob of his stereo violently forward. Def Leppard's *Hysteria* exploded forth at top decibel.

"Pour . . . some . . . sugar *on meeeee*!" the giant lineman sang.

"In the name of *love*!" added Peter. The twins shared a long, silent moment of fraternity, followed by a sweaty embrace.

"Love you, big dog," Kevin sniffed.

"Love you, too, baby bro."

I winced. *Fuck. This.*

I hefted my book bag over my shoulder and scuttled down the hallway, toward any kinder fate. For example, swallowing a box of razor blades.

Outside, away from the chaos, I felt more sane. I tried to assess the situation with some calm: this was college, or close enough, so the library might be a relatively okay place to be. There would be books there, and comfortable chairs to lounge in. I hadn't started my classes yet, but being in an environment where the smart kids hung out might make me feel like I hadn't deliberately stationed myself in a sea of degenerates for the remainder of my education.

I hoofed it to the library and made my way to the bottom floor, where I collapsed in an uninhabited corner. Feeling the strong need to rinse the last vestiges of Def Leppard from my eardrums, I pulled my Walkman out of my backpack and popped in one of my favorite albums, Slayer's *Hell Awaits*. Pulling the plastic headphones over my ears, I settled back happily in my chair, where I closed my eyes and let the music flow over me.

My peace was short-lived.

"Motherfucker, *hey*!" A brisk knocking on my desk interrupted the music. A huge black dude with a shaved head and a gold front tooth swayed over me. "Turn off that shit."

I slipped the headphones off my head, angrily. "Why should I?"

"Because this is a *library*," he said. "You have the volume up so high, I can hear every last goddamn drum solo."

"Oh," I said. "I didn't realize you could hear it."

"You should have, with those cheap-ass headphones," the giant said, laughing. I realized this guy was a football player, too—I'd seen him at the meeting, but we'd never talked. "You got those for free, huh? Found 'em in the trash?"

"I bought them." I scowled.

"Well, you overpaid, tell you that much," he said and laughed cheerfully. "Man, that's not even Slayer's best album. All that Satan shit? Corny as a *motherfucker*!"

I inspected him more closely. "What do you know about Slayer?"

"Oh, because I'm *black*, I can't know metal?" His thick eyebrows knitted together, and suddenly, he looked annoyed. "Are you for real, man? Are you actually *saying* this shit to me?"

"Calm down," I told him. "I just didn't expect it. That's all."

"I guess we're all just some Run D.M.C. fans to you, huh?" His gargantuan head bobbed in front of my face, eliminating all other fields of vision. "Man, I *know* Tom Araya. I *feel* his pain."

"Shut up already," I said. "You just caught me by surprise." I looked him over. "You play football, right?"

"Yes. And so do you, I believe." He grinned and extended his hand for me to shake. "My name's Josh Paxton."

"I'm Jesse James," I said, taking his massive paw in my hand.

"Like the outlaw?"

"Just like," I said.

Josh made a finger gun and shot me with it. "Well, it's a pleasure to meet you, you weakass-headphone-wearing punk."

"Pleasure's all mine," I said.

We became instant friends. Josh was smart, funny as hell, and best of all, he seemed to hate everyone on the football team even more than I did.

"Every motherfucker's out for himself," he complained.

"I hate it," I agreed.

"These chumps all think they'll be suiting up in the Big Ten two years from now," Josh said. He looked at me. "What do you think?"

I said nothing for a moment. "I'm here to play football the way it's supposed to be played."

"Course you are," Josh said, laughing. "You wouldn't leave even if they begged you, would you, Outlaw Jesse?"

"Well, I didn't say that," I admitted. "If a scout comes up to me and wants to talk, then we'll talk."

But the scouts were precisely the problem. There was always a murmur going around our locker room: *Scouts are coming to the next game! Scouts'll be at practice on Thursday!* Talent snoops for big colleges became these mythical figures who could deliver us from our drab lives.

Discontent isn't necessarily a bad thing when it comes to football. A talented coach would have harnessed our resentment at being outsiders, hitched it to our physical brutality, and made us into a fearsome squadron. But our head coach was trying to get out, too. He'd had offers at UNLV and UTEP, and by God, he was going to sniff them out. Everyone wanted to get out of Riverside and the bush leagues once and for all. That's the universal dream of junior college, after all: to *leave* junior college.

And I was as guilty of entertaining those fantasies as the rest of them. Each morning I got up thinking I *should* be at Pitt, or Hawaii, or Iowa, or U of Colorado—any of those teams that recruited me. I was a talented athlete and a leader, but due to my own idiotic lack of foresight, I had ended up going to junior college in the same damn town where I'd gone to high school. We even played our games on the same *field* I'd played on in high school. I felt like I was on the hamster wheel, running faster now, but in the exact same spot.

It felt even more like that when I found out that Rhonda had enrolled as a student at Riverside Community. She and I ran into each other several times, shared several awkward glances, until one day, she finally approached me.

"Jesse," she said, "I just want to let you know how sorry I am about the way things turned out."

"Doesn't matter," I mumbled. "I'm over it."

She looked down. "No, I'm serious. I really . . . I really loved you." Rhonda touched my arm. "I've never felt the same about anyone."

I fell for it, of course. Soon, we were dating again. On Sunday nights, I'd drive us downtown, to get a pizza and a couple of Cokes. But I was ridiculously poor.

"Hey," I said, "I hate to ask, but . . ."

"It's no problem," said Rhonda, smiling, taking out her pocketbook. "You can get us next time, okay?"

I felt embarrassed, but the constant practices and classes kept me so busy that I didn't have any time to work a job. Stealing was kind of out of the equation nowadays, so pocket cash became hard to come by. I had a beat-up car, but I lacked the money to drive it very often. More than once, I found myself scrounging around in the backseat, digging for seventy-five cents so I could put enough gas in my car to go home.

All the players seemed to be poor. The locker room was falling apart. Only two out of the four showers worked. Our quarterback's shoes were covered in duct tape. One day, after a particularly grueling practice, I dragged myself up the steps to the parking lot, only to find one of my teammates breaking into my car.

"What the *fuck* are you doing?" I said, stunned.

He looked up at me sheepishly. "Oh, is this your car, Jesse?"

"Yes, *asshole*." Immediately, my jaw clenched.

Sensing impending harm, he extricated himself with a quickness. "Look, guy, I'm leaving, okay?"

"See ya!" I said, fake-smiling.

The whole thing made me tired. Being broke and without allies could wear the strongest guy down. One evening, after another interminable practice, I pumped the last three dimes I had in the world into the candy machine in our dorm. I was tired as hell. My stomach was growling. All I wanted was a candy bar. I was going to eat it in two bites and collapse into bed.

My money in the machine, I stood in front of the window, sizing up the selection carefully. My eyes fell on a Whatchamacallit, and suddenly, I grinned. Whatchamacallits reminded me of being a kid: when I was nine or ten, my dad had gone to one of his auctions and returned home with a truckload of them.

"What's *that*?" I asked, my young eyes bugging out.

"Fuckin' candy bars," he said.

"Who . . . who are they for?" I asked, breathless, hoping against hope.

He looked at me as if I were stupid. "You. Me. Have as many as you want. Hell, eat 'em all, get 'em out of my life."

There was something fishy about the boxes upon boxes of candy bars, of course: they were probably stolen from some cargo truck years earlier, then bought for pennies on the dollar by my dad, who didn't know what the hell to do with them. But for his giant, hungry, ten-year-old son? Absolute heaven. I ate Whatchamacallits that summer until I couldn't stand them. Until I was straight pooping Whatchamacallits.

I had not tasted a Whatchamacallit in almost a decade. But locked in this dorm of loud, delinquent football drunks, broke beyond belief, suddenly, I desperately needed one. I needed something that reminded me of home. I put my change in, pressed the button on the machine, and waited. Nothing happened.

"Goddammit," I growled.

I tried again: nothing. The Whatchamacallit, encased in its tan and brown wrapper, hung on its hook, smugly.

"Come *on*," I groaned. I shook the machine, then kicked it. The candy bar wobbled, but remained in place. *Where was my goddamn Whatchamacallit?!!*

"Yo, yo, Outlaw, what's the problem?" said Josh Paxton, approaching on deceptively quiet, graceful fat-man feet.

"This machine, man!" I pointed at it, outraged, near tears. "It stole my money!"

"Calm down, calm down." Josh patted me on the back. "Go to sleep, Jesse. You'll have a candy bar in the morning. I promise."

I looked at him and nodded. He was right. I was having an episode. It was, after all, only a candy bar. The next morning, I awoke early. Opening my door to the hallway, I was surprised to discover a small pile of assorted sweets scattered right outside my room. Whatchamacallits, Twix, Bonkers, Hubba Bubba Bubble Gum, about ten or fifteen packages of candy in all. Slowly, I walked down the hallway to investigate. The candy machine's plastic casing was completely shattered and open to the public. I laughed and patted the ruined machine softly. Some punk must have murdered it for me. Now, that's a real friend.

———

Football remained my principal reason for being alive. Yet for the first time, I was beginning to entertain tiny shreds of doubt in my own ability. In high school, I'd always been the most physically gifted guy on the field at any point in time. Being six foot three and 225 pounds means quite a lot in high school. At RCC, every single player was big. To a man, we were lean, healthy young animals.

My biggest problems arose when we began running the slant, a defensive lineup designed to help more agile players like myself use raw speed to combat the strength of giant offensive linemen. When you run the slant, instead of hitting the opposing players straight up when they snap the ball, everybody on your line all lunges in one direction. I thought it was a great strategy: if I tried to butt heads with big, fat, tub-of-lard linemen, I'd lose every time, but if we ran the slant, often I'd be past them before they even got their hands off the ground.

The only catch was, I had to be really fast off the line. And for one reason or another, that wasn't happening.

"What's up, James?" Coach Meyer asked me after one game.

"What do you mean?"

He stared at me. "Zero sacks tonight. Only a couple tackles. That's not your typical performance, is it?" He frowned and pointed to my knees. "Are you having issues, son?"

"No," I said, surprised. I wore a knee brace in every game, but only as a preventative. I'd worn them all throughout high school, to the point that it felt totally natural to me. "I'm fine."

"Then why aren't you *coming off the line*?" he snapped.

After staring me down for a few more seconds, Meyer put up his hands in frustration, turned on his heel, and left.

I couldn't figure out why, but all that week in practice, I was slow off the line. I just couldn't dig in the way I used to. The other guys had an edge on me. I felt useless.

"Damn, Jesse, you suck," Anton Jackson said. He clapped a hand on my shoulder. "Time to quit, man, don't you think?"

I racked my brain for reasons for my demise. Maybe it *was* the knee brace? It was technically possible. Maybe it was slowing me down, impeding my natural first step. Perhaps my only recourse was to play without it. It was risky, certainly, but it might be worth it. My head reeling, I walked all over campus. Finally, I headed back to the dorms to change for dinner.

As I returned to my room, I found Josh Paxton slipping a note under my door.

"What the hell are you up to?" I demanded.

"Oh," Josh said, whirling around to face me. "This ain't nothing."

"Bullshit," I said, annoyed. "What's on the note?" I pushed past him to pick it up. *"To whom it may concern?"*

"I was gonna leave it anonymously," Josh explained.

"Yeah, I can see that," I snapped. I read aloud: "To whom it may concern. Your girlfriend is seeing Dan Konte behind your back."

I stared at the big man. The two of us were alone in the hallway.

"Man, I *wish* you hadn't come around," said Josh sadly. "I was trying to leave that anonymously."

I felt numb. Dan Konte was a teammate of ours, a huge lineman who had a stereotypical lineman dumbness to him. "Should I take this seriously?"

Josh nodded mutely. "Konte told me," he said, finally.

"Seriously?"

"Yeah," Josh said, looking down at the floor. "He said . . . well, he said she's real sexy."

I stood there, trying to get a hold on the emotions that were running over me.

Finally, I managed to nod. "Yeah," I said. "I guess that's true."

That next Saturday, for the first time in five years, I played a game without a knee brace.

Trust no one, I thought. *Fuck 'em all.*

My knee felt light. My whole being felt light, in fact. The anger ran in me like a fever, and I absolutely dominated. I got three sacks in the first half.

"Killing!" Coach Meyer exclaimed at halftime, shaking his fist joyously. "That's cold-blooded *killing,* son!"

It was true. I was out there murdering everybody. The second half began, and we continued to destroy them. All the life and enthusiasm drained out of the Long Beach City College football team like a warm, gentle piss. *Can't stop me,* I thought, deeply vindicated. *You might as well go home . . .*

"Killing!" Josh Paxton screamed, as we ran up the score on them, ran their hopes and dreams into the muck.

With four minutes remaining in the fourth quarter, I sacked the quarterback for a final time. Standing up, I raised my arms up to celebrate. It was the best I'd felt on a football field since arriving at Riverside Community Shithole. No adversity could stop me. Not poverty, not drunks in my dorm, not Rhonda, not my deadbeat dad.

Meanwhile, the hugest lineman on the Long Beach team sped toward me.

I am Jesse James, I thought with satisfaction, my helmet tipped down over my eyes. *And I am headed for greatness!*

Just then, the lineman drilled me right in the knee. My pain was so immediate and so intense that I puked in my helmet even before I hit the ground.

"FUGGGHHH!" I wailed, vomit spraying out of my mouth and coating my chin.

It was a crippling hit. The force of impact folded my leg up completely, until my ankle touched my hip. In a single instant, I realized what had happened. Staring at my leg in disbelief, the adrenaline took over, and I went crazy with rage. I was well beyond livid: I needed instant revenge. But unfortunately, I couldn't stand up. My knee was totally shattered.

"YOU *MOTHERFUCKERS!"* I screamed, trying to hobble my way toward anyone on their team. Unable to move, in desperation, I heaved my vomit-smeared helmet toward the other coach. "YOU CHEAP FUCKING BASTARD!"

Emergency attendants dashed onto the field and strapped me to a stretcher, dodging my blows as I swung at them. I strained against the taut nylon restraints of the stretcher, tears involuntarily streaming from my eyes. "No. No."

I was rushed to the hospital, and they performed surgery that night. I don't remember much of the operation. They knocked me out pretty good for most of it.

But when I woke up that night, I was more afraid than I had ever been in my whole life.

———

I lay in my hospital bed in a white gown, sweating and staring up at the ceiling. My heart was trip-hammering a million beats a minute.

I have to get out of here, I thought. *I have to leave here.*

I tried to propel myself out of my bed but, to my dismay, found I couldn't move. My leg, packed into a huge fabric splint, felt like it weighed a thousand pounds.

I cannot be here, I thought. I looked straight up above me, into the faintly glowing fluorescent light fixture. An industrial hospital aroma, part antiseptic, part flower-scented air freshener, surrounded me. The faint yet constant noise of beeping machines emanated from all corners.

Terror gripped me full force, and with a start, I wrenched myself out of my bed and hopped to the floor. Horrible pain stabbed through my knee. I opened the door, and pulling my hospital gown around me, began to inch my way down the hallway.

An hour later, I awoke on the floor of the men's bathroom, covered in piss. As I struggled to get to my feet, an orderly opened the door and found me.

"Come on, son," he said kindly. "Let's get you back to your bed."

He must have told a doctor, because I remember waking up several hours later with my attending surgeon shaking his head over me. "I hear you were up last night roaming around." He clucked his tongue. "Seems a little early for that, don't you think?"

I cleared my throat. "No, I'm fine, sir. Can I go home now?"

"You are most certainly *not* fine, Mr. James," the doctor said. "You had a complex surgery last night, and you will be recuperating here for the rest of the week, is that clear?"

"No," I said, "I mean it, I'm good to leave. Seriously," I assured the surgeon, "the knee feels good. You did a great job."

"You are not listening, Mr. James. I am telling you, stay put, right here, in the hospital."

"You can't make me stay," I said, the panic gripping me again. I had to leave. It was the only thing I cared about. "You can *advise* me, but I know my rights. I can leave if I want to."

The doctor looked at me, annoyed. "All right, Mr. James," he said finally. "I'll tell you what: there's a flight of stairs at the end of this hallway. If you can go down those stairs all by yourself, I'll feel confident in letting you go. How's that?"

"Fine," I said.

By this time, the sedative they'd used in the operation had worn off completely. There were no painkillers left in my bloodstream, but I inched myself off the bed and, wobbling badly, tried to stand.

"How about some crutches?" I asked, wincing.

"Certainly," the doctor said, and he fetched me a pair. I braced them under my arms, and started off down the hallway. Each time I made an impact into the slick tile, my knee would jostle. It felt like knives twisting into my flesh. Slowly, I approached the stairs.

"Mr. James, this doesn't seem wise," the doctor said.

Stiffly, I jabbed the plastic tip of a crutch onto the first step, and pushed off with my standing foot. My body hovered over the wobbly padding. With great effort, I managed to straighten my body, and I came to rest one stair lower.

"All right, son, that's quite enough. Back to bed."

I ignored him. Sweating hard, the pain surging through my entire system, I jabbed again, this time using the opposite crutch. I pushed off. All my muscles seized, as I wobbled down another step safely.

I repeated my movements, over and over, the muscles of my neck and back clenching awfully, sweat pouring down my brow, the fabric of my flimsy hospital gown flapping behind me. After a hellish, painful eternity, I arrived at the landing.

My shirt was soaked. Panting, I looked up at the doctor.

"So?" I gasped, my heart pounding. "Can I go?"

He looked at me with some sympathy. "Yes, son," he said quietly, after a moment. "I'll sign the release document."

———

I went to my dad's place. It was two weeks before I could get up and move around the house comfortably. Each day was a struggle with pain, a test of my will to even make it through the day. But it was worth it to be home. The hospital had frightened me badly, though I did not at the time fully understand why.

Slowly, things got a little easier. Over the next two months, I worked diligently to rehabilitate my shattered knee. The surgeon had done his job well. If I brought everything I had to the table, there was a good chance I would play again.

"Hey, look at this, you're *alive*!"

"Josh," I said, grinning. "What are you doing here?"

"My moms made you some cookies." The mammoth man held up a dinner plate in his hands. It was covered in aluminum foil. "I told her I had a friend who was a weak little bitch, he needed nourishment before he passed away completely."

"Gee, that's nice of you." I laughed, taking the plate from him. "Tell your mom I'd like to thank her in person, okay?"

Josh walked slowly around my homemade gym, taking in the weights and straps I'd scattered around my backyard. "Nice little setup you got here."

"I want to get back on the field," I told him.

"Rhonda's been asking about you," Josh said.

I waved him off. "That's way over, man."

Josh shrugged. "Good for you," he said. He lowered himself to the ground and opened up the foil that covered the dinner plate to seize a chocolate chip cookie. He popped the entire cookie into his mouth, crumbs falling down the front of his shirt.

"I thought those were for me."

"I need *something* to cheer me up as I watch your sad little comeback workout, don't I?"

"Make yourself useful, dude," I said. "Throw on some tunes."

He reached around in his pocket, and with some effort, managed to pull out a cassette tape. "Time for some Joey Shithead!"

Music blasting, we sweated in my backyard.

"YOU CAN'T DO IT!" Josh screamed, as I lifted up a thirty-pound weight with my left ankle. My knee shook with the effort. *"Too weak!!"*

"QUIET, BLACK PUNK-ROCK MAN!" I shouted, trembling with the effort. "No one can crush me!"

It took immense effort, but finally, I was ready to head back to school. My rehabilitation had been so thorough that my hurt knee had actually become stronger than the good one. My crutches were a thing of the past. I walked almost completely without a limp.

I got my bag ready excitedly. It was like summer vacation in reverse: I was returning to the one place I felt at home.

"Heading back today?" my dad asked.

"Yep," I said. I checked myself out in the mirror. I'd probably lost some weight, looked a little gaunt around the face, but overall I was still looking all right. I cracked a grin at the old man. "Hope you won't miss me too badly around here."

"Nope," he said.

I didn't let his shitty mood deflate me. Nothing could touch me, today.

"Can't wait to get back to that team, huh?" he asked.

I looked at him. "I'm excited, yes."

"You just remember something, Jesse." He nodded his head at me, seriously. "You're nothing but another body to those people. Much as you think you're using them, they are using *you*."

We stared at each other for a second.

"You know," I said slowly. "You're just an old, pissed-off man who hates the world. You always have been."

He snorted. "But am I *wrong*?"

"Yeah," I said. "You are wrong, okay? The whole way you see the world is totally skewed."

My dad waved me off. "Go on. Time to get back to your fantasy world. I'll be here when they use you up and spit you out."

I pushed past him and stomped out the door.

I was returning just in time to catch the tail end of our season. Our schedule was nearly completed: we had a single remaining regular season game, and then the playoffs. Steadily, I walked through the campus, down toward the stadium.

Coach Meyer and Coach Brown, our defensive coordinator, were waiting on the steps to greet me when I arrived.

"Well, if it isn't Jesse James," Coach Meyer said. He stuck out his hand for me to shake. "How goes it?"

"Really great," I said.

"That's what I've been hearing," he said. "Paxton said he's been visiting you at home, supervising your progress. He says you're ready to rock."

"Josh has been a terrible distraction, sir."

"That's what I figured," Coach Brown said, laughing. "You look good to me, son! Stand up, so we can take a look at you."

I stood up for them.

"Take a deep-knee bend for me?" said Coach Brown. I did it. "No pain?"

"None," I said, breathing deep.

"You got hit hard as hell."

"This is one tough kid," Coach Meyer said, looping an elbow around my neck. "My sense is, he's ready to play."

They both looked at me, waiting for me to speak.

"That'd be a quick damn rehab, Barry."

"Let's leave it to the boy to make the decision," Coach Meyer said. "He knows what his body can do." He turned to look at me. "How does that knee feel for you?"

"Nice," I said, flexing it. "It feels pretty strong."

"You see?" Coach Meyer said. "He's ready. I tell you what, Jesse, those four sacks you got against Long Beach were un-fucking-real. We could use some more of that in the playoffs, I'll tell you that much."

I said nothing, just sitting there, looking at the ground.

"Well?" Coach Meyer prodded me. "Everybody says you're ready to play. *Do* you want to play?"

It was a beautiful fall day. The sun shone down on our faces, and you could smell the cut grass on the field. I was an athlete. This was what I had been born to do.

I looked up at my coaches and told them, "No, I'm done."

Both of them looked shocked.

"Excuse me?" Coach Meyer asked quietly.

I shook my head firmly, feeling more sure of my decision. I had never liked to side with my father, but in this case, I couldn't help it. He was right. I was a commodity to these people. I'd been broken, but now I was fixed. They'd changed my flat. Now they wanted me to head out, full throttle.

"You know," I said, "someday I might have some kids."

Meyer stared uncomprehendingly, as if he was listening to a foreign language. "And?"

"Well, I was just thinking," I continued. "Someday, I might want to pick them up and run with them."

I picked up my bag, nodded respectfully, and left them sitting there.

6

As soon as they found out that I'd quit the team, the school stripped me of my scholarship. That was that—I was gone. As relatively cheap as RCC was, I couldn't afford to be there if I had to pay for it myself.

I set out to scrub my dorm room of my existence. Pants, socks, undershirts, cassettes, toothbrush: I stuffed them all into two green army duffels. The job took me about ten minutes to complete. I had nothing, really.

"I'll see you again," Josh said.

"Nah," I said.

"Sure, I will. You'll be that guy out there on the freeway, begging for cash," Josh said. "I'd always give you a nickel, Jesse James."

"Cool, I'll remember that." I stripped the cheap, dirty linens from my bed and, after looking at them cheerlessly for a moment, crumpled them into my duffel.

"You'll have a bitchin' homeless tan," Josh continued. "All brown and healthy-looking."

"Hey, look. Thanks for helping me out with my rehab and everything. I appreciate it."

"Can't have you out begging with a broken knee," Josh said. "Good luck, Jesse."

I headed back home to my dad's place, dreading the homecoming. I knew he'd make me eat some crow for coming back. Sure enough, the knowing grin that spread over his face when he saw me just about made me sick.

"Well, what now?" he said, hardly even trying to hide his smile.

"I'll figure something out," I muttered.

"Stay here as long as you need," he said magnanimously.

Right off the bat, we started butting heads. About a week after coming back home, we got into a fight concerning some car parts that I'd sold out of the garage.

"Where's my cut?"

"What are you talking about?" I said, outraged. "What does this have to do with you?"

"You stored 'em in my garage, didn't you?"

"Yeah, but . . ."

"Are you paying rent around here?"

"No, but . . ."

"Yeah, I didn't think so!" His eyes blazed. My dad's temper had been ignited by the subject of money. All his attention focused on me now. "You come here whenever you want, and you use this house as your own personal storage bin . . ."

"I won't anymore," I said. "I'm gone."

". . . you're making deals on my damn front steps and paying no rent? No, no way. Not in my house."

"I told you I'm leaving." I pushed past him. "So stop fucking talking."

He laughed rudely. "Oh, I'm sorry! I didn't realize you had so many places to go. Tell me, Jess, where are you headed? Back to school? Oh, no, they didn't want you there."

"Get away from me."

"How about to your little friend Bobby? No, wait a second, he sold you down the river once already. Better not go there."

My temper was rising, and so was my frustration. "I'm telling you to *shut up,* man."

"You think you can get away from all this shit, don't you? But the truth is right here. *You can't run.* This is your goddamn *life.*" He stood for a second, his hands on his hips, a smug expression on his face. "Sooner you figure that out, the better."

I looked at him—at the pitiful specimen that was my father. His bald head sprouting stray hairs. The beard he had always been so proud of was more gray than black, now. His 1970s big-collar print shirt looked faded and out of date, and a potbelly bulged out from beneath the lower half of it. The sags of age had added rings beneath his eyes, and crow's-feet poked from the corners of them. He looked tired. When he smiled, his teeth looked worn down. It was a grim sight.

"I'll clean out the garage this afternoon," I told him. "You won't see me after that."

He scoffed. "Son, that's what you said last time. That's what you say *every* time."

I looked at him. "This time, it's real."

He laughed, then walked back into the house, slamming the door after him.

I stood there for a second, listening to the silence.

"Dick," I muttered. Then I packed up the garage. Then I left.

—

My mom hadn't been in my life for several years. But there weren't any options left. So I came begging.

"You want to stay here . . . with *me?*" she said doubtfully.

"Just for a while, Mom," I assured her. "Just till I get my shit together."

My mother lived alone in a house in Long Beach. Aside from the drunk boyfriend she'd had when I was just a little kid, right after my dad and her split, she'd never gotten another partner. You could tell she was really used to living the solo life, because every time she opened a cabinet, she slammed the crap out of it. Same with every door.

An earsplitting rattling of plates awoke me the first morning I was there.

"*Mom,*" I grumbled. "What's the commotion?"

"Oh, hello, son," she said, still a bit surprised to see me in her house. "You're up early."

"Didn't really have much of a choice," I mumbled. Rubbing my eyes, I came into the kitchen to make myself a cup of coffee.

My mother gave no indication that she'd heard me. A bowl smashed down powerfully on the countertop: "Oatmeal?"

"No." I winced, putting a hand to my head. "Mom, do you get the paper delivered here?"

"No, sweetie. Not much call for me to read the paper these days."

"All right," I said. "I'll go out and get one."

"What's the hurry?"

"I need a job, Mom," I said. "Don't know if you've figured this out yet, but I'm kind of penniless, right now."

She looked at me, unsure of how to take my comment. "Do you need some money for lunch, sweetie?"

"It's all right." I kissed her on the cheek. "I'll see you later, okay?"

I headed to the closest diner and bought a paper and a cup of coffee with change. Perusing the want ads, I saw nothing but a whole bunch of low-paying crap: carpet cleaners, fast-food cashiers, busboys, and hotel clerks. I sighed, depressed. Maybe my dad was right. Maybe I was fucked in the water.

Then I saw an advertisement that said, "Skilled Welders/ Fabricators Only."

I looked closer, and was greatly encouraged by the next line: "Earn $1,000 a week! Immediate openings. Exp. required."

Now, *that* looked interesting. I'd learned to weld in freshman shop class, and I'd always been pretty good at it. Consistent practice had eluded me to this point—I'd always been too busy with sports—but I'd kept up on my skills here and there. And I'd certainly cut up enough cars to know my way around a blowtorch.

Nevertheless, there had to be a catch—and there was. The job wasn't local: it'd be in Seattle, up at a shipyard, near Puget Sound. Still, I took down the number and called up a manager, who described the job responsibilities to me. It was aluminum TIG welding, which I'd never done before. But there didn't seem to be many other jobs out there, so I lied to him and told him no problem. "TIG welding? My favorite!" He replied that he liked my initiative, and that I should report to work the following Monday.

"I'm thinking about going up north," I told my mom. "I found a job, and it pays really good money."

She slammed the refrigerator door. Pickles shook. "Really? You just got here."

"I know, Mom." I gave her a hug. "I think I need to make some kind of new start."

She nodded.

"Be good," my mom said. For a second, I imagined asking her if she wanted to come up there with me. We could start some kind of new life together, have the lovable, kooky mom-son relationship that we should have had all along, but didn't. But she was already looking at her hands blankly, forgetting I was even there.

I wasn't angry at my mom. I didn't disdain her, like I did my dad. She wasn't a bad woman. But she had never tried very hard to be part of my life. It was sad, but by now, we'd sort of missed our window. Neither of us really had the inner resources or the drive to fully connect.

I had never been out of California in my entire life. I had nowhere to live, and no money. The prospect shook me a little. *How the fuck was I going to survive?* Fortunately, my mom wouldn't let me go before she'd stuffed a couple hundred bucks in my pocket. I tried to refuse, but she could probably tell that my heart wasn't in it. She wouldn't let me say no.

"Thanks, Mom," I said, embarrassed.

"Write me when you get there," she said.

I found a Greyhound going north and bought myself a ticket. As soon as I boarded, an ancient wino plopped down next to me, reeking of whiskey. Immediately, he passed out on my shoulder. I looked out the window, watching the highway pass by blackly.

When we finally pulled in to Seattle, it was early evening, and very cold. I still wore my Southern California uniform: a pair of cut-off Dickies and T-shirt. Shivering, my heavy bags on my back, I bounced from motel to motel, unable to find a place that fit my budget.

Exhaustion threatened to undo me. In desperation, I found a phone book and called a Red Lion Inn in Kirkland, Washington. They had a single small room that was going for fifteen bucks a night.

"Where's Kirkland?" I asked.

"Oh, just about fifteen minutes from downtown."

"How am I supposed to get there?"

"Bus?" the night manager suggested, perversely.

One interminable city bus ride later, and I arrived at the Lion, sweating and clammy in the cold night air.

"I'm the guy you spoke to on the phone," I announced. "You said fifteen, right?"

"Sure, fifteen bucks. But you gotta stay a week." The dumpy woman gave me a quick once-over. "You *got* a week's rent?"

I gave her the money, and lugged my two duffels up to my room, where I sat down heavily on my bed. The bedsprings creaked beneath me. A feeble lamp cast a putrid yellow light around the room, displaying a small, grayish dorm-style refrigerator, two rolls of toilet paper, and a plastic bath mat that lay coiled on its side in the grim tub.

It would have to do. I rolled over, listening to the creak of the bedsprings. My clothes were filthy. Sadly, I realized that I didn't want to go to my first day at work smelling like a bum. Though I was dead tired, I forced myself to go down to the front desk and ask the night manager if by any chance there was a Laundromat nearby.

"Down the road, half a mile on the right," she grumbled. "Bring your own soap. Their machine's busted."

I didn't have any laundry soap of my own, but I set off anyway, hoping she was wrong. Soon, I realized that the night manager had underestimated the distance greatly. A good mile and a half had passed before a strip mall appeared on my horizon.

It was winter, Seattle, 1988—grunge was being born, but I barely noticed. Sweating and tired, not to mention mildly freaked out to be in a new place, I struggled under the weight of my tramp bag. Vaguely, I fantasized about heaving it into traffic and letting the oncoming cars maul my overripe clothes into oblivion. But then I'd have to buy new ones, and I couldn't afford luxuries like that at the moment.

Finally, I saw the strip mall. As I walked toward the Laundromat, a guy came out the door and passed me, nodding in a pleasant, friendly manner.

"Hey, man, how ya doing?" he said.

"Fuck off," I barked instinctively.

A confused, fearful look passed over the guy's face, and he quickly scurried off.

I muttered "sorry" under my breath, but the dude was long gone. *Dammit!* I thought. He'd taken me by surprise. Where I came from, you didn't talk to people you didn't know on the street. This Seattle shit was going to take some getting used to.

The next day, I rented a car for work. "What's the cheapest thing you've got?" I asked the guy working the counter.

"Try this on for size." He tossed me the keys to a Chevy, a

no-frills piece of crap. It had almost no suspension at all. I felt like I was riding on a set of Tonka wheels. But the price was right. It was going for about ten bucks a day.

Now I would just need food. I lurched to the grocery store, where hungrily I seized a towering stack of lunch meat, three loaves of white bread, and a bottle of ketchup. I moved toward the checkout, but then, reconsidering, I turned to my right and added a stack of pink wafer cookies to the pile: a fourth food group.

—

"So, you *definitely* know how to TIG weld. Is that right?" my boss asked me on my first day at work at the shipyard. It was seven o'clock in the morning in December off of Puget Sound. The wind coming off the water was absolutely freezing.

"Definitely," I agreed, shaking from the cold.

"Where'd you learn?" he asked dubiously. "Tungsten inert gas welders are pretty rare in this day and age. And, well, no offense, but you're just a kid."

"My dad." It was the first thing that came to mind. "Welder."

"Well, all right, then." He seemed satisfied. "Go over to the office, get your torch and your helmet. Tell 'em to give you a work jacket, too. You don't want any of those fucking sparks gettin' on you, am I right? Burn the goddamn skin right off your face!" He cackled alarmingly.

It didn't take me long to realize the job I'd taken was slow, repetitive, and dangerous. Even more, it was *difficult*. I'd considered myself a good worker with a torch, but in this shipyard, I found it surprisingly challenging to execute my tasks. In the most basic terms, we attached and repaired the metal appendages of giant crafts: one of my first jobs was to construct the munitions racks for the USS *Camden*, a guided missile frigate. The scale and importance of the work inspired me, but the job required me to regularly worm my way into tiny spaces. Often, I was caught in between bulkheads so tight that I literally couldn't wear my welding mask.

"I can't fit it on my head!" I complained to my boss. "There's no room!"

"Well, wear this!" he yelled to me. He tossed me a little leather hood with goggles on it. I looked at him.

"This is . . . a gimp hood."

"Okay, go in there with nothin' on your fucking head, I don't care!" He stomped off to troubleshoot the next battery of problems.

Despite the challenges that came with the work, I caught on pretty quickly. I labored completely alone, every day, and immediately I loved that. I *welded*: that's what I did. The simple realization that I could come to work, get out my torch, and start blazing away for hours and hours, and then receive good money for it, well, it felt great. I took chaos and made order of it. That was my job.

With bright bursts of electricity, I jointed aluminum and steel. Soon, a vague realization came over me that I might actually be good enough at this to do it as a career. Maybe it wasn't curing cancer, but I was contributing to the world. One way of life, football, had disappeared for me. But just as quickly, another had arisen to take its place. I felt grateful for the turn my life had taken.

The jury was still out on Seattle as a city, though: it was absolutely freezing there. After years of the mildest Southern California winters, I'd been dropped face-first into a never-ending drizzle that went from cold to gray, and back to cold. My Chevy bombed its way through flooded highways at seventy miles per hour, its shoddy tires spraying up huge arcs of water. I remember the windshield wipers of that car vividly, because I never actually turned them off. They batted back and forth so continually that I'd wear them out by the month, and had to fork over eight bucks for new ones.

"You want the regular model, or the double-arm blade?" the lady behind the counter asked me.

"Give me the doubles," I said. "I've never seen anything like this in my life."

The people mystified me, too. Seattle was in the dawn of its

Plaid Shirt Era. This wasn't the preppy California plaid I had grown up with, either. Dudes wore goatees, sideburns, and beanie caps pulled down over their eyebrows. Meanwhile, chicks went for chokers, ripped jeans, laced-up Docs, and pale makeup. Apparently, a mutant gang of ex-hippies with seasonal affective disorder had taken control of the city's fashion scene. No matter where you went, you could never really get away from the plaid.

It wasn't that I hated grunge; in fact, quite the contrary. I just liked to laugh at the people who thought it was so hard-core. These folks had never been to a Circle Jerks show, I can tell you that. When it came down to the music, I actually liked a bunch of the bands and their sound. In Pike Place Market, there was a Sub Pop record store, where they sold singles and EPs and limited edition stuff by cool new bands like Tad, Mudhoney, and Soundgarden. I happily threw my money down for those records.

The welding money came through as promised. For the first time in my life, I had cash to burn. The dumb part of me wanted to blow it all on toys, of course, but something inside me told me not to be such an asshole. Getting a better place to live would be way smarter.

"Your week's up," the night manager at the Red Lion Inn coughed, irritably. "Whatcha gonna do?"

I decided to stay put. It was the easiest thing to do, and broken mattress springs be damned. The shipyard had me working fourteen-hour days, so I wasn't inside that motel room very often. Also, this was the first time I'd ever had a pad of my very own, and hence, I had nothing to compare it to. The lukewarm shower, broken mirror, and trashy courtyard view were just so much gravy to me.

Each month I sent off some cash to my mom to help her with her rent, but beyond that, I didn't have that many expenses. On weekends, I'd make myself a bag lunch and drive to downtown Seattle, where I'd end up at the Aquarium or at the Ballard Docks, watching the sea lions play. I'd park myself with my bag of sandwiches and laugh as I watched the sea lions swim around and poach the world-class salmon. They'd take one huge bite, and then just toss the rest of the fish away. Kings of all they surveyed. I dug them a lot.

There was a secondhand bookstore downtown that I grew fond of, and I took to wandering around in there and exploring their shelves. No one had ever told me I was smart when I was in school, but I had always liked reading, even if I'd spent more time on the football field trying to shake the life out of people. Now I had ample time to sift through the piles of good-smelling old books, pick up the ones that looked most interesting, and bring them back to the Red Lion to pore over more carefully.

One book I got in Seattle was *The Old Man and the Sea*. For some reason, I really got into the image of that old man out there on his skiff, fighting for his giant catch. I found myself going over his fate again and again as I was welding. Everyone said it was a sad book, but I thought it ended pretty happily. After all, he'd knocked off three or four sharks with his own hands, hadn't he? That old man was a badass. At night, I read that book in my bed, falling asleep with the lights on, exhausted from work.

Thinking back, it was an odd period of my life. I was totally alone and, surprisingly, I had no desire to be with anyone else. Something was happening to me, with all the isolation and hard work I was doing. It truly solidified my sense of being and what I was capable of. It was as if my body was absorbing the solitude like sunlight, synthesizing something powerful from it. I don't recall making a single friend during the ten months or so that I spent in the Pacific Northwest. But I don't recall ever being lonely, either.

———

Eventually my stint in Seattle came to an end. I had to get out. The weather was making me stir-crazy and nuts. When April came and it was still dreary and gray, I simply couldn't handle it. And although

I continued to gain competence in my job, I didn't quite see where it was going. Welding paid great, and I could feel good about being a craftsman, but where was the future in it? I didn't consider shift leader the highest goal I wanted to strive for.

The other guys at work didn't dig me all that well, either. I was the youngest kid, by far, and I never paid much attention to them when I came in, just put my head down and got straight to work. It made it that much worse that I'd received several promotions since joining the shipyard.

One day one of the guys asked me, point-blank, "Who do you know?"

"I don't know anyone," I said.

"Come on, don't be a wise guy," he said. "You related to the boss?"

"Yeah, he's my mother." I glared hard at him. "Anything else you need to ask me?"

He shrugged. "Nah." As I walked away, I heard him mumble, "Wiseass."

I called my mom from a pay phone at the Lion that night, and told her I was coming back to California.

"Oh, sweetie, that's great," she said.

I cleared my throat. "Can I stay with you for a little while until I get my own place?"

Long Beach had not changed much in my absence. In fact, it was precisely the same as I'd left it. In a way, I felt oddly insulted, like, how could this place function without *me*? I *was* Long Beach! On the morning of my arrival, I walked down the street to get a gallon of milk, passing at least ten people on the street on my way. Total poker faces. Nobody acknowledged my existence, much less said "hi." I sighed, relieved. I was home, all right.

I had some cash, so I wasn't too concerned about how I'd survive. More than that, I had a trade now. I figured that if things got tight, I would be happy doing some welding work in the surrounding area.

There were plenty of jobs in Southern Cal for a blue-collar guy who kept his eyes fixed to the metal.

I was also kinda psyched to put together another motorcycle. Up in Seattle, when I'd started to accumulate money, I'd gone by a Harley dealership to see how much a brand-new chopper would cost.

"Oh, not too much. Twelve thousand should get you most of the way there."

I was taken aback. I was making good money, but twelve *grand*? Just for some bike that every other corny dude with a fringe vest and leather chaps was riding? I said thanks, but no thanks—it was too damn rainy to ride a bike every day there, anyway—and I resigned myself to the rented Chevy for a while longer.

But now that I was home and had access to my mom's garage, I started to dream again about putting together my own model. In high school, I'd made Rhonda's Volkswagen for almost nothing by being creative, doing the paint and body work myself, and haggling for parts. Maybe with my new welding skills thrown into the mix, I could create a cool-looking custom bike that would blow the local pigfuckers right out of the water. At the very least, it'd do for a hobby.

Meanwhile, I was enjoying being back. My cousin Dave showed up at my mom's soon after I got back, asking me if I wanted to head into L.A. to go hang out at Golden Apple.

"Yeah, man, sounds like a plan." I was always up for more comics.

We tooled down in his car and when we went to the store, the owner recognized me right away.

"Fuck, kid, you just keep getting bigger and bigger. You frighten the shit out of me, do you know that?"

I laughed. "Whatever, man."

"Whatever, nothing! Listen, our security guy is shit. How's about you come back and work some gigs for me? You were the best guy

I ever had, seriously. *No one* stole anything on your shifts, swear to God. Not even the schmucks working the register!"

I thought about it for half a second. "Yeah, sure."

I mean, why not? I didn't have anything better to do. After all, it would get me out of the house, push me to be a little more social, which was probably a good thing. I didn't want to become a total recluse at the age of nineteen.

Crossing my arms at Golden Apple wasn't a particularly fascinating endeavor, but I tried to be responsible, and as friendly as a security guard probably can be. I must have looked all right doing it, though, because before too long, other folks started asking me to work security for them, too. And because Los Angeles is an industry town above all else, I quickly found myself around celebrities.

I met Rick Rubin through a friend, and that led to a ton of work for me. Rubin had just parted ways with Russell Simmons, the cofounder of Def Jam, and was on his way toward establishing Def American, his new label. Rick dug me a lot, and the feeling was mutual.

"Got a great job for you, Jesse," he'd say. "How'd you like to work Sir Mix-A-Lot's record release party? Everyone has to enter the club through a giant ass, you'll love it."

"Sure thing, man."

"*Jesse!* We need you to follow Flava Flav around today. Please, make sure he doesn't smoke any crack, okay?"

"I can do that."

Anything Rick would ask, I'd do. He was hilarious and ridiculously talented as a producer. He just had that golden touch. Everything seemed fun coming from him or his crew. Rick got me a gig working as a bodyguard for Debbie Harry when she was making a comeback album at the Variety Arts Center, down on 9th and Figueroa. Downtown L.A. itself was a real entertaining shithole way back then. Crackheads ruled the street night and day. Etched into my brain is an image of a completely nude guy strolling down the street, reading a paper, right in the middle of the afternoon.

Almost against my will, a career began developing for me. I went to a Vandals show at Fender's Ballroom in Long Beach, which was kind of like the CBGB of the West Coast. You could always count on Fender's to supply a psychotic punk experience for you— they booked some of my favorite bands, like 7 Seconds, Uniform Choice, and Bad Religion, all super-intense, sweating, straining bands with power to spare. That night, the place was packed and rocking. You didn't exactly have a mosh pit in Fender's; it was more like the entire venue was just this giant, swirling mess, and if you didn't want to be in it, well, you shouldn't have come, you pussy.

I felt bodies smash up against me, arms whacking my face and shoulders. Their drummer was totally beating the shit out of the skins. I felt the high-energy music pump into my bloodstream, and I was enlivened by the collective energy of a thousand screaming fans. Just for the fuck of it, I pushed the giant, red-bearded monster standing next to me in the small of his back.

He stumbled forward, crushed two smaller dudes in his attempt to regain his balance, then pushed me in the chest. "FUCK ARE YOU DOING??" he bellowed.

"HAVING FUN, ASSHOLE!" I screamed, pushing the guy next to me so hard he fell on the ground and was trampled by tens of dirty boots in the beer puddles.

"TOUGH GUY, HUH??" With a crushing forearm, the red-bearded pirate bowled over his three nearest neighbors.

We continued to fight with each other by proxy. As the Vandals whipped the crowd into greater and greater frenzies, we continued to smack unsuspecting punks in the throat, balls, and breasts, knocking the wind out of them, boldly spinning them into unknown corners where no punk had gone before.

I was crying with laughter by the time the set ended, even though somebody's fingernail had somehow managed to cut the side of my face open.

"What's your name, man?" I said, extending my hand, blood dripping liberally off my forehead.

"Dimwit," he answered. Ignoring my hand, he drew me into his huge body for a sweaty, disgusting hug.

"Dimwit?" I said, my bloody face pressed into his giant, jean-jacketed vest. "*The* Dimwit?"

"I'm him," he answered proudly. "Drummer for the Four Horsemen. Legend in my own motherfucking mind."

I probably should have known. Dimwit and his brother, Chuck Biscuits, were cornerstones of the hard-core movement. They hailed from Vancouver, British Columbia, but had risen to SoCal fame throughout the 1980s. Chuck, in particular, had been in an assortment of the most important punk bands of the decade: the original drummer for D.O.A., he had played with both Black Flag and the Circle Jerks in following years.

"What do *you* do?" Dimwit asked me, the sweating crowd slowly filing out beside us. A few of them, who we'd injured, shot us dirty looks. "Beat up on people, I guess?"

"I'm a welder," I answered. He looked at me incredulously. "Though lately, yeah, I've been beating up on people."

Dimwit stared at me, still confused.

"I'm security," I explained. "For a comic book store."

"You should talk to Chuck," Dimwit said. "He's playing with Glenn Danzig these days—you know him?"

"Sure I do," I said. "I like Danzig."

"Well, they're about to go on tour to Europe and shit. I think they're still looking for security."

"I don't know," I said carefully. "I'm not so sure I want to make a whole life out of this."

"You got something better lined up?" Dimwit asked.

"Nope."

"Tour life's *very cool*," he confided. "Just trust me, dude, it's one hell of a party. Music, chicks, Scandinavian punkers who are, like, just *begging* you to laugh at them. Great times."

Fender's Ballroom had almost emptied by now. The coarse floorboards were littered with spent cups and broken glass. The manic swirl of energy that had occupied the club was gone, but something still rang there, a certain power and meaning. One lone punk kid who appeared to have drunk a bit too much was still on the floor, crawling painfully across a small pool of vomit.

Dimwit gestured grandly at the garbage all around us. "I mean, what *more* could you want?"

7

The next morning, the phone rang at my mom's place.

"Jesse?"

"Yeah?"

"This is Dimwit. Listen, man, I talked to Chuck about you," he said. "And he's definitely interested. Danzig's playing tonight at the Palace, so if you want, you can meet up with Glenn."

I decided not to dress up for Glenn Danzig. I wore a wife beater. In fact, I probably *looked* like a wife beater. My face was still all scabbed from the previous night's show, and I had the beginnings of a shiner going from a random punch in the face that I couldn't even remember. In Seattle, I'd gotten even bigger: I was 240 pounds of pure muscle.

Yep, I thought, looking in the mirror, *I'm going to get this job.*

Still, there was competition. A big tattooed black dude, about thirty years old, was already in the room with Glenn when I came in. Danzig looked us over, one to the other.

He began with my competition. "Bill, you've got the leg up on experience," he said. "You've done tours, correct?"

"I've been doing concert security for ten years," he explained. "Been all over the U.S., Europe, and South America. I know this job inside and out. That I can guarantee you."

Glenn nodded. "Jesse?"

I raised my eyebrows, giving him a blank look.

"Do you have much experience in concert security?"

I shook my head. "No."

He grinned. "So, why should I hire you, you think?"

I looked him over and shrugged. "Don't know."

Glenn looked at me hard. "Chuck Biscuits says his little brother saw you at a show at Fender's last night."

"Vandals," I confirmed.

"What did you think?" Glenn asked.

"Pretty okay," I said. "They play music you can fight to."

Glenn laughed. "Music you can *fight* to?"

My rival scoffed. "Real mature attitude for a security guard."

"No, I'm curious," said Glenn. He looked amused. "Tell me more, Jesse."

I cleared my throat, shifted in my seat. "Well, I just think punk, it's about letting off steam."

"True," Glenn said.

"You gotta pump people up," I continued. "Otherwise, I mean, what's the point? All this hair metal crap—Def Leppard and Guns N' Roses and Skid Row—it's just *soft*. It's a waste of time, if you ask me."

"Makes me sick," Glenn agreed.

"I like intense music," the black dude interjected. "Just with soul. That's all I ask."

Glenn ignored him. "What's your take on Danzig?" he asked me. "Are we tough enough for you?"

"I've always dug your music," I said, honestly. "I was listening to the Misfits when I was twelve."

"Gee, thanks for making me feel like an old man," Glenn said, laughing. "Well, okay. You wanna come aboard? We have a few shows left in the U.S., then a European tour right around the corner."

"Fuck yeah," I exclaimed. "I'm ready to go."

The other candidate crossed his arms sourly. "I like to fight, too, okay? It's just not, like, my first option."

———

Doing security was a lot like being back on the football field—only with a super-intense sound track.

"Just make sure no one touches Glenn," Chuck Biscuits told me. "That's your main challenge. Glenn whips everyone into a fucking frenzy, and for some reason, his fans always want to fight him."

I laughed. That made sense to me. "Keep them off the stage, huh?"

"Yeah, keep us safe. Keep the crowd safe, too—scare people, but don't touch them unless you have to." He grinned. "Basically, make sure no one gets too bloody."

My first Danzig show, in Portland, Oregon, was unbelievably loud, and almost comically intense. I spent two and a half hours on stage, hovering nine feet above the writhing masses, watching them fight and bash one another like enraged beasts. Standing directly in front of the speaker, the deep bass vibrated through my body as the barricade pulsed with the force of a thousand death-metal punks.

"I can feel it jabbing!" Danzig screamed.

The near-delirious band beat the shit out of their instruments, as if they never intended to use them again. The music was so deafeningly loud, it made my brain itchy inside my skull.

"Make me—come alive!" he screamed.

Glenn Danzig was a monster on stage. Every lyric of every song, he growled forth a primal howl, whipping his long black hair around his head like it was a rabid animal he was trying to shake off. His front-row fans emulated him: they screamed at him, challenging him to fight, giving him the finger, and showering in the nasty sweat flying off his hulking, compact frame.

After the show, we headed to a Portland strip club to unwind. The Acropolis was kind of a dive, but I suppose it could have been worse. At least no one was wearing plaid.

"So what'd you think, Jesse?" Chuck asked me.

"Blew my mind," I answered, truthfully. "My ears are still ringing, man."

"Pretty easy?" Danzig asked.

"Definitely."

"Well," Glenn said, "I don't mean to nitpick, but I think there were a couple of things you could have done better. I was getting some bad vibes from this one shithead right in the front row. He looked dangerous, like he was getting ready to jump the barricade and come on stage."

"That one kid with the tats on his face?" asked Eerie Von, their bassist.

"Exactly." He turned to me. "Did you see him, Jesse?"

"No," I admitted. I had been too involved with the overall experience: the music blasting relentlessly from the speakers, engulfing my body and my head.

"So, you gotta have better eyes, okay? Remember, we're all depending on you. I'm sure you're great at reacting—you got awesome reflexes and everything—but paying really close attention is even more important," he said. "Instead of dealing with problems, *anticipate* them. It's better that way."

I nodded. "Yeah, man, I'm really sorry. You're right."

"No problem," Glenn said. "You're learning. I think you're gonna be really good at this."

Encouraged, I ordered another beer. We sat back and drank, and idly, I wondered whether the stories I'd heard about bands on tour were true—was it all a bunch of sex, drugs, and rock 'n' roll? If so, when was it going to start?

I began to get a nice little buzz going. In my little personal haze, I stared up happily at the gyrating dancer on stage.

Just then, I noticed Glenn, who was up at the bar getting a beer. An older dude appeared to have recognized him. He was leaning over him, harassing him, and Danzig seemed totally uninterested. Immediately, I saw that I'd been given the perfect opportunity to redeem myself. *Anticipate!*

Popping out of my seat, I strode quickly toward Glenn and the older guy.

"Yo, jerk-off," I growled. "Take a step back."

"Jesse, it's . . ." Glenn began.

"Not a problem, Glenn," I said, turning to the older dude. "Are you *deaf*? My friend doesn't want to talk to you. So take a fucking step back."

"You telling *me* to step back?" the older guy said, amazed. "Why, you stupid lunkhead, I should . . ."

He never finished his sentence. I stun-punched him in the face, and his head snapped back into a glass stuffed-animal vending machine. The plate glass of the machine cracked, spiderwebbing.

The rowdy Acropolis suddenly fell completely silent. I could hear the record screech to a halt. The house lights came on. A blond, leggy stripper, who only moments before had been grinding lustfully on stage, covered her huge breasts with her hands.

"Jesse," Glenn said quietly. "You just punched the manager of this club in the face."

"I should send you to jail, you bastard," he mumbled from the floor. The machine's metallic claw wobbled unsteadily.

"I'll pay for the damage," I mumbled. "I'm really sorry."

"You'll be reimbursed for your machine, Jack," Glenn said, shooting me a dirty look. "Not to mention a trip to the doctor. It'll come out of our new security guard's first paycheck."

Our bus ride back to our hotel was somber.

"So . . ." Glenn began.

"Yeah," I said. My head was already hurting from the alcohol. "I know . . ."

"You really can't *do* that, Jesse."

"I know. I know."

"We have to find a middle ground, man," Glenn said, laughing. "I need to know that you're one hundred percent behind me, so I can be as crazy as I want to be. But I don't actually want you to, you know, incur bodily harm on anyone."

I sighed. "I'm sorry, Glenn. I was just trying to do my job right."

"Just remember this," he said. "You are the biggest guy in the room. You can make people do your bidding, simply by standing there. So watch your temper. Be *nice*."

"Be nice," I repeated.

"People *want* to obey you," he said, smiling. "So let them."

With Glenn Danzig's words echoing around in my head like a confusing Zen koan, I took to the remainder of the tour with a newfound determination to execute my job like a pro. Again, I was reminded of playing outside linebacker: you used quickness and intelligence, not brute force, to anticipate the rush of the crowd. There was always going to be more of them than you, so you had to learn to watch them carefully, and let *them* expend their energy, instead of wasting yours. Being a bodyguard was not about crushing heads. It was about creating an impression of yourself that was bigger, calmer, and more woefully dangerous than anyone else in the world.

Of course, theories didn't always translate to the real world, and they didn't always save your ass from taking a beating every once in a while. As much as people liked to pick fights with Glenn, even more they liked to shout at me, insult me, and tell me to go to hell. Punk crowds were unified by a hatred of authority—and, as odd as it was to realize, I was that now. At one of my first shows, a quick *"FUCK YOU!"* alerted me to a Newcastle bottle spinning quickly toward my face.

Transfixed, I watched it come closer, unable to move. It made a curious humming sound as it spun. And then it smashed into my head. The bottle didn't even break, but my head got a dent.

This job, I thought, *is going to cost me some brain cells.*

On the brighter side, Glenn and I grew close pretty quick. Both of us were fighters. We bonded around that.

"Come do this Muay Thai thing with me, man," he'd say, all excited. "I want to show you how they box in Thailand, it's *super* violent!"

We checked out all kinds of martial arts together, spurring one another to do more and more intense trainings. We must have made a funny pair: I was a six-foot-three, blond, and wide-eyed twenty-year-old. Then here was Glenn, this little black-haired Italian dude with a wrinkled forehead and tiny black boots, whose attitude was so relentlessly aggressive that half the time I felt smaller than him. On stage, Glenn was so full of testosterone and rage, he reminded me of some kind of mutant superhero.

He took the music real personal. Metal at that time really *had* gotten kind of soft and mushy, with glam acts like Poison and Warrant getting crazy airplay on MTV, filling arenas with their diarrhea power ballads and capturing the hearts of thirteen-year-old girls. To real punks like Glenn, it was insulting. And that came through in the focused rage of his performances.

Somewhat disappointingly, the sex part of this rock 'n' roll dream never seemed to materialize. Maybe because we were mired in the late 1980s. AIDS was a real threat. It seemed like everyone knew someone who had died of it, and that took a lot of the zip out of casual sex. Plus, I was always skeptical: if I was at a show, and met a girl who immediately offered to give me head, well, then what did that make me? Nothing more than a guy who could get her backstage.

Glenn had pretty much the same attitude.

"Dude, you know what I always ask myself?" he said to me one night in his office.

"What's that?"

"This groupie chick who wants to sleep with me, what was she doing last week?"

"I don't know. What's the answer?"

"Pantera."

So Glenn was a rocker who didn't fit that lecherous mold. Most of the time I knew him, he had a long-term girlfriend. She'd even come on the road with us occasionally. Slowly, as I observed Glenn and the way he treated people, he sort of grew into a role model for me. It wasn't that I wanted to be a rock musician or live that lifestyle; far from it. But there was a type of dignity to him, the way he carried himself, that I hadn't been exposed to before.

In due time, I became quite serious about being top-notch security. In order to get my band from the hotel to the show, on stage and off, then backstage, onto the bus, and finally rushed through the lobby to their hotel room without anything happening to them, every single movement had to be calculated. I had to be watching over my shoulder the entire time. I was kind of a mother hen to them, which was funny, since I was all of twenty years old.

Life was exciting. But due to my responsibilities, I rarely let loose all that much. For the most part, my rock life was wound up real tight. Stressful, even. And I still had a furious temper that would explode when I was challenged.

One night, at a show in Hamburg, Germany, a bald-headed punker in the front row began to go ballistic when the band shifted into the song "Mother."

"Die you freaking cocksucking prick!" he screamed at Glenn. That in itself wasn't really a problem, since everyone screamed at the band. That was just part of the scene. But this dude was also spitting: sending gobs of saliva into the air, with great distance and accuracy. And that pissed me off.

"Knock it off!" I yelled, coming down to the barricade, spearing him with my meanest look. "Quit spitting at the band."

"FACK YOU!" he screamed at me, his beer-breath exploding all over my face. He continued to scream maniacally at Danzig and the band, then leaned around me and launched another huge hawk of spit at the stage.

"Stop *fucking spitting*," I demanded, furious. "Or I will kick your ass!"

"FACK! YOU!" he cried again, and, hocking up the thickest gob he could muster, he spat directly into my face.

Disgusted, I snapped my head back and head-butted the punk in the face as hard as I could. In an instant, I had split his face from the bridge of his nose to his hairline. Spraying blood like a burst water balloon, he crumpled backward into the crowd. Immediately, the pit turned on him like deranged wolves and began attacking him with crazed vengeance.

Sheepishly, I looked up to the band. Danzig was shaking his head, bemused, like a dad finding his kid fucking up, yet again. I shrugged my shoulders apologetically. I still had a few things to learn.

———

When Danzig's tour ended, I headed back home to California. My mom's house was still open to me, and I intended to stay there for a while.

But soon the word got out to other bands that I'd done a pretty good job for Danzig. They started to woo me into working for them. Part of me wanted to say no, but the money and the adventure were just too intense for a young punk to resist. Working a Slayer/White Flag/Social Distortion show? I couldn't pass that up even if I tried.

I had the good luck to work with some pretty amazing bands in those days. In 1991, Rick Rubin hooked me up with the Red Hot Chili Peppers. They were recording a new album, and Rick had the weird idea that they should do it as recluses in this funky old mansion that he'd rented. I lived there with them for about a month, helping them out and doing their errands, since it was clear they never wanted to step outside for even an instant. It was a legitimately spooky house, which made sense: it had been Harry Houdini's once upon a time. It fit perfectly with the name of the album, *Blood Sugar Sex Magik*.

I got along pretty well with everyone in the band, especially Chad Smith, their drummer, who liked bikes, so when the Chili Peppers were about to go on tour to promote the album, they asked me along to work it.

"Of course," I agreed.

What was especially memorable about that tour was not just that the Chili Peppers were performing an awesome album, finally coming into their own as superstars, but that Pearl Jam and Nirvana were the opening acts. I remember watching from the side of the stage as Kurt Cobain broke into "Smells Like Teen Spirit" for the first time on a national scale. I had never heard of this guy before, but instantly, I recognized that he meant something. The crowd always went nuts for Anthony Kiedis and Flea—those guys owned every audience they'd ever met, make no mistake about it—but during the shows I worked, they *loved* Cobain. The entire audience hung on his every word.

Slowly, over the next several years, I grew into my gig. I became fairly well known among rock groups, recognized as someone who took his work seriously and commanded respect. I had no interest in drugs, and I think that, too, was attractive to the groups. Cocaine and heroin had savaged so many of their talented members. Gradually, I let my flattop grow out. I did a tour with Soundgarden. Slayer was next. White Zombie followed.

Bit by bit, I was becoming part of the scene. It was a peculiar little world that I had stumbled into, and certainly an interesting one for a young man. I was proud of being an insider, and if mine wasn't the most glamorous of all jobs—I mean, I wasn't exactly invited out on stage during encores—well, then, neither was welding.

I was getting to see places I'd never even considered visiting. The blue-collar kid from Long Beach had somehow managed to get over to Europe.

"Let's go out, let's walk around, man!" That was my chorus. I'd rather have died than sit around in my hotel room at any given moment. I felt it was a terrible waste of time.

Almost all the bands had been to Europe before, though, and hence they were a little bit more reserved.

"We got a show tonight, Jesse. Ever heard of a nap?"

"You guys are practically in your coffins," I said. "It's sickening. Don't you want to go out and *see* stuff?"

"You're *security*, dude. Watch some TV. Start working on your potbelly."

That wasn't going to be my fate, though. I might have been hired muscle for a punk band, but I'd be damned if I was going to let a whole continent's worth of sights go unexplored. With the enthusiasm of a total nerd, I began seeking out all the Italian frescoes and Renaissance museums I could find. No matter where I went, I couldn't get enough of the architecture and the incredible attention paid to detail.

I wasn't all about the high art, though; sooner or later, I'd inevitably find myself at a bookstand, leafing through European motorcycle magazines. I wanted my next cycle to be bitchin', blow everybody else out of the water. And to do that, I needed it loud, fast, and most of all, unique. Because I was overseas, I felt like I had an advantage over the rest of the cats stuck stateside—cycles were more popular over here, and they had much more stylistic variance. I pored over hundreds and hundreds of motorcycle magazines in Sweden, France, Italy, and Spain, often purchasing them to examine more closely backstage or on the bus. I received a per diem for food, but I never used it. I filled up on apples and oranges at the hotel, and usually copped a free dinner backstage. I put all my money toward bike magazine research.

Backstage, when I had a free moment, I enjoyed talking shop with other bodyguards.

"I have patented the absolute *foolproof* way to remove a groupie from a hotel. No fuss, no hassle."

"Do tell."

"Well, you know how it is, man," I said. "Your bass player was all stoked to get this chick inside his suite at midnight. But now it's three in the morning, and he's had his kicks. He wants her out."

Sympathetic nods all around; clearly, this is familiar grist within the security guard community.

"So you're stuck. Obviously, she doesn't want to leave—no groupie worth her stripes is gonna leave without being told flat-out. I mean, she's done *her* job, right?" I said. "Any decent human being would let her rest in his bed till morning. But remember, we're not dealing with human beings, we're talking about musicians."

"Preach it."

"So all of a sudden, she becomes *your* job, right? 'Jesse! Get rid of her for me!' You can try reasoning, but that almost never works, and you can't touch the girl. No way. Then you've got a drama on your hands."

"Can't have that."

"Of course not. So what *I* do," I said, lowering my voice to a confidential whisper, "I breeze into the room, and before anyone can say a word, I grab the groupie's handbag, and I fling it into the hallway. She'll run after it like a poodle. At that point, I slam the door shut behind her."

"No!"

"Yep. She'll immediately start banging on the door like some psycho, but you have to ignore that. Then you just call down to the front desk, say there's some crazy woman trying to break into your room—and if you wouldn't mind, could you please have her ejected, immediately?"

"Genius," my compatriots said.

"Give me a little credit here," I said modestly. "I'm very good at what I do."

When I was back in the States, I spent almost all of my free time in my garage, trying to get better at building motorcycles. Progress came slowly. I could slap a whole bunch of cool parts on my bikes, sure, and make everything kind of function as a whole, but from a design perspective, it didn't feel like I was doing anything earth-shattering.

Still, I kept riding Harleys as fast as I could around Riverside and Long Beach, rattling my teeth, blowing off steam, having fun. Random security gigs continued to come my way. If they appealed to me, I'd accept them. When a dive bar in Anaheim called the Doll Hut requested my services, being the generous soul I was, I decided to appease them.

God bless the bar. Working security at one of those places was like a paid vacation. I was too tightly wound to take a night off—already, in my early twenties, I was well on my way to becoming a workaholic—but folding my arms in the fun, stupid, party atmosphere served fairly well as a social event.

After a few weeks of working at the Doll Hut, I got to be friends with a few of the people there. One chick, Kelly, and her rockabilly boyfriend, Mike, had grown up right around the corner from me. They were neighborhood folks, real cool people.

"Jesse, tomorrow night, I want you to come with us to Captain Cream's!" said Kelly. That was a club in Mission Viejo where she worked. "There's this *super*hot chick working there, and guess what? She's *single*. We'll introduce you!"

I agreed, and the following night, we all tooled over to the Captain's together. As we came in the door, Kelly nudged me, pointing a lacquered nail toward the stage.

"There she is," Kelly proclaimed, gesturing toward the sexy blonde on stage, who was writhing rhythmically in a red bikini. "Didn't I *say* she was hot?"

I nodded, impressed, and waited for the bikini to come off. But Captain Cream's was only a bikini bar, and the girls didn't do full-on nudity. The suit stayed on.

"Geez, what a tease," I sulked.

But I continued to watch the girl on stage. After only a few moments, I had to admit, she had it going on. I'd gotten used to the ultra-slutty, over-the-top, almost comic sexual pantomime that they served up everywhere else. But there was a kind of class to this woman. She had the perfect body and the perfect moves, but somehow she danced to entertain. By the end of her set, I was hypnotized.

"Let's give it up for *Karessa*!" sang the DJ, as she moved off the stage.

"*Karess-a?*" I laughed.

"What?" Kelly said. She looked at me, confused. "Her real name's Karla."

"Oh, okay," I said, still smiling.

"Karessa's a very good name," Kelly said, eyeing me distrustfully.

"Yes," I agreed. "Very classy."

Later in the week, Mike called me up and said a double date was in the works; was I interested?

"Heck, yeah," I said. "I'm all about it. Just tell me where and when."

The four of us went to a Mexican restaurant in Long Beach. I was very nervous. At that point in my life, I hardly even knew how to function around real women. I just had no game at all.

"Tell Karla about what you do, Jesse," Mike prompted me.

"I'm . . . I'm on the road a lot. With bands," I stammered.

"Jesse's friends with all these famous dudes," Mike said, talking me up. "He's in security. Keeps everyone safe and sound."

"Sounds like a real *mental* workout," Karla said, smiling. She was so pretty, she looked even more amazing in clothes than she did in the club. Her skin was tan and her hair blond. Every inch of her was confident and impeccable.

"Are you . . . making fun of me?" I asked, reaching for a handful of tortilla chips and stuffing them in my mouth, embarrassed.

"No *way*," Karla said, smiling even bigger. "Why would I do that?"

Over the course of dinner and our subsequent conversation, I realized that Karla was mature and well-spoken. She was a dancer, sure, but she obviously had her shit in line, and knew who she was. With a tingle of excitement, I thought to myself, *Jesse James, you're officially on a date with an* older woman.

I ended up dropping Mike and Kelly off first. Then I took Karla to her apartment in Huntington Beach.

"Do you have roommates?" I asked.

"Nope," she said. "I live by myself."

"I guess you have your own wheels, too, huh?"

"Brand-new Mustang," Karla said. Proudly, she pointed to her car in the lot. "*Well,* Jesse?"

"What?"

"Aren't you at least going to come up and take a look at my place?"

I smiled, embarrassed. "I was sort of waiting for you to ask."

We made out rather drunkenly for a few minutes at her place, but it was very late, and another tour was beginning for me early the next morning.

"I better go," I said regretfully.

"Too bad," Karla said, smiling. "I was just beginning to like you."

"Do you . . . want to hang out when I get home from Europe?"

"Maybe," she said, smiling slyly. "I'll consider it."

"All right," I said. "What's your number?"

She scribbled it down on a piece of paper and handed it to me. "Are you really going to keep this?"

"Sure," I said. "Just ask for Karessa, right?"

She socked me in the arm. "That's *so* funny."

We kissed a final time, and then I made for the door. My hand was on the doorknob, when she cleared her throat.

"Hey." I turned my head to look back at her. She shrugged, kind of shyly. "I really do want you to call me," she said, finally.

I grinned. "I will."

Karla stayed firmly in the forefront of my mind, and as soon as I returned home from my tour, I asked her out on another date. She accepted. That evening, over drinks, she regaled me with the latest tales from the bikini bar.

"A guy this weekend tried to get kind of wise," Karla said. "I had to do *your* job, Jesse."

"How's that?" I asked, laughing.

"I had to beat the shit out of him!" she said.

"You're kidding, right?"

"Not at all," she said, cheerily. "Look, this jackass was trying to feel up on my friend Paulina, just being real rude and stupid. When she pushed his hand off, she spilled his drink all over his suit."

"Criminal," I said, taking a long pull on my beer.

"Isn't it? So anyway, he got all pissed, and *backhanded* her!"

"Ooh," I said. "Unwise."

"Unforgivable. I punched him right in the head. And man, I about broke my hand! This idiot had a *really* hard head."

"Try not to use your knuckles on somebody's skull," I advised, as I motioned for another round for both of us. "Recipe for pain."

"So I'm a rookie," Karla's voice lowered conspiratorially. "Want to hear what happened next?"

"There's more?"

"Yes! This jerk freaking punched me in the *face*. Broke my fucking nose," Karla said, proudly. "That was the end of my night! I had to go to the hospital and get my nose set, so I can stay pretty. There was blood all over my bathing suit. Pretty sick!"

I was speechless for a second. "Yes," I said, finally. "That's frightening."

She was an outlaw; that much was clear. And it became clearer, the more time we spent with each other. Karla had grown up an orphan in Pennsylvania. Her adoptive mother, whom she'd loved, had died when she was just seven years old, and from there, she had bounced around to a bevy of foster homes. Unsurprisingly, she had failed to make deep connections there. At eighteen, she'd come to California. When the opportunity came up to start dancing, making real money, she had taken it.

"How, um . . ." I didn't quite know how to phrase this. "How . . . um . . . ?"

"How old am I?"

"Yes," I said, relieved. "How old are you?"

"Thirty," she answered. "And how old are you, Jesse James?"

"Well . . . twenty."

"Does the age difference bother you?" she asked. "Do you envision it to be a *problem*?"

"No," I said honestly. She was a woman, in every sense of the word. Self-sufficient, strong, experienced, and totally gorgeous. I had no problems.

"Great," Karla said, shortly. "Got any more questions?"

I began daydreaming about Karla when I couldn't be with her. On tour, I often found myself smiling, thinking about the odd stories and adventures that she'd gotten herself into. And when I was at home in Long Beach, there was just no one else I wanted to be with.

"How about taking me out in that cool-ass Mustang of yours?" I asked her one day. "I'm in the mood to joyride."

We drove out into the traffic, letting the warm Southern California air hit our faces. Normally, I hated to be in the passenger seat. But next to this exciting new girlfriend of mine, it felt perfect.

"Hey, let's pull in here and get a Coke," Karla said, hooking a quick right into a parking lot.

She spied an unoccupied space in the otherwise packed lot, and made for it. But as Karla swung into the spot, an older guy in the space next to her opened his car door.

"Karla!" I yelled. But she didn't stop. Instead, she *increased* her speed, drove directly into his door, and smashed it hard enough to nearly rip it off the hinges.

"What the *fuck*!" I yelled.

"Crap," Karla said. "Let's get out of here, quick!" With a glance behind her, she threw the car into reverse, peeled hellacious rubber, and took off screeching out of the parking lot.

"What the fuck did you just *do*?" I yelled.

"Hit that guy's door," she admitted, adding, "that was probably my fault."

"You *think*?" My heart was pounding.

"Don't have a heart attack." Karla laughed. "Gosh, you need to unwind a little bit, Jesse. I think maybe you work too much."

Karla wasn't pretending to be tough—she *was* tough. She was a hothead, sure, but her pugnacity was tempered with enough maturity and smarts that it came off as impressive more than anything else. *Together,* I thought secretly, *we make a pretty great package.*

———

Glenn had remained a friend over the years. One afternoon, he approached me with a proposition.

"Jesse," he said, "how about you come back to work for me for a while?"

"What's the gig?"

"Just a U.S. tour. Simple as can be. What do you say? Are you there?"

"Oh, why not?" I said, shrugging. "You guys suck pretty bad these days, but I suppose I could do a few shows just for old time's sake."

Danzig had been steadily gaining in popularity, and by the early nineties, they'd begun to play larger arenas. Instead of working clubs with two thousand or three thousand kids, now they were playing in ten-thousand-seat arenas, and as usual kicking huge mountains of ass. The crowds were harder to control at big shows, though, and more security was necessary. Arenas had to hire their

140 ✠ JESSE JAMES

own team of guys—locals who didn't necessarily have experience or any sympathy with the punk scene itself.

One night in Orlando, Florida, I had a very bad feeling that something was going to go wrong. All of the security looked like meathead ex-football players, which kind of made me hate them right off the bat. Then I saw that they were being really aggressive to the kids who were slam dancing and crowd surfing. Whenever a kid got up on someone's shoulders, they'd pounce on him and wrestle him to the ground.

"Assholes," I mumbled to myself. The fans were just expending some energy. If they tried to touch the band, well, then that was one thing. But crowd surfing? That was part of what they paid for.

"Tell your children not to hold my hand," Glenn screamed.

I stood there stewing, but then the music punched into me, making my hair stand on end. I had been doing this for several years, but it still thrilled me to be on stage, watching the barricade pulse, feeling the manic energy of thousands of punk elbows and knees flying.

"Tell your children not to understand!" he cried.

Just then, I saw a very tiny kid get up on someone's shoulders in the first row. He looked like a little twelve-year-old punker, with a shaved head and maroon lace-up Doc Marten's that were about three sizes too big for him—a little mutt of a kid. He was tossed backward and started to surf the crowd. They passed him from hand to hand. He looked surprised and ecstatic. I grinned. He was having his time.

"Hey, get the *fuck* down from there!"

Out of nowhere, a beefy security guard came stomping toward him, salivating—this kid was easy meat. The guard pushed three kids out of his way, and then seized the little twelve-year-old by the scruff of the neck and slammed him down to the ground.

I watched it happen, and again it pissed me off. *Let the kids mosh. That's the whole point.* After a minute, I realized something was wrong. The runt wasn't getting up. He had been down there too long. Immediately, I jumped down from the stage into the crowd. It was an eight-foot drop. My boots hit the floor hard, stinging.

"Move! Get out of the way, *now*!"

I pushed everyone away from the spot where he had landed. They cleared.

And there, on the ground, lay the small punk, completely motionless.

I picked him up in my arms. He weighed almost nothing. I felt some kind of convulsing in his chest.

"Wake up, kid," I said. There was no response. "Come *on*!"

He gave no acknowledgment that he'd heard me, though. Scared, I hefted him up and placed him on stage. I jumped back up, and, picking him up, I ran through the side doors to get us into the fresh air.

"Please, kid," I said, crying. "Hey, wake up, man. Don't die on us, okay?"

At that moment, I felt him go completely limp in my arms.

8

I was just so devastated. I had never felt anyone die in my arms before. He was such a skinny little kid, tiny. More than anything, he was so incredibly *young*.

"It never should have happened," I said hoarsely that night on the phone with Karla. I tried to express the grief that was overwhelming me. "They didn't have to pull him down like that."

"I'm really sorry, Jesse," she said. Her voice was soft. "I'm so sorry that happened."

"The *worst* case should have been to take that kid and throw him out of the show, you know?" I choked.

"Yes," Karla said.

"He's listening to his favorite band, crowd surfing, going nuts— and then suddenly, he's outside, listening to the show. That'd be enough of a lesson, wouldn't it?" I sniffed. "Instead, they broke his neck and he's fucking *dead*."

Karla was quiet for a moment. "Is there any way you could change things?"

"Meatheads rule this job. I can try to tell them to use less force. But I don't know if they're gonna listen."

"Jesse, you are so gentle," Karla said. "You look like such a big, tough guy. But you're just this little gentle guy inside. Aren't you?"

"Yeah, right," I grumbled. "Whatever."

"Hey, wait a second," Karla said, seriously. "I *love* that about you. You understand that, right?"

I didn't say anything.

"I love *you*, Jesse."

I didn't respond. Just listened to the hum of the phone. "I better go," I said, finally.

"I *said*, I love you," Karla repeated. She waited. "Got anything to say to that?"

———

From that day on, I made sure that if I was going to work, part of my job would include training the arena security on the day of the gig.

"These kids are going to mosh," I told everyone. "They're going to look like they're killing each other. But they *aren't*. If anyone's fighting for real, drawing blood, or actually posing a real threat, just grab them and escort them out, and shut the door behind them."

I was greeted by nods and affable shrugs.

"Do not *injure* anyone," I said.

But it's tough to change the way aggressive men operate. Aging jocks with pale-yellow security jackets and thick beer bellies continued to break punk heads all across Ann Arbor, Boston, and New York City. I probably even broke a few myself. Bit by bit, I felt myself growing disgusted by the entire enterprise.

"I'm thinking about turning in my stripes," I confessed to Eerie Von, Danzig's bassist.

"Yeah," he said.

"You're not surprised?" I asked.

"Jesse," he said, "you are way too smart for this."

"Ah, shut up."

Eerie shrugged. "I don't see you being sixty years old and still knocking people on their heads." He took a long pull at his beer, and stared at me incredulously. "Do you?"

With Eerie and Glenn's encouragement, I segued into tour management. Now, instead of being in the front lines, I was handling the day-in and day-out needs for the bands. I was accountable for an exhausting litany of tasks, including but not limited to: checking the musicians into their hotel rooms, getting their keys, producing a reliable itinerary, schmoozing the front desk, standing up to the concert promoters, and making sure there was Jim Beam and not Jack Daniel's in the dressing rooms—or Gummy Bears and not Jujubes.

This is totally fucking absurd, I realized in no time at all. Rock stars were very talented at what they did, to be sure, but they were also coddled little children who were generally used to getting their own way. I was not very good at coddling. It was not part of my skill set.

I was pretty damn proficient at collecting the money, though. Concert promoters, notorious for lying about the gate, often put their heads together with sleazy tour managers to stiff the record companies and skim great profits off the top. I was a record company's dream—no concert promoter in the world was going to swindle me. I looked way too scary. At the end of the week, I'd fly out to the record executives with a big briefcase full of cash, feeling like a Mafia don.

But the thrill of transporting someone else's hundred-dollar bills was fleeting. I wasn't quite dumb enough to think there was a future in what I was doing.

Then one day Eerie came to me, looking low.

"Jess," he said glumly, "you're going to have to book Chuck a flight back home."

"Why's that?"

"Dimwit, man. He's dead."

Chuck Biscuit's little brother had died of a heroin overdose. Dimwit had been a one-of-a-kinder, a great talent with a huge personality, not to mention the guy who'd hooked me up with touring in the first place. He was one of the most brutal drummers punk had ever seen, but he wasn't invincible. The lifestyle had kicked his ass, and I saw it as a sign.

What finally pushed me over the edge, though, wasn't the death and drugs surrounding me. Instead, it was a simple videotape.

I was working for White Zombie at the time. We were all sitting on a tour bus, headed into Detroit, when Rob Zombie leaned over to me and said, "Jesse, you like bikes, right?"

"Yes, Rob," I said patiently. Rob knew I liked bikes. Everybody who knew me at that time understood it was all I could stand to talk about with any kind of interest. He was just giving me the needle. "Yes I do."

"Then you'll get a *huge* kick out of this." And he flipped on the *Easyriders* tape.

Easyriders Video Magazine—not to be confused with the famous Peter Fonda movie of similar name—was a cheesy promotional vehicle that focused on the bearded dudes and jean-shorted chicks who inhabited the bike world. This particular episode featured some geriatric biker who apparently had done security for the Grateful Dead for about twenty-five years.

"This right here's my *baby*!" said the roadie proudly, thumbing toward a decrepit Harley panhead that leaned next to a brick building, a ramshackle police-service sidecar attached clumsily to the old machine.

I squinted distrustfully at the television screen, inspecting that roadie more closely. A dirty red bandanna wrapped around his head. Beard stubble sprouted from his chin and cheeks, grizzled and irregular.

Shit, I thought to myself. *Is that going to be . . . me?*

Outside my window, Midwest scenery whipped by. I envisioned myself twenty years from now, with cracked teeth and flabby arms, going out on midnight runs for the band: *Jess! Pick us up some speed, would ya, man? Haw haw haw! Roadies rule!*

I knew I had to get out. And fast.

That night, Rob and I were screwing around backstage before the show, and he started teasing me again.

"For a big, rugged fucker, you sure are a big *softy,*" Rob said. "Aren't you? I mean, tour manager? Booking rooms, are you serious?"

"I don't have to bust heads to be a *man,* Rob," I said gently.

"Scared of the crowd." He shook his head sadly. "Man, I never thought I'd see the day!"

"Unlike your typical rock star," I said, "I was not born with a tiny dingle."

"Beg your pardon?"

"All I mean to say is that I have a normal-sized penis. Unlike your typical singer for White Zombie, I don't feel the need to continually assert my masculinity in public."

"Oh *bullshit!*" Rob laughed. "You've gone soft, Jesse. Man, you would not even *stage dive* now, given the chance. You old woman!"

"I'd stage dive," I countered.

"You would not."

"Absolutely. It'd be fun."

"*Really?*" Rob said wickedly. "How about tonight?"

"How high is the stage?"

"Fifteen feet." He laughed. "Big drop! But I mean, if that's too high, you could wait until our gig this spring at the La Jolla Senior Center."

"Fuck you," I said. "Tonight's the night."

"When I go into 'I Am Legend,'" Rob said, "that's your cue. You dive right into the crowd and start surfing. That work for you?"

"I'm Jesse James," I reminded him. "Original head-buster. In some circles, I am still 'the man.'"

"You are so not doing this," Rob said, laughing.

I watched the whole show excitedly, like it was my first. When White Zombie finally thrashed the opening chords to "I Am Legend," I took a running start. My big steel-toed boots smashed hard onto the boards of the stage. At the last possible moment, I pushed off the steel lip, and, jumping as high as I could, soared directly over the crowd like a huge, ugly eagle.

Detroit fuckers aren't stupid, though. The crowd parted like split shit, and I smashed directly down onto the concrete floor. I dislocated my elbow, shattered my radial head, broke my thumb, my nose, and my cheeks.

"Christ," I mumbled weakly. "Can somebody call a doctor?"

The band wailed on unrelentingly. Some punk's boot came down smashing on my busted thumb, shooting waves of awful pain. A knee slammed into my back, and for a moment, I lost consciousness. I was twenty-four years old, and I was done with this shit.

———

When I arrived at my mom's house the next day, I had a cast on my arm, a bandage on my head, and a perfect imprint of a Nike tennis shoe on my chest, where a doctor had stepped on me to snap my arm back into place.

"Jesse!" my mom said. "What on earth happened to you?"

"Don't ask," I said. My head pulsed with pain. "But I'm getting out of the security business."

"Well, I'm glad," she admitted. "Those people weren't good company for you. What do you intend to do?"

"Oh," I mumbled. "I've got a plan."

I'd been working on a little shovel pan straight-leg frame-custom Harley for about a year in my mom's garage. I'd taken my time on it, spared no expense, and in my opinion, it had come out really good. Whenever I'd take it out, people would really dig it, ask me questions about it. I decided the bike might serve me well as a kind of portfolio piece, and I started to take it around to shops to see if I could get a job on the strength of the work I'd done on it.

Performance Machine was the biggest Harley custom brake manufacturer in Long Beach. The owner, Perry Sands, knew my dad, so it was a natural that I'd ask him for a gig.

"Take a close look, man," I said, after introducing myself and telling him what I had in mind. "This bike has Performance wheels and Performance brakes."

"Sure," Perry said, looking it over carefully. "I can see that. But which shop put this together for you?"

"Nobody," I said proudly. "I did it myself, in my own garage."

He gave me a doubtful glance. "Uh-huh. I bet you did. And I guess you painted it yourself, too?"

"Yes, I did," I said stubbornly. "I can do all this stuff. If you give me a chance, I'll show you. I'll work hard as hell."

Frowning, Perry gave me the quick up and down. "How about that busted arm?"

"I heal quick."

Eventually, Perry offered me a job in the back of his shop, installing brakes and doing whatever dirty work needed to be done.

"Pay's twelve dollars an hour to start. How's that sound to you?"

"Kinda shitty," I admitted, "but I'll take it."

"Good." He laughed. "You start tomorrow."

Performance Machine was just like the shipyard. I came in early and left late. When I was in the shop, I put my head down and worked like an animal. Soon, the great feeling that I'd had in Seattle returned. I was using my hands and my mind to make something beautiful and functional and cool. The work gave me a natural high, every single day, even though I was just pretty much a grease monkey there.

Soon, Perry and his brother Ted took a shine to me, probably because I was so serious about the whole job, especially for a kid.

"You actually *like* this crap, huh, Jesse?" they said.

"It's okay," I said nonchalantly.

"Get a load of him!" Ted said with a laugh.

Being back in Long Beach had another advantage: it helped me focus on my relationship. Karla and I were still going strong, and as each day passed, we seemed to get more serious.

"Jess, your hair is getting so *long*," she said one evening, as we were drinking beers together in the hot kitchen of her cramped Huntington Beach apartment. "It'll be longer than mine soon."

"Just working up the nerve to apply to Captain Cream's," I explained.

"You are a weirdo!" said Karla, laughing. "Oh my God! I'm dating a freak." I drew her closer to me and kissed her on her pretty, tanned shoulder. She took a long pull at my beer. "Who lives with his *mom*."

"My mom's all right," I said, defensively.

"But as a roommate?" Karla wrinkled her nose. "You can do better than that, Jesse."

"I doubt it," I replied. "I don't think anyone else would put up with me."

"Oh, I'm not sure," Karla said quietly. She ran her fingers through my hair thoughtfully, from my scalp to the back of my neck. "I think I might be able to do a pretty good job."

So that was that: Karla and I decided to take the plunge. Together, we pooled our money and took out a six-month lease on a little house up on Hackett Avenue. It made for very humble beginnings. I brought my Harley, a beat-up pickup truck, and all my tools. Karla had her swimsuits, her high heels, and an old dinner table. That was about it. For some reason, we did the move at night.

Maybe we thought it was safer or something. It wasn't a very good neighborhood.

"Well?" she asked me on our first night there. "What do you think?"

We lay in bed next to each other, and I could hear the traffic whizzing by outside. It sounded like the ocean—if the ocean had an old internal combustion engine.

"This place is a dump."

"*Jesse,*" Karla said, outraged.

"Oh, hell, I sort of like it," I admitted.

"Man," Karla said, snuggling closer to me. "We are going to be *happy* here. I know it."

I'd never really had a home of my own in my entire life. It had always been my dad's place, or my mom's, or Rhonda's mom's— and it had always ended badly. That night on Hackett Avenue with Karla, I felt the oddest sensation of safeness.

My natural inclination, of course, was to celebrate the occasion with some violence.

"I've decided to teach you how to kickbox," I told Karla, the next morning. "That way, you can keep safe when I'm at work."

"I am *perfectly* capable of taking care of myself, Jesse," Karla assured me.

"Well, now you'll be even more capable," I said.

We sparred for a few minutes. I showed her how to throw a cross.

"Not bad!" I said. "For a girl, you have pretty good form."

"Oh, for a girl, huh?"

"Don't get all offended," I said. "Here, let me show you some combinations."

I hooked a short left into her chest, and followed with a right jab. But Karla darted away from the left, and in so doing, she stepped right into my jab. I bipped her good, right on the chin.

"Oh, shit!" I laughed. "Sorry, honey, I didn't . . ."

I never got to finish my sentence. Karla socked me in the face with her gloved fist, as hard as she could.

"*Fuck!*" I cried, holding my eye in pain. "What the hell did you do that for?"

"Instinct," Karla snapped. She was still holding up her dukes in front of her. She stared me down like a boxer. "Reflexes took over."

I tried to open my eye, but already it had begun to swell. "Instinct. Got it."

"So what's next?" she said cheerfully. She bounced nimbly from foot to foot.

"You're done," I said very quietly, unlacing my gloves. "Flying colors. You passed."

We had tons of love for each other. But we were not a perfect couple. Adjusting to regular life after having been on the road for so many years proved a bigger challenge than I had anticipated. It wasn't that I had been so wild on tour; quite the opposite, actually. As security, I was so used to constantly sweating to ensure that no drummers got stabbed and no groupies got pregnant that I'd rarely had the chance to blow off some steam. Now at long last, it was *my* time to be a shithead.

"I don't like you going to strip bars," Karla informed me.

"I don't even speak to the girls, honey," I told her. "Honest, no one gets a dime from me."

"Then why are you even *there* if you don't talk to the girls?"

"My friends make me go," I swore. "I try to steer us all over to the library, but you know, they just won't have it."

I took Karla seriously, but I also felt like it was my God-given right to run around, talk shit, get into fights, and get drunk with my friends. I knew she couldn't press me too hard about going to strip clubs; after all, hadn't she been doing pretty much the same thing for years now? I guess it was kind of rotten of me to use that against her, but I did it anyway. I didn't know any better.

"Let me be my own fucking *man*," I demanded, coming home

drunk in the middle of the night. "Just because we live together doesn't mean we're married. All right?"

"Yeah, you sure are a big man," she said. "I love the way you're acting, it's so *adult* and *cool.*"

"I told you, you're my woman, and that should be enough for you."

"It's not that, Jesse. I don't like you running around with that crowd . . ."

"Okay, Karessa," I grumbled. "Just let me get some sleep, how's about that?"

"How *dare* you call me that in this home!" she snapped. "You want to *sleep*? Go sleep on the fucking couch."

Despite my growing enthusiasm for drinking and carousing, I somehow always managed to be on point for work. Within a short while, I'd become the go-to guy when anything special came up for Perry or Ted in terms of custom design. One day, a customer named Bob Bowder came in to buy some wheels and brakes. He'd been a famous hot-rodder from Southern California in the fifties.

"Hey, I know who you are," he said with a smile.

"What do you mean?"

"I've been hearing about this long-haired kid who practically *lives* in the back of Performance Machine nowadays. You're Jesse James, aren't you?"

"That's me," I admitted, wiping my hands on a grease-stained rag.

"Look," Bob said. "I don't want to get you red in the face, but Boyd *Coddington's* been asking about you. Did you know that?"

"Nope," I said, truthfully. Coddington was in the hot rod business; I was a motorcycle guy, not a car freak, so I'd never really taken the time to pay too much attention to his shop.

"I believe he's interested in getting you to come work for him," Bob said, casually. "The way I hear it, Boyd's saying that if you're half as good as what people have been saying, he wants you on his team."

"I do bikes," I said, shrugging.

"Well, don't you see, that's just it," Bob said, lowering his voice to an excited whisper. "Boyd's been trying to make some custom motorcycle wheels and parts, but he's not having much luck with it."

"Ah," I said, beginning to understand.

"He needs someone who really knows his way around a Harley." Bob looked at me. "Are you that guy?"

I wasn't quite sure what to do. The only person I knew to ask was an old fifties greaser named Doyle Gammel, who I'd gotten to be friends with through the shop. He also happened to know my dad from back in the day. Doyle was savvy, but he was also Perry's best friend, so I knew I was sort of taking a chance by asking him for advice.

"Are you fucking KIDDING me?" Doyle roared. "*Boyd Coddington* is asking *you* to come work for him?"

"Yes," I said. "What should I do?"

"Do you have *any* idea how hard it is to get into that shop?" Doyle's eyes flashed, and he leaned up so close to me that, for a moment, I was sure he was going to clamp his teeth onto my face. "Boyd's the *best*! If you don't take that job, *I'll fucking kill you!*"

With that even-keeled recommendation in mind, I went to Perry the following day and gave him my notice. A week later, I was working for Boyd.

"You're going to be my wheel guy," Boyd explained to me. "Understood? You are going to eat, shit, and breathe *wheels*."

Boyd was the biggest custom-car wheel manufacturer in California. But he hadn't been able to tap into the market for bikes yet.

"Motorcycle geeks are finicky," he explained to me. "Man, if they give me a call, and they get a sense I don't know what I'm talking about? They're *gone*." He stared at me. "What I need is an expert. Can you build me some bitchin' wheels, and talk about them to customers?"

I cleared my throat nervously. "I can try, that's all I can promise." I motioned to the workers who walked confidently around the shop. "Some pretty intimidating company I have here."

"Ah, you'll be fine," Boyd encouraged me. "You got some hot rod in you."

The talent Boyd had amassed was truly staggering, though. I couldn't help but take a tiny step back when I walked in for the first time. Twelve of the most talented dudes on the planet had been assembled together to build custom cars from the ground up. They were the all-stars of the hot rod world: Chip Foose, George Gould, Steven Greninger, Roy Plinkos, from El Paso, Texas—they were simply world-class. Each painter, each upholsterer, each fabricator sat at the very top of his field. And I had been brought there to work with them.

"Hey, everyone," I said, on my first day on the job. I gave a small wave, then pointed to myself. "I'm Jesse James."

No one even raised his head. The shop continued to hum along with its steady, patient buzz of activity.

"Great to meet you, too," I mumbled, and set about my work.

For my first few weeks, I spent literally every second of my time welding in the back room. No one spoke to me. It figured: I was a tattooed kid in my mid-twenties, and the next youngest guy there was probably about forty. A couple of master metalworkers from Sweden were in their eighties. I just didn't fit in.

One afternoon, I was sweating over a wheel, a split spun hoop, adding material to it to enlarge its circumference. I was all folded over my work, my welding helmet over my head. With no warning at all, Greninger walked up and pounded on the table as hard as he could with a hammer. *WHAM!*

I jumped about a foot and dropped the welder on my pants.

"AAAHHHH!" I screamed involuntarily. "What the fuck are you *doing*?"

"Just making sure you were paying attention," Steve said quietly. Walking away, he added thoughtfully, "Shithead."

After a second, I laughed. I knew then that I'd been accepted.

Things were pretty cool after that. I'd come into the shop with a metal tape, and fast-talk all the old guys into letting me blast it through the morning. "Yeah, you like Slayer, dontcha, ya Swedish motherfuckers?" They had no idea what to make of that music, except they were pretty sure they hated it. I made some good friendships with the old weirdos, though. Roy Plinkos quickly became a teacher to me. As long as I brought him a pint of peppermint schnapps, he'd show me all kinds of cool stuff. You wouldn't want to get his breath near any kind of open flame, though.

Everyone did impressive work. We built beautiful 1932 Fords literally from the ground up, making the tubes, the wheels, the frame, and the suspension all by hand. We constructed a car for Wilt Chamberlain. Boyd quickly decided he liked me, probably because it was clear that I was superstoked to be there. I was making very little, maybe $700 a week, a fraction of what I had earned while on tour, but I didn't care. I knew the experience I was getting was rare and valuable. My own work was a success, too. Wheels were flying off Boyd's shelves as fast as I could manufacture them. The custom motorcycle movement was well under way, and Boyd, savvy businessman that he was, had gotten in at just the right time.

"You know," I said to Karla thoughtfully, "I just might be able to tap into this market myself. I mean, I could probably make some bike parts right here at home."

"Well, why don't you?" she asked me. "You have the garage space."

"Boyd probably wouldn't want me making wheels," I said. "He'd see it as competition."

"Then how about making something else?" Karla said reasonably. "Something he's not doing as much."

I thought about it for a while, and then it came to me: *fenders*. When I'd been at Performance Machine, one of my occasional jobs had been to take Harley fenders and widen them. In the early nineties, a lot of people liked to have a big back tire for their Harleys—that was just the prevailing style. That meant fenders had to be bigger, too, so they could fit over the large back tire.

Enlarging factory fenders was a bum job, though. Performance Machine had their fenders manufactured in China, and working with that cheap steel was a total mess. The metal would bubble and spatter terribly under a welding torch as I attempted to split them, and then rejoin them with new steel. But, I reasoned, if I started from scratch, with better metal, I could make a really cool-looking fender. High quality, durable. Generally kick-ass.

A name had been kicking around in my head for a while, too, one that I thought had a certain ring to it.

"What do you think of the handle *West Coast Choppers*?" I asked Karla. "For my business, I mean."

"Wow," Karla said. "I like it. It's catchy."

We made a good team in those days, at least when we weren't squabbling. Karla was still dancing then, had been doing it for going on a decade. Eventually, though, she came to an impasse, because the swimsuit dancing that she had grown up on had sort of started to go out of style.

"They're all little sluts," Karla said, crying, one night when she came home after work.

"Hey," I said. "What's wrong? What happened?"

She buried her head in my chest. "The other girls I work with . . . I don't want to talk about it."

"Come here." I got up and got a glass of water from the kitchen sink for her. "Stop crying and tell me what's going on."

She sniffed, and wiped away the tears from her eyes. "My boss . . . he says I have to go topless."

"I thought they didn't do that where you worked."

"We *don't*!" Karla spat. "But my boss says all the other places are doing it these days. He says the customers expect it."

I sat there for a second. "What do you think you're gonna do?"

She shrugged and looked so helpless. But then she screwed up her face, and gave me that determined kind of look that I had come to associate with Karla. "I'll just go topless, then."

And she tried, for about two weeks. But it was awful to see. Every night, Karla came home from work bawling her eyes out, pissed at the rude crowd, and incensed at the younger girls who were cutting into her money.

"I was so close to punching that Jezebelle tonight, I swear to God!"

"Honey . . ."

"I mean, I am like this far from *wrapping up her hair around my fist* and *yanking* her down to the floor!" She paced back and forth across the linoleum of our kitchen. "Tell me that I won't! I've done it before and I am FULLY capable of doing it again!"

"Karla." My voice was loud. "Just stop for a second."

"What?"

"I don't want you doing this anymore."

"Who cares what *you* want?" She looked at me incredulously.

"Come on," I said. "Give me a break. What I mean is, I don't think *you* want to be doing this anymore."

She bit her lip stubbornly. "Oh, believe me, I do. I'm better than any of those little tramps."

"I know you are, Karla," I said. "You have class."

"Yes, I do," Karla sniffed.

"But you've done it. You've lived it. It's enough. It's time to move on."

She stared at me for a second, helplessly. "But what else can I *do*?"

"Work with me. Help me get my business off the ground."

She was quiet for a moment, considering. "Not the worst idea I've ever heard."

"Right?" I asked.

"You could use a lot of help, is what I really mean," Karla said. "You've got no sense of how to balance a bankbook, for one thing."

"Well, see, there you go."

"Not to mention you know nothing about marketing."

"Right," I said, clearing my throat.

"I've always wanted to try to learn about business accounting," Karla said, excited all over again. "I think I might have some talent at it."

"You'll be just great. Let's move on to the next stage, okay?"

She came closer to me, and I wrapped her up in my arms.

"I got your back," I said. "I promise."

She kissed me and we hugged. It felt really good, to have her heart up next to mine, to have her little body sitting up on my thighs, clutched close to me.

"You really think I was good?" she whispered. "I mean . . . at dancing?"

"Karla," I said to her, truthfully, "you were the best I ever saw."

9

My life felt full and busy. I was trying to figure out how to get my own business off the ground, but I continued to work at Boyd's during the day, knowing I'd never find myself in the company of so many experts again. Unbeknownst to me, though, my life was about to get even fuller.

"Hon?" Karla said to me one morning as I was getting up and getting ready to ride to work. "Can I talk to you?"

"Sure thing," I said. I buttoned the top button of my Dickie's shirt, letting the others hang open in my Long Beach gangbanger fashion. "What's up?"

"I . . . I think I'm pregnant."

I was stunned.

"Are you serious?"

"Yes," she said, looking pale.

I waited, mulling the news over. After a moment, I was able to let the news sink in. "Well, that's good."

"*Good?*"

"Yeah," I said. I came nearer to Karla and put my hands on her shoulders. "Aren't you happy?"

"*I* am," she admitted, blushing. "I just didn't know what you were going to say."

"I've been *hoping* we'd have a kid."

"Really?" She looked at me happily. "Man, you never told me that! You're always surprising me, Jesse."

"We need another welder around here," I continued.

"That's very funny," Karla said.

"What?" I said, smiling. "A little fella with a strong set of hands is just what I need out there in the garage."

"How do you know it's going to be a boy?" Karla asked, her hands on her hips.

I looked at her quizzically. "I'm Jesse James. Of *course* it's going to be a boy."

When I let Boyd in on the news, he grinned real big at me.

"Congrats, kid. And listen, if that girlfriend of yours wants another baby, just let me know."

Boyd reminded me of my dad sometimes. He was a good hustler. I think out of everyone I've ever met, he was just the master of massaging money out of people. I can't even count the number of times people came into the shop all pissed, threatening to sue him, because their superexpensive custom car had some imperfection in it, or wouldn't be ready on the agreed-upon date.

"You *promised*!" they'd scream, red-faced, spitting into Boyd's face.

"Listen, can I talk to you?" he'd ask them seriously. "I'd like to tell you precisely what occurred with your car; I think you'll find it very interesting." And he'd shoulder them into his office, like they were the last friend he had on the earth. Forty-five minutes later, the pair would walk out arm in arm, and Boyd would escort them to the parking lot, where he would bid them a respectful adieu.

"What happened?"

"Wouldn't you know?" Boyd would say to me, shaking his head, impressed with himself. "That fucker just sprung for two more cars."

Boyd had a softer side to him, too. He was dedicated to employing developmentally disabled adults in his shop. The whole time that I worked there, Boyd had three or four of these guys in there, working alongside his team of seasoned pros to churn out hot rods. I didn't quite get it at first—obviously, they slowed down our production schedule to some degree, and I was always a stickler for moving fast. But after a very short while, I discovered that I loved working and learning alongside these guys. They just had the biggest hearts ever. One really special worker was named Gregory. Boyd tended to coddle Gregory, but I treated him just like any other coworker.

"Yo! Gregory. Come here for a second. I got something to tell you."

He would put down his tools and look at me, interested.

"Hey man," I'd whisper. "*Fuck* you."

Gregory's eyes would get all wide. "Fuck *you,* Jesse!"

I was never happier than when I was buying Hershey bars and Dr Pepper's on my breaks, and trying to feed them to Gregory to get him all wired on sugar. He also loved Power Rangers, so I'd always wind him up good by starting conversations about them.

"Boy, you like those Mighty Morphins, huh, don't you?"

"Yes," said Gregory, looking excited. "Goldar!"

"Goldar's one of the bad guys, though, isn't he? Are you a bad guy, Gregory?"

"*Yes.*" He squinted at me, giving me his best impression of an evil villain.

When Gregory celebrated his fortieth birthday, I bought him a big Power Ranger glove, one that made all these electronic sounds. Man, his eyes sure did get big when he unwrapped that glove.

"For me!" he said, cradling the glove possessively.

"Now, hold on, that glove is not for *Gregory*," I said, "it's for a badass *Power Ranger*, okay?"

His birthday was on a Friday. The following Monday, bright and early at seven a.m., his parents showed up with him at work. They were very old, and this morning they looked very tired.

"Are you Jesse?"

"I am," I said.

His mother handed me back the box gently. "Thank you very much, but we're going to have to return this to you." She cleared her throat and looked sideways at her son. "Gregory hasn't been to sleep yet this weekend."

"Whoops," I said, reddening, as I accepted the box. "Hey, Power Rangers have to sleep, too, Gregory," I reminded him.

For a while, Boyd's was like home for me. But then things started to get bumpy. I was making the shop a ton of money with the wheels, and Boyd started to treat me with favored son status. The grumbling started then, and it only worsened when Boyd gave me a new van to drive around.

"Really, Boyd?" I said, impressed. It was a brand-new Astrovan, lowered, with cool seventeen-inch wheels. "I *dig* it."

"Something to drive that hot pregnant girlfriend of yours around in," Boyd explained.

"Gotcha," I said, laughing.

"It's not a fucking present," Boyd said. "Just so you know. It's on loan, so get that through your head. But you're doing real good. Just look at it as a small bonus, to let you know my heart's in the right place."

Unfortunately, the word got around real quick that the boss had given me a car. Right away it started getting a little political and cliquey in there. Guys who'd started to open up and accept me clammed right up.

"Boy, I wish *I* had a new car," one of the guys complained loudly, as he passed by my wheel station. "That'd be pretty sweet."

"Yup," said another guy, shooting me a hateful look. "My Jag's about dead. I guess we'll all have to hitch rides with Jesse James. That is, if he'll be so kind as to pick us up in that shiny new van of his."

"It's ridiculous," I complained to Karla, that evening. "Why should I be putting my energy toward a team that actually resents me for doing the best job I can?"

"Maybe you should give notice," she suggested. "That doesn't sound like a very healthy environment."

"I'd love to," I said. "But we're not exactly doing a million in retail yet, are we?"

I'd set up a space in the garage where I could build my fat fenders, and I'd manufactured a few of them from raw material. My design was good, and my craftsmanship looked up to par; I'd put one over the rear wheel on my Harley and to me, it looked pretty damn cool. But a nagging problem remained: Who was I going to *sell* them to?

I was stumped. On top of the issue of sales, my problems seemed magnified by a shadow of doubt: try as I might, I couldn't quite accept the idea that I could actually become a successful person by starting my own motorcycle business. When we were growing up, the biker world simply wasn't respectable—it was for Hells Angels and speed freaks. Even though I loved this work, the thought of a man working steadily at this particular craft to support his family still seemed a bit foreign to me.

And I wasn't the only one having doubts.

"Please don't take this the wrong way," Karla said. "Because, I'm actually curious. But I mean, why would anyone pay so much for a motorcycle *fender*?"

"Well, I don't know," I admitted. I placed my hand on her growing belly to soothe me. "It is kind of odd, when you stop to think about it."

"I mean, why do guys care so much about bikes in the first place?" Karla wondered, her arms folded.

"Beats me," I said. "One of life's greater mysteries."

But somewhere in the back of my mind, I knew that there was a pretty good answer to Karla's question. Motorcycle fans saw themselves as rebels, just like punks did. Rejecting the status quo of society generally takes a certain kind of courage, but more than that, it takes *style*.

I was a jock turned delinquent turned bodyguard turned welder. I knew my market: men. They were ex-cons, trespassers, and reprobates; but more, they were guys who saw themselves as fitting in somewhere outside of normal. A fierce-looking chopper was their indispensable outlaw badge. When they thought about peeling out, riding into the desert, boots smoking with the speed of the ride, I wanted Jesse James and West Coast Choppers to be the first name off their lips.

"Yep, honey," I said to Karla, affectionately running my hand over her stomach once more. "Pretty weird. I really have no idea why anyone gives a damn."

———

So for the time being, I stayed on at Boyd's, ignoring the dirty looks my coworkers sent my way. Fuck them, it wasn't like Boyd had given me a Porsche. At night, I hung with my lady and teased her about being pregnant.

"Hey, you want one?" I asked, motioning to my beer.

"Real funny, Jesse," she sniffed. "God, I wish you could be pregnant for just one day, and see how easy it is."

"I got troubles of my own," I cried. "I'm out there trying to start a business! Make a buck for this little baby!"

"Who are you trying to sell your fenders to, Jesse?" Karla asked.

"Well," I said, "I took a few to the swap meet last weekend."

"Are you serious?" Karla laughed. "The *swap* meet? Did you actually sell any?"

"One," I admitted, embarrassed. "Look, I understand the swap meet, okay? That's where I grew up."

"Okay," Karla said, looking serious. "No more fooling around. It's time for us to get cracking. What we need to do is go around to some *shops*. We need to get you to a place where someone might buy, like, *ten* of your fenders."

"Maybe Performance would want some," I mused.

"There you go," Karla said. "We'll start there. Where else?"

"I don't know," I said. "There's probably about ten bike shops in the area we could try."

Karla grinned. "So what are we waiting for?"

Karla was right. Most of the bike shops we talked to liked fenders, and agreed to take on a couple right away, to see if they'd sell to customers. And immediately, they did. I started receiving progressively more excited phone calls from store owners, demanding that I furnish them with more custom fenders.

"This is incredible!" I told Karla. "I mean . . . I can't believe it. People really like these things!"

"Of course," Karla said, sounding authoritative. "A chopper really looks good with a wide back wheel, covered by a fat fender." She giggled. "Don't it?"

Soon, the orders began piling in. From one week to the next, they doubled in size. Then tripled. My margin was great: I was selling each fender for several hundred dollars, and reaping a nice profit on each piece.

One day, Karla approached me with a snooty look on her face.

"As West Coast Choppers' official business manager," she announced, "I request a meeting with our chief Grease-Monkey-in-Charge."

I laughed. "What is it?"

"Jesse, I've been looking over the books," Karla said, her voice filling with rising excitement. "You're making more on your fenders than at the hot rod shop."

I was completely taken aback. "That must be a mistake."

"It's not, babe. I checked the numbers three times. Honestly, it almost doesn't make sense for you to keep on working there."

"But I *like* those guys," I said, after a second. "And I owe a lot to Boyd."

"And we have a baby on the way," Karla reminded me, patting her stomach. "Just think for a second. Imagine how much we could be earning if you decided to put all your time toward your own business."

I was silent for a moment. "I'll think about it."

But the breaking point came soon. One evening, when Karla was nine months pregnant and huge, she approached me cautiously. "Hon," she said, "do you know how much West Coast Choppers cleared this week?"

"Nope," I said honestly. But I knew it had to be a lot. I had stayed up most of each night working to fulfill massive orders from independent bike shops, then rising early as usual to get to Boyd's. I was beyond exhausted.

"Ten thousand dollars," she said quietly.

I was amazed. I stood there and said nothing.

"It's time for you to resign, Jesse," she said gently. "Like, today."

———

So I quit. Our garage up on Hackett Avenue wasn't going to hold me anymore. It had gotten so full of tools, it'd take me forty-five minutes to move everything around before I could even have a space to work. I had a mill, a lathe, and a paint booth, all smashed together in a two-car garage.

"Do you think you might help me find a space?" I asked Doyle Gammel, a few days after I left the hot rod shop.

"Kid, you are truly an idiot to leave Boyd," he sighed. "But yeah, sure, I'll help you if you want."

I let out a breath, relieved.

"Hell, I'll even *rent* to you," Doyle said. "Look, I got five thousand square feet on Minnesota Avenue, and about half of that's going to waste. My weight machines aren't moving like they used to."

Over the years, Doyle had shifted gears, moving from constructing hot rods to making custom gym equipment for the California prison system.

"You do great work," I said. "The felons of our society thank you."

"Fuck you, okay?" Doyle replied. "There's money in prisons."

To start, I rented a single carport from him—an area about as big as a patio.

"What do you think?" Doyle asked, watching me load my tools and workbench into the space.

"It's great," I said, enthusiastically. "But watch out. I won't be in just one carport for long, you can bet on that. Soon I'm gonna be taking over your whole shop, Gammel."

"I'll believe it when I see it, Jesse. But you're a good kid. You remind me of your dad. Always working," Doyle said. "He stored his antiques and furniture across the street from here, way back in the seventies, do you remember that?"

"Sure, I remember," I said.

"Now, that was a *greasy* sonofabitch!" Doyle laughed. "Man, that guy had so many swindles going, it was incredible. Do you remember the time . . ."

"Doyle?" I interrupted. "Do you ever talk to him? I mean, like, these days?"

"Nope," Doyle said. "I haven't spoken to him in years." He looked at me. "You guys aren't in touch very often, then, I suppose?"

"Understatement." I laughed bitterly.

"Well, you know, maybe there's still hope. Reconciliations can happen at the oddest of times."

I just shook my head. "Doyle, my girlfriend's nine months pregnant, and he doesn't even know her name."

Two friends of mine from the neighborhood, Fast Eddie and Jim Lillegard, came over to keep me company at the shop on one of the first days I was there. Although the new shop was pretty tiny, it still felt vast and empty compared to my own garage. I didn't have any orders for the day, and the shop was barren of activity. My tools, scattered all over the place, looked silly and useless to me in their inactive state.

I couldn't help but think: *Man, what if I've bitten off more than I can chew?*

Jim leaned over to Eddie and chuckled. "He'll be out of business in a month."

I cleared my throat. "Yeah, we'll see," I said, finally.

Maybe I'm a stubborn sort of guy or something, and maybe I'm a little too sensitive for my own good. But that particular comment has stayed in the front of my mind for the better part of twenty years.

I'll show you, motherfuckers.

I had no marketing team, and West Coast Choppers had zero name recognition. My only ace in the hole was *quality*. If the motorcycle scene had a dirty little secret, it was this: ever since the 1950s, Harleys had used great motors in their bikes, but their accessories were just sort of shoddy. They cut corners and had as much of their manufacturing done overseas as they could possibly get away with. A few other builders had made a name for themselves producing quality peripherals, but for the most part, no one was very dedicated to making motorcycle components that looked really stunning.

"I don't care how much this costs to make, or how high the final price is," I told Karla at home that night. "I am gonna make *bitching* stuff. That's all I care about."

"Uh-huh," she said, breathless.

"I'm going to put my name on it," I promised. "Jesse James and West Coast Choppers. Hey, did I tell you, I want to use this Maltese cross as our logo? People are going to go crazy, it looks so hard-core."

"Jesse," Karla said, her voice taking on a warning tone that, in my enthusiasm, I completely ignored.

"I mean, if people want good stuff, they should have to pay for it," I said. "And I think they're gonna cough up the dough, no problem! This is the right stuff, at the right time. Don't you think?"

"JESSE!" Karla yelled. "The *baby* is coming!"

We jumped in the car and sped down to Long Beach Medical. With me having quit Boyd's, we had no health insurance, but I had fender money.

"How will you be paying for the room, sir?" a nurse said to me snidely, looking at my long greasy hair and tattooed arms. "Medicaid, sir?"

I showed her my wad. "Cash."

Funny how good they treated us after that. Karla got the biggest room around, and when her labor continued late into the evening, I was allowed to stay there with her overnight.

"Don't leave me, okay?" she said, gripping my hand.

"Hell, I thought you were tough," I chided her. "Thought I had a wildcat for a girlfriend, but I guess I was wrong."

"Don't leave," she whispered.

"I won't," I promised her. "I'm not going anywhere."

Karla suffered through twenty-six hours of labor, through screams and grunts and sweats. And I stayed right there with her. I was by her side when the doctor helped a baby out from within her.

"It's a girl," he announced, holding her up for me to see.

I almost fainted. *A girl?* I thought. *Couldn't be.*

But then a feeling came over me, the strongest feeling I'd ever felt. I looked at my baby, and it was the oddest thing: I loved her instantly. I loved her more than anyone I'd ever met in my life. I was a father. Instantly, my life had changed. I had a daughter.

———

We named our daughter Chandler. Suddenly, I had two strong new forces in my life: a new baby and a new business I was trying my damnedest to grow. The challenges of both made me very happy.

"Let's take her up to the Laughlin River Run," I said to Karla.

"Jesse!" she said. "She's just an infant."

"Yeah, but she's a *badass* infant," I said, matter-of-factly. "And I'd like her to come to a motorcycle show with her dad."

So Karla and I drove up to Laughlin, Nevada, with Chandler in tow. She was so small that we strapped her down to a seat with a motorcycle tie-on. I was nervous on the way up: I wanted to hurry up and get our brand out there. We set up in our booth and for the entire first day, attracted very little business.

"Is this even worth the trip?" I grumbled.

"Patience, sweetie, patience," Karla advised. But I could tell she was feeling nervous, as well.

The second day began in much the same fashion: as they passed by, customers looked with interest at the wide fenders we had out on display, but not a single soul plunked his money down to purchase one.

"This is bullshit," I said, slamming my hand on the table. "I'm gonna break us down early. We're heading back to Long Beach."

But just then, a guy named Skeeter Todd, who worked for a distributor named Custom Chrome, stopped by the booth. He looked the merchandise over with a discerning eye.

"You know what?" Skeeter said, finally. "I'll buy as many of these as you can make."

"Are you kidding?" I asked him, laughing, unable to believe my ears.

"No, these are great. You gotta come to Morgan Hill, though, and meet the distributor, Steve." He looked at me seriously. "I think we can make you a hell of a lot of money, Jesse."

Custom Chrome, at the time, was the biggest motorcycle parts distributor in the world. It was a very big deal to get an appointment with them. Karla and I celebrated hard that night.

"I wish to make a toast!" I cried, holding up a beer in our seedy Laughlin hotel room. "To good ol' *Skeeter*!"

"What's his last name?" Karla asked. Chandler was cradled in her arms, and she slept soundly. "You shouldn't toast someone without putting his last name into it."

That stopped me. "Man," I said. I thought as hard as I could. "I can't remember that dude's last name."

Karla remained unfazed. "To Skeeter," she announced regally.

"Hey, no!" I cried, remembering: "To Skeeter TODD!" I swigged my bottle of Coors, putting it down easy. Then, in victory, because I was feeling so good, I cracked open a fresh one.

———

The following Monday morning, I headed up to Custom Chrome to talk business with Steve Fisk, their head of distribution, a big guy who had been around forever. You didn't get as high up in the food chain as Steve was without being sharp as hell. He was quick-talking, crude, and was said to be fluent in Mandarin and Cantonese.

"You do excellent work, Jesse," Fisk said.

"Thanks a lot," I said. "Skeeter was telling me you might want to buy a good number of pieces."

"That's right," Fisk agreed. "I'm thinking a hundred dollars a fender, too."

"A hundred dollars a fender seems a little low, Steve," I told him calmly.

He shrugged. "Well, that's your opinion, Jesse. But keep in mind that we have suppliers over in China, and they're very capable of duplicating an oversized fender like yours."

"No, they can't," I said, just as calmly.

He stared at me. "And what makes you say that?"

"Just a hunch," I said. "I mean, why would we be standing here and having this conversation, if you could get my product in China, for less money than I want?" Keeping my voice at an even keel, I continued. "You're trying to okeydoke me, Steve, but I'm sorry to tell you—I'm not that guy."

Fisk said nothing for a moment. Then he spoke. "What is it you want?"

"I want three things," I said. "I want two-fifty per fender. I want a minimum initial order of one hundred pieces of each size. And the biggest thing, I want my name on each of my fenders: Jesse James, West Coast Choppers."

He snorted. "Why would we do *that*?"

"Cause it's no deal if you don't," I said. "I'm not stupid, Steve. These fenders are gonna sell like crazy for you—they're gonna make both of us a lot of money. And if my product's out there, I want it advertising *my* brand, not yours."

We stared each other down for a few moments. "You're a cocksucker," Fisk said.

"Yup."

He sighed, defeated. "I'll call the legal department. We'll get the papers drawn up."

From that moment on, West Coast Choppers became a recognized entity. We never looked back. Our logo was part of it. Some people thought it was like a swastika, but it wasn't, it was a Maltese cross, a symbol of valor and strength. Besides having been popular with hot rodders and motorcycle enthusiasts for many years, the symbol happens to be on every fire truck in the nation.

I didn't mind the controversy, though. Whatever brought us more attention, I was for it. We were a new company, and we needed brand recognition. And after a very short amount of time, it began to happen for us. My fenders sold swiftly for Custom Chrome, and soon, other distributors began to knock on the door with increasing interest. I was able to take on my first employee, a welder-fabricator friend of mine named Rick Henry. He tried to help me shoulder the increasingly large load. But demand just kept on growing.

One morning, I received a phone call from a guy named Jay Sedlicek. Jay lived in Iowa. He'd gotten to know me a few years back when he'd bought some products from Performance Machine.

"I called Perry today and asked for you," said Jay. "He said you'd gone into business for yourself."

"True enough," I said. "I'm doing custom fenders, mostly. Need some?"

"Actually," Jay said, "I need a whole *bike*. Can you do that for me?"

"Man, that sounds like fun."

It was precisely the challenge I'd been waiting for. I'd done paint work, exhaust pipes and wheels, and of course, by this time, I had fenders down pat. But Jay Sedlicek was the first guy who wanted a whole bike made to order.

"Great," Jay said. "What's the deposit you need?"

"How do you mean?"

He laughed. "How much *money* do you want in advance?"

I thought it over. "If you send me a check for twenty-five thousand we can get this thing popping right away."

To my utter surprise, he did it. Jay Sedlicek was customer number one. He wanted a flat-track Sportster, a modern XR-750 with big brakes and cool wheels. Beyond that, all the design specs would be up to me.

Hmmm, I thought. *Let's see . . .*

I bought a used bike and tore it down completely, right down to the bare frame. From there, I began to carefully build it up from the ground, constructing a gas tank, fashioning a dual stainless exhaust system, and forming custom wheels and fenders. I even designed a shaped aluminum exhaust cover, using old-school methods: hammer and mallet. It was the first time I'd tried to make an organic shape out of metal. In the end, it looked pretty gorgeous.

Of course, me being me, I wrecked the bike on its first test drive, trying to pop a wheelie at breakneck speed.

"You freakin' idiot," I mumbled, lying on the ground, dazed and bleeding.

So I had to start from square one and bust my ass again to

rework it in time for the deadline. But in the end, the job got done. The check stayed cashed. Jay never knew.

The orders kept coming—at a pace that surprised even me.

"Shit, you think we can keep up?" I asked Rick.

"I don't know, Jesse," he said doubtfully. "If this keeps up, you gotta let *me* hire someone."

Our turning point was the day we installed a fax machine in the office. Now distributors could simply fax me purchase orders for the parts they wanted, instead of calling up and haggling with a human being.

"Goddammit!" Rick would cry, frustrated, every time he'd hear the mechanical screech of the fax machine go off, followed by the sounds of an order being printed. "How are we ever going to get ahead?"

That thing used to go all day. Orders for tens of thousands of dollars used to stream in, hour after hour. It was almost magical. But I was working constantly, and it was wildly stressful. I was sleeping about three hours a night. Still, when I was building a crate in the driveway outside of Doyle's to ship a $20,000 order that I did in one week, it made it all worth it, and then some. For the first time in my entire life, I truly felt successful.

"You're looking good," Karla told me one night when I'd finally dragged myself home to our tiny house. "Tired, but good."

"I'm happy," I told her.

"We're really doing it, huh?" Karla asked.

"Yeah, I guess we are. It's kind of amazing." I opened up the refrigerator and took out a beer. I took a drink from it, and looked my girlfriend over for a long second. "You know, you look really good, too. I think being a mom agrees with you."

"You really think so?"

"Definitely," I said. "Are you the hottest mom in Long Beach?"

She socked me on the shoulder. "Jesse, you're such a sweetheart."

I opened up the refrigerator again and stared into the pale light. "We have anything to *eat* in here?"

"Oh," Karla said. "I made some pasta. Chandler and I ate earlier. But I think it was mostly her eating, and me cleaning up." She laughed. "Go on ahead and take a shower. I'll heat it up."

I kissed her. "Thank you. You're the best."

"I know," said Karla, moving past me, lighting the gas on the stove. "Now, if you will *please* go wash yourself, I would be eternally grateful. You smell like burned tires or something."

I kissed her on the back of her neck. In the next room, our baby daughter slept an untroubled sleep. In my heart, I knew things could never get better than this moment. Somehow, we'd made it to the top.

10

We just got bigger and bigger.

Orders piled up. I hired another welder, a dude from El Salvador named Eduardo. He had attitude: "I can weld all day, so just watch me." I watched him. I purchased another planishing hammer, so me and Rick could both work on shaping metal at the same time. All day long, the pneumatic hammers would pound metal . . . *BAMBAMBAMBAM!* It was a fine orchestra: the *sssstth* of the welding torch, sending sparks flying up over Eduardo's darkened helmet, the constant *crreeeeecch* of the fax machine . . . plus the Circle Jerks and Bad Brains and Suicidal Tendencies . . . I brought a huge Peavey amp and a pair of thousand-dollar Pioneer speakers . . . a finger touching the dial delicately . . . music smashing up against my eardrums . . . the din hurting my head . . .

"Turn off that *fucking music!*"

"Oh, sorry Doyle," I said, laughing. "I didn't see you there. This is how my team works, man!" I turned down the tunes and shut down my planisher. "That better?"

"No," he shouted. "My ears are bleeding. Your music *sucks*."

"Aw, stop moaning, you big baby," I said. "Hey, Doyle, I think I'm gonna need to hire some polishers soon. This is way too much for me and Rick to handle. You know anyone?"

"How much you paying? I might take the job on myself. My weight machines aren't selling for shit," he sniffed. "This is crazy, what's going on here, Jesse."

"Told you, Doyle," I said modestly. "Didn't I say I was gonna need more space soon?"

"Well, do you?"

"Yes," I said. "I've been thinking about what direction I want to go in. This fender shit pays the bills, but I want to shift over to making whole bikes."

"Better money?"

"Better everything," I said. "See, I got a picture in my head of the kind of bikes I want to see. No one's making them. Everyone's caught up on that same old shit—"

"Grandiose fucker," Doyle interrupted me. "Sure, I'll rent you some more space. Take over this whole building for all I care, man."

Shifting over to creating entire custom bikes seemed like the next natural step for West Coast Choppers. I didn't see a future in building fenders and exhaust pipes for the rest of my life. I might be able to make a living at it, but if I limited myself to making parts, then I might as well be a machine. There was probably more money in selling customs, anyway. You involved the buyer in the decision-making process, and then charged him handsomely for the privilege of weighing in on the particulars of the design.

But even more than making a bundle, I was attracted to the idea of the bike as sculpture. Harleys were gorgeous machines, but if you bought them from a dealer, they all looked the same. You plunked down fifteen grand as an expression of your own individual badass nature, and then you lost it in the parking lot among dozens of identical copies.

It didn't have to be that way. I had ideas for elongated handlebars, dynamic frames, silvered gussets, and chromed-out wheels. We'd capitalize on the momentum we'd generated thus far; our guerrilla advertising and enthusiastic word of mouth would do the rest. It would take a huge amount of effort, dedication, and talent, no doubt. But I was beginning to believe that I might have enough of all three to succeed.

—

As I began to spend more and more time at the shop, Karla was not pleased.

"I never see you anymore," she said.

"Honey," I said, "West Coast is at a fragile point. You understand that, right?"

"No. Explain it to me."

"I just took on two more guys," I said. "They need my guidance."

"You just got a pool table in there, too."

I laughed. "Well, Doyle about rented me the whole place, and we needed to fill a room. Look, can't I blow off some steam after I get done slaving? You know, I'm working fifteen-hour days."

"You have a daughter, Jesse. You have responsibilities at home, too."

"I know," I said gently. "I will try harder to make time for all of us. I promise."

But even as I said it, I knew I was lying. The momentum was building for West Coast Choppers, and it was just too damn exciting to be away from there even for a minute. With more employees around to work the hammers, I was freed up to do design work, and I wanted to seize on it.

"What's that?" Rick said to me, looking over my shoulder in the small office I'd converted into a drawing studio.

"A frame I'm working on," I said. "See how it's gonna be all elongated and smooth?"

"You think people will want to ride like that?" asked Rick dubiously, staring at the long, curved backbone and the intricate piping I'd drawn.

"I don't know," I said calmly. "I guess we better build one and find out."

I slaved over the shop jig, welding the tubes for a week, failing at the work, frustrated, then coming back time and time again to correct it. Finally the piece was born: a complicated but ultimately very functional elongated custom frame that would hopefully serve as a structural base for a beautiful motorcycle.

"I'm going to patent this," I told Rick proudly. "My CFL frame."

"How's that?"

"Choppers for Life."

Slowly, I was becoming better at my craft. Projects I'd seen as overly complex or simply too intimidating seemed wholly within the realm of possibility. *Hell, I might as well* try, *right?* I spent a full fourteen-hour day attempting to handcraft a gas tank out of aluminum sheeting. I hand-pounded the metal, softening it, shaping it, coaxing it underneath the foot-tensioned planishing hammer. Back and forth, back and forth, I ran the metal, until it was butter-soft and shining. I welded the partitions together, coaxing shape, form, and function out of what had previously been dull and flat.

I can't believe this! I laughed to myself, when I was done. *It actually worked!*

It was addictive. I wanted to do it all the time. Thinking back to the years I'd spent running around with rock bands, knocking people's teeth out, I could hardly believe I'd been that person. This was so much more fulfilling. It was a completely encapsulating existence, creative while still being badass, and littered with wads of money around every turn.

Local fame was even part of the package. As our brand grew in recognition, the Long Beach and Riverside motorcycle freaks began to talk to one another, and I had gearheads coming by every day, just to hang around the shop.

"Whattaya say, Jesse, you got a job for me? I'm a dynamite painter, man, I can make candy flames shoot up at a moment's notice! That gas tank of yours would look pretty fuckin' bitchin' with some custom flake, tell you that!"

Everybody seemed to want to be included. We were growing at such an absurd rate, with so many new orders coming in for custom bikes, that I was actually able to employ some of the more talented guys who came by. Again I expanded into Doyle's studio, taking over another nice-sized chunk to use as a paint shop.

"Dude, you ever think about making *T-shirts*?" my friend Chino asked me one day. Chino was a fixture in the low-rider world, the accepted master of hydraulics and lowered Impalas with crazy rims. "Put that cool-ass logo on there, and I bet you could sell a load, man . . ."

So T-shirts with our Maltese cross got thrown into the mix, too. Right off the bat, they went like hotcakes. I'd pictured making only enough for the guys at the shop to wear, so we could be our own little gang, but the locals clamored for them, and we sold out our first thousand-order run in under two weeks.

I was feeling hot. The energy of success ran over me constantly, like a current of electricity. I wanted to work all day and drink all night. Sleep just didn't interest me, and after a while, neither did home. I dug up a few friends from around the way who were still stoked to go out and get drunk on weeknights. Mike Newman, Baby Hud, Paul McFadden—they were all six foot two or bigger. Nobody fucked with us. If they did, it got ugly real quick.

"Let's get us some beers," Mike said.

"Let's get us some *trouble*," I countered.

Mike had a real saucy mouth on him. He was the worst fighter in our group, but for some reason, he was always the one starting shit. One evening, we were at a bar on Bayshore and 2nd, when he overheard some Long Beach City College football players doing some drunken bragging about their schedule.

"Hey, what was that team that fucked your knee up, Jesse?"

"Long Beach City College."

"Yeah, that's what I thought," said Mike. "Hell, they were punks then, and obviously, they're punks now."

They looked at him, irritated. "And who are you, tough guy?"

"John Madden," said Mike, pushing his bar stool out from under him and letting it thud onto the floor. "Can't you tell?"

"Well, come on," said their biggest guy. He swung at Mike, just missing smacking him in the mouth with the meat of his fist. When Mike tried to swing back, another football player clocked him in the side of the head. His head hit the bar with a dull thump.

"Oh, boy," I said, putting down my beer and cracking my knuckles. "This just got fun."

Hud, Paul, and I dropped into fighting stances and began to trade blows with the other players.

"Fellas, fellas!" cried the bartender. "We just freaking *redecorated* in here!"

My sparring mate was a big, baby-faced lineman. His skin was peachy-soft, blotchy from the alcohol. He couldn't have been more than twenty.

"I'll give you one chance to turn around, sonny," I told him gently.

Instead, the baby lineman gave a guttural war cry.

"*GRRRRRRRRAAAAAAARGGHH!*" He came flying at me, his fist cocked back, the weight of his huge gut and man-tits all packed behind a big haymaker.

I dropped to my knees and punched him hard in the crotch. His face went purple. When he bent over, I kneed him hard in the face. Blood spurted up from his lips and nose. "I said you could leave. That's really what you should have done."

Our fight spilled out into the street. A random drunk jumped in, and hit me hard from behind with a forearm shiver. I collapsed to the ground, laughing in the excitement of the brawl.

"Hey, somebody's *watch* is down here!" I yelled. I slipped the metal cuff over my wrist, and rubbed the back of my head absently. "Man, finally. I've been *needing* a cool watch."

We always seemed to run away just before the cops came, protected by the magic of youth, stupidity, and success. Long Beach was an industrial wasteland, but we ruled it. The Reno Room knew us well. Strip clubs let us sit in the corner, form our own little men's club. I was never there to hit on the chicks. I just liked to get nice and drunk there. Felt right. I needed some time to be stupid, to be irresponsible. To not worry about shit.

"Jesse, dammit, if you're going to come in at three in the morning, at least be quiet about it!" Karla hissed, as I stumbled into our bedroom late one night.

"Sorry, sorry," I mumbled drunkenly. "Go back to sleep."

"I can't go back to sleep!" she said, pissed. "It's not that easy. I'll be up for at least an hour now."

"Try harder," I responded, collapsing into my pillow heavily.

"You smell like a goddamn pack of cigarettes," Karla said, sitting up angrily. "Where were you? Gold Club? The Rio? The Fritz?"

"Leave me *alone*," I mumbled. "Just let me do my thing."

"I don't *see* you!" Karla said, crying. "Chandler's learning how to walk. Did you know that? You've hardly even been here for it!"

"I'll do better," I said. My head was throbbing painfully. "I swear, okay? So do me a favor. Lighten up."

"Jesse," Karla said, "we gotta talk."

Slowly, I lifted my head from the pillow and looked at her.

"I'm pregnant again."

"Oh, boy," I groaned. "Listen, let's talk about this in the morning . . ."

"I want to get married."

"But why?" I protested. "I mean, I just don't see . . ."

"No more, Jesse, okay?" Karla said, cutting me off. "I mean, seriously. We gotta get married. If you can't do that for me, then, I'm gonna leave you." She stared down at me seriously.

Both of us stared at each other, and after a second, I just broke out laughing. Karla shook her head.

"I mean, what the *fuck*?" she said. "We're gonna have another *child*, honey. I think we need to do a little better than this!"

"I'm kind of a mess, huh?" I admitted.

"Oh, just *kinda*," she said.

"So you wanna get married, huh?" I groaned softly, pulling the pillow over my head, hiding under it.

"*Yes*." She pulled the pillow off me. "It doesn't have to be any big ceremony. But I want a ring on my finger, Jesse."

"Well," I said, "let's talk more in the morning. It doesn't sound completely out of the question."

Karla stared at me. She folded her arms.

"All right, all right!" I cried. "Damn, no one ever won an argument with you in your whole life, did they?"

"Nope," said Karla, smiling proudly. "No one ever did."

———

We were married in a very small ceremony in Long Beach, and some six months later, our second child was born—a boy. We named him Jesse Jr.

"Look at this *punk*," I said, holding him to my chest, marveling at his small fingers and tiny nose. "This one's gonna be trouble, I can tell."

"No, he will *not*," Karla said. "I want my son to be a sweetheart."

"He's another Jesse James, hon," I said to her. "You don't have much chance, I'm afraid to tell you."

It was thrilling for me to have another child around. I loved Chandler and Jesse Jr. so deeply, and so totally without effort. I received a deep kind of satisfaction from spending time with them, a glow that I couldn't put into words. It was a bit like when I'd gone up to Seattle, and entered the shipyards for the first time; this sense that I had been born to do this. Experiencing fatherhood was like sinking neatly into a hole that had been bored out especially for me. I felt so incredibly thankful for the fact that by coming into this world, my kids had changed my life.

Yet at the same time, I remained totally driven. It's a paradox that all successful men who have families must deal with: they love their kids completely, but at the same time, they are addicted to an idea of "making it" that forces them to go out into the world and do battle. In my bones, I knew that West Coast Choppers was on the cusp of becoming something huge. And that notion excited me greatly. It got me out of bed in the morning with a frenzied sort of nervousness that demanded I head over to the shop.

"We have someone on the line who would like to speak with you about purchasing a new custom, Jesse."

Melissa was my new secretary, a tattooed chick in her thirties who sported a Bettie Page hairdo and fit the image of our upscale-yet-down-to-earth Long Beach bike shop.

In recent months, I'd hired on more than ten new employees, including a team of polishers, two master painters, more welders, and now a woman to work the phones. Karla took care of payroll. That left me captaining the ship, which recently seemed to be sailing at a faster speed every time I looked up.

"Okay," I said, sipping my first cup of coffee of the day, scanning over an inventory sheet. "Who is it?"

"He says he's Tyson Beckford," Melissa whispered. She covered the phone. "Oh my God, do you think it's *the* Tyson Beckford? That man is the most beautiful human being on the planet."

Of course, it was him. Word of mouth was beginning to make

our brand well known across the United States and Europe. The custom choppers we were producing were loud and brash-looking. They often inspired a kind of double take by random passersby. "Who the hell *made* that for you?" they asked. Through excited discussions in parking lots and at parties, West Coast Choppers had slowly begun to amass a list of wealthy clients who were very interested in seeing if they could get one of our custom bikes.

"Tell Mr. Beckford that I'll build him a bike, but only if he takes you out to dinner," I joked.

Melissa blushed and handed me the phone. "You better talk to him."

Simply put, we were rolling. The shop felt like a team, and I was the natural leader. It felt like being back on the field for La Sierra—I was so serious about what I did, people naturally fell in line behind me.

Then one afternoon, Doyle approached me and asked if we could have a little talk.

"I'm gonna have to ask you to move, Jesse."

"What the hell are you talking about, Doyle?"

"I'm sorry, kid." He shrugged. "But I'm selling the building."

"Why?"

"The weight machine business is bullshit," he said. "I'm too old for it anyway. Look, a guy gave me a real sweetheart buyout, so I have to take it while I can." He clapped a friendly hand on my shoulder. "You need more space than I can offer, anyway."

"But Doyle," I said, "I have all these employees. I'm putting out thousands of dollars every week just to keep them coming in to work, and . . ."

"Hey," he interrupted, "life is not fucking fair. The deed's already signed. You got thirty days."

That afternoon, I rode my bike all over Orange County. *Maybe I should find an upscale location in Redondo or Manhattan Beach,* I thought, *rich clients might dig it.* But nothing looked right to me, and after a while, I realized I would never feel comfortable in the high-income tax-bracket neighborhoods. I was a roughneck. Long Beach was my home.

After days of searching, I found an absolutely massive space in Long Beach, at 718 Anaheim.

"This is as big as a city block," Karla said, shaking her head. "You can't afford it."

"Yes, I can," I said.

"Jesse," she said, warningly. "It's risky. Think of the overhead."

"I can do it," I told her. "With more space, I'll be able to take on more projects. I can make more bikes. We'll manufacture more fenders."

"Who will make them?"

"We'll hire more staff."

"And pay them how?" Karla cried.

"*Trust* me," I snapped, annoyed. "I can pull this off."

The building at 718 Anaheim was totally trashed when we moved in, and it took two solid weeks of cleaning and construction to get it into even rudimentary shape to support a motorcycle shop. The tension mounted. Again, I had to wonder if I'd bitten off more than I could chew.

Thank God for my son and my daughter, who brought things back to such an elemental level.

"Daddy," Chandler said, "can you make me a toy?"

That, I could do.

"What do you want, sweetie?"

"A *frog*!" she announced, hugging me.

Holding Chandler in my arms or listening to my infant son's heartbeat . . . it awed me. I had basically stumbled into having kids, but now I couldn't imagine being away from them for even a day. Anything they needed from me, I tried to give to them. And they almost always needed only my love.

Being a dad, I couldn't help but reflect on my own relationships with my parents, who had never really seemed interested in giving me this kind of physical closeness. Remembering made me bitter. I couldn't help it.

"I just can't believe my dad doesn't know his own grandkids."

"It's a lost cause, Jesse," Karla said. "Forget it."

It blew my mind, because I saw how adorable and how perfect my kids were. I couldn't understand how people who were flesh and blood weren't willing to make the effort to know them. I took the rejection personally, as if it was happening to me all over again, instead of my kids.

———

Months passed, and my shop and my kids grew. Unfortunately, so did the differences between me and Karla. Though we functioned as a team, the tension between us was mounting. The more we squabbled, the more I retreated into booze. The more I drank, the madder Karla seemed to get. It was a vicious cycle, and I didn't know how to make it stop.

Then, in the spring of 1999, an event occurred that would change my life. A producer from the Discovery Channel, Thom Beers, called and proposed making a documentary about our shop.

"But why?" I asked, honestly flummoxed.

"Have you been watching TV lately, Jesse?"

"Not really," I said. "I don't have much time for it."

"Reality TV's hit," Thom explained. "And it's here to stay. Have you heard of *The Real World? Survivor?* These kinds of shows are leading the pack, nowadays. Viewers are starting to expect shows about real people."

"I know what *Survivor* is, Thom," I said, looking down at the long to-do list I had in front of me for the day. "And we're definitely not that. So, unless you got something else to tell me . . ."

"Jesse," Thom interrupted me, "we think that what you're doing is absolutely unique. West Coast Choppers is very popular among a certain segment of the American population."

"Gearheads, bike freaks."

"Sure, gearheads. But with an hour-long show, the rest of America gets to see what you're doing. It'd be great exposure. Come on, what do you say?"

I thought it over for a while. I still didn't see what was going to be compelling enough over at our shop on Anaheim Avenue to rivet the American public to their seats—our high drama was going to consist of watching an average white boy try to make payroll at his greasy garage. But, I reasoned, Discovery was probably good at what they did. It couldn't hurt to try.

The shoot was a disaster, though.

"You could not have come at a worse time," I told Thom. "I'm getting ready to take five brand-new custom choppers to a huge annual bike rally in Daytona Beach, Florida."

"Yeah, and?"

"We got a ton of work to do," I snapped. "I don't need any distractions!"

"More drama equals better ratings," Thom said. He held up his hands. "Just saying."

I almost eviscerated the camera crew. For two weeks, they lived in our shop, asking so many questions and being so invasive that I almost lost my temper several times. They seemed dead set on capturing every single step of what we did as a custom shop, from manufacturing the wheels to welding the frames to painting the flames on the metal.

They filmed us riding around Long Beach; filmed us talking with customers; filmed me feeding the sharks that I kept in a tank in the shop. They even filmed me squabbling with Karla over payroll, and by the time they got done with their work, I felt like an animal in the zoo who'd been prodded with a stick.

"Look," I grumbled. "Can you explain to me why the hell you have all this footage of my dogs fighting each other?"

"Shows a deeper portrait of who you are?" replied a cameraman.

"No," I disagreed. "And I don't think footage of dogs trying to bite each other is important enough to be in the final cut of this show."

"I'll make a note of that," he said drily.

Even though I hated the process and resented the strangers who had busted so rudely into my shop with their lights and cameras, I had to admit that secretly I dug the attention a little bit. Who wouldn't have? I craved respect and acknowledgment just as much as anyone else, maybe a little more so.

Some months after the crew had completed their work, Thom invited me to Los Angeles to view a rough cut of the piece. I watched with a mixture of alarm and pride as the film slowly unfolded in front of me.

The version of myself on the screen rode his motorcycle to a beachside cliff in San Pedro and overlooked the Pacific Ocean wistfully.

"I feel like I spent more than half my life trying to kick the world's ass, fight everybody, and stuff like that . . . and I'm not even really into it anymore. I just want to trip out, make the stuff I make, hang out with my kids."

"This is cheesy," I said to Thom. "Cut this part, okay?"

"Hold on," he said, shushing me. "I love this section."

"But don't get me wrong," the me up on the screen continued, *"I'll still punch someone. If they start shit with me, I'll finish it."*

Beside me, Thom laughed. "You come off so real, Jesse!"

"I don't even remember *saying* that," I complained.

"We think that's precisely what people will enjoy about you." He turned on the lights. "You're spontaneous, unguarded."

"Thom," I said, rising to leave, "I appreciate your enthusiasm. I really do. And I apologize in advance because, dude, this thing is gonna tank."

The next two weeks were about the most nervous weeks of my life. I felt totally exposed by the footage that was going to air, and my temper was at its absolute worst. I sheltered myself in my office, alone, as I waited for my national exposure and subsequent humiliation.

On the evening the show was to air, I was sitting in my office all by myself, my stomach clenched in a knot.

"Go home, Melissa," I said.

"Really, Jesse? There's some more . . ."

"I said *go home,* please," I snapped.

She saw from my face that I meant business. "Uh, okay," she said, grabbing up her bag and beating a hasty exit.

I wondered how I could have been stupid enough to allow a TV crew into my private life. How could I have been so prideful and naïve, to think that anyone would actually care what happened in the day-in, day-out life of a motorcycle shop?

Just then, the phone rang.

"Yeah?" I said.

"Is this Jesse James?"

"Yeah. Who's this?"

"My name is Jim Newsome. I live in Detroit. I just saw your show on TV!"

"What are you talking about?" I growled. "It hasn't aired yet."

"It has over on the East Coast! Man, I just had to call you—I *loved* it!"

"What?" I said, stunned.

"Sweet work, man! *So much* love going into those bikes!"

"I'm . . . glad you liked it," I mumbled, still shocked.

"Like it? Goddamn, man! I *loved* it!" he exclaimed. "You know when you were on that bluff, looking out over the ocean, saying you didn't want to fight anymore? Dude, that's *me*! That's how I feel every *day.*"

"Really?" I said.

"Keep on doing what you're doing, man. You're the best."

As I hung up the phone, my jaw dropped slightly. There were people out there who related to me.

"Jesse," Thom told me the next day. "The ratings are insane. They're through the *roof.*"

"Are you kidding?"

"No, I'm not. Look, this show went crazy. So many people checked into our website, it melted our servers."

I laughed. "That's the weirdest thing I've ever heard."

"Enjoy the success," Thom said. "And rest up, because Discovery is going to want to work with you again. I can *guarantee* that."

The aftershocks were immediate and massive. Requests for custom bikes absolutely went through the roof. In the space of one week, I had a yearlong back order, with clients from around the world begging to be included at the end of the list.

"I think *I'm* going to have to hire an assistant," Melissa told me. "I can't deal with talking on the phone this much!"

"Hey, everyone," I announced, "my *secretary* needs a secretary."

Suddenly, the activity around our shop was like a beehive. We had visitors every day, folks from the Southern California area who had seen us on TV and wanted to be part of the gang.

"So this is the scary-ass dog I saw on TV!"

"That's Cisco," I said proudly. "Nobody mess with that pit!"

The prices for a West Coast Chopper bike rose. Now I could get away with selling one of the specials for well over $100,000.

"And see, our bikes work to showcase our products, too," I explained to Hud. He'd come by on his way home from work to grab a few beers with me and the new hangers-on, who'd posted themselves up in the corner to ride the wave of our local celebrity.

"How's that?"

"Well, man," I explained, "think about it. You see some fool driving around in a crazy-looking bike, with a sweet-looking custom fender, a custom gas tank, and custom air filter. Maybe you can't afford the bike, but you could throw down for a part or two, make your own chopper look smooth."

"Genius!" somebody said.

I nodded, proud. Slowly, I was getting caught up in the success. It felt impossible not to. I was a homemade superstar, after all; a minor-league celebrity who'd somehow managed to hit a huge home run. I could drink in local bars for free on this for the rest of my life, probably!

But the best party was at West Coast Choppers. We had crowds at all times of the day, and especially after hours. The local Harley association annually put on something they called The Love Ride. I thought it was just dumb—a bunch of yuppies with their factory Harleys with tassels on the handlebars and all that crap.

"I wanna have the *No-Love* Ride," I announced. "Let's invite all the bikers around here and have a huge kegger at the shop!"

The No-Love Ride attracted fifteen thousand people. It was just madness. I bought a hundred cases of beer and we went through them in twenty minutes. The city of Long Beach had snipers on the roof before I was able to tell the police department what was going on.

I was married to the shop, and I loved it. I sat back just like Boyd Coddington, wheeling and dealing, taking outrageous offers for custom bikes well into the evening.

"Jesse?" Melissa said. "Karla's on the line."

"Oh," I said frowning. "Well, yeah, put her through."

"Hi there, moneyman," Karla said. "Are we going to see you, tonight?"

"What do you mean?" I said. "Sure. I'll be home later."

"I mean for dinner."

"Well, no," I said slowly. "I have to work a few more hours, Karla. Look, I've got about a million things to take care of . . ."

Click.

"It was nice talking with you, too," I said to the dial tone.

Our brand had gone crazy. Motorcycle magazines began calling with offers for photo spreads.

"Jesse, we want to have you on the cover of *American Iron.*"

"Yeah, I'd love to have a West Coast Chopper up there," I said. "It'd be a great honor."

"We want to have *you* up there with it, Jesse. How's that sound?"

My first thought was to refuse, but then I just shrugged. *Hey, why fight it?* "Yeah, sure," I said casually. "Whatever you need."

Within a few months, my bikes and I had graced the covers of five different motorcycle magazines. A handful of writers hailed me as the wunderkind of the chopper world. I half believed them. It was heady stuff. Heady as hell.

"Think we might sell a few more T-shirts this year down in Daytona?" Rick asked.

"Dude," I said, "I would not be surprised."

I wasn't ready for the craziness, though. People were literally knocking over other vendors' booths to get to us. It was a sea of utter biker madness, and when the smoke cleared, we'd sold $680,000 worth of T-shirts in just under three days.

"Are you fucking *kidding* me?" Rick asked.

"Nothing would surprise me now," I said. "Come on. Let's celebrate."

We headed to a bar and started slamming the brew. Straight away, I got a nice little buzz on. *Everything I've worked for all my life is coming to fruition,* I thought. *I'm on the top of the heap.*

"Dammit, Rick, let's walk the strip!" I cried. "Take in all the beautiful people, those who have made us rich!"

My eyes danced. The street felt hot and humid and bright. Sweating, I walked tall through the pack of revelers, my head turning to take in the jean shorts and elastic tops, women with boa constrictors wrapped around their thin shoulders, men with ferrets perched atop their heads elbowing aside brothers with gold teeth peeking out of broken mouths. A fat Jesus with a shower cap carried his cross through the mob.

"These are my people," I explained to Rick.

"I may need a few more beers to deal with them," he said.

We ducked into a strip bar, where I switched to vodka and cranberry. "Make it strong," I warned the bartender, "or I'm leaving." I frowned, watching an elderly-looking biker slut doing a full split on the filthy, beer-stained floor. *Hey, nice leather thong,* I thought, feeling the flush of the alcohol in my face.

We sat back in the corner, our backs pressed up against vinyl cushions, progressively getting drunker and drunker. Strippers with flabby stomachs circulated through the bar, proposing lap dances. We waved them away impatiently.

"I'm feeling sick," I told Rick. "I need some dollar bills to throw at people."

Rick handed me a handful of dollars. Slowly and carefully, I folded them over, twice, then three times.

"I used to play football." I hefted them up toward the stage, one hand on my drink. "Watch me go."

Drink after drink, I drained sweet liquid through thin red bar straws, laughing, as my dollar bills hit blond strippers on top of their hair. The grimy dollars fell to the floor, looking diseased in the purplish neon of the Daytona nightclub.

The phone in my pocket rang. I looked at the number. It was Karla.

"Hi, *honey.*"

"Where are you?" she said.

"We're at the club, baby," I said. "Me and Rick."

"What a surprise," Karla said, annoyed.

"Baby, do you know how many T-shirts we sold?" I began, triumphantly.

"I don't care, Jesse, I really don't," Karla said. She sounded exhausted. "Look, I'm just calling you because I need to know, are you coming back to Long Beach tomorrow, or Tuesday?"

"Call the shop." Rick goosed me in the side, pointing out a very fat dancing girl. I stifled a giggle. "Because right *now,* I just don't have any idea."

"Yes, I'll call the shop," Karla hissed. "*They'll* tell me when my husband is coming home. That's just *great.*"

"You're killing my buzz, Karla," I said, pronouncing every word carefully. "*Murdering* it."

"Well, I won't do that anymore," she said, furious, and hung up the phone.

I held the phone up to my face for several seconds longer, though I knew it was dead.

"Who was that?" Rick asked, not taking his eyes off the stage.

"My wife," I said. "She was curious to know if you and I are going to have another vodka and cranberry here, or move on to the next bar."

"Next bar," Rick said.

The street was a blur. We stumbled down it. For shits and giggles, I pushed a big meathead-looking jock in the back.

"Watch it, douche bag!" he yelled.

"You want to throw down?" I mumbled. A sour taste came up in my mouth and I vomited in front of me, coming about an inch away from ruining my jeans.

"Let him go," the guy's girlfriend told him. "He's totally wasted."

Rick steered me into another club. We sat behind the bar and listened to heavy metal on the shitty speakers. I looked at myself in the mirror behind the bar. A douche with leopard-spotted hair sat next to me. I waved at him in the mirror.

"Hi!" I said. "You have a lot of earrings, don't you?"

He frowned at me. "Whatever, dude."

"No, really," I cried, "your earrings go all the way up to the top of your ear! Did you even *see* that? Hey Rick, get a load of this feller's sexy little hoop earrings!" I laughed uproariously.

"Calm down, Jesse," Rick said.

"I am calm," I told him, calmly. "Waitress," I said. "Oops. I mean, *bartender.* Barkeep! We'd like a bottle of vodka, over here."

"A bottle?" she said.

"An entire bottle, miss," I answered. "Your best stuff. I want to show you a secret talent of mine."

The bartender sighed. "Sure." She placed a half-filled bottle of Smirnoff's in front of me. "What's your talent?"

"This," I said. "Duck."

I picked up the bottle by its neck, and, as hard as I could, hurled it into the mirror. The mirror and the vodka bottle exploded into a spray of glass shards. Rick and I winced.

"What the fuck was that!" the bartender cried.

I sat there and swayed sickly in my seat in the silence that ensued. "I'll . . . uh . . . pay for that mirror."

"Jesse," Rick said, hooking an elbow around my midsection, hoisting me to my feet. "I think it's time to go."

11

✦◆✦

"Sir? *Sir?* Is everything all right in there?"

Each brisk rap against the airplane's restroom door felt like an ice pick jabbing into my brain.

"Sir? Excuse me?"

In response, I vomited loudly and explosively, spattering the small stainless-steel toilet with a frightening-looking gush of phlegm and blood. Turbulence rocked the plane and, sweating, I let my forehead play back and forth against the cheap industrial mirror, trying to find some coolness there.

"He's been at it for half an hour," I heard the stewardess complain to a coworker. "It sounds like he's dying in there."

I groaned. "I'm fine," I mumbled miserably. My voice was so low, I knew no one had heard me. "Honestly."

But the saliva was building up in my mouth again, acidic and nauseating. An icy shiver surged through my arms and chest, and I knew what was coming next. I positioned my mouth over the toilet and once more retched convulsively, my eyes tearing up, my diaphragm clutching, tight and miserable.

I squinted down at the toilet. It was filled with vomit.

This isn't me, I thought. *This isn't how I want to live.*

"*Excuse* me." The stewardess knocked relentlessly, annoyed. "Sir, is everything all *right* in there?"

"Yup," I gasped, leaning up against the wall. I pushed the flush button with my knee, and tried to steady myself. "I'm coming right out."

———

"I made a decision," I told Karla on the ride home from the airport. "I'm quitting drinking."

She said nothing, just gripped the steering wheel tightly.

"Seriously," I said. "I know I can do it. Will you support me?"

She remained silent, staring instead into the thick traffic as we weaved our way down the 405 South, toward Long Beach.

"Well, hell," I said, slightly offended. "I knew you wouldn't be *happy* to see me, but I guess I was . . ."

"Jesse!" Karla cried. "Shut up! Just shut up!"

My insides curled up inside me. I could tell something bad was about to happen.

Karla began crying. She sobbed softly, as she gripped the wheel, her forearms tensing.

"This traffic," she whispered finally. "It's ridiculous."

"Karla," I said. I put my hand on her knee. "Karla, please stop. What's going on? Tell me."

"I just . . ." she said. She sniffed, shaking her head. "I just can't live like this."

"But I'm going to stop boozing, I told you. I promise."

"It's not the drinking, and you know it." Her face was the picture of exhaustion and resignation. "You're not here for me. You haven't been for years."

I sunk back in my seat.

"I'll try harder."

Karla shook her head. "Jesse, our marriage hasn't worked for a long, long time. You're obsessed with your business. And when you want to have fun, you choose going out with your friends over spending an evening with me, every time."

"But I can *change*," I protested. "We could go to a counselor, or something like that . . ."

She gave me a tight, sad smile. "I'm sorry—it's just too late. It's over, baby. And you know it."

I sat there in silence, absorbing the news. The wheels of our big black truck rolled across the pavement quietly, sunlight streaming into the cab, harsh and unwelcome.

———

Only a few days later, I moved out of the house. At first I slept at the shop, but soon I was able to find an apartment down the street from Karla and the kids. No matter what happened between us, I wanted the kids to have both of their parents nearby.

I felt awful, like I'd failed. But I knew Karla was right in ending it. I had never prioritized her needs. Though in my heart I'd known our marriage was falling apart, I'd never attempted to fix it. My own desires had always come first: work, partying, getting fucked up with my friends. Deep down, I felt ashamed, and I promised myself I would never make that same mistake again.

I consoled myself by vowing to be a better dad—there, I could still redeem myself.

"Why are you picking me up from school, Daddy?" Chandler asked me.

"I want to spend some more time with you, honey." I gazed at her in my rearview mirror, strapped into her little car seat. "I miss you a whole bunch."

"Why aren't you sleeping at our house?" Chandler asked suddenly.

"It's kind of complicated," I began. "Mommy and I are taking some time off from each other. You know how you get mad at Jesse Jr. sometimes?"

Chandler nodded.

"And you don't want to be around him?"

Chandler nodded again. "Because he's a butt-head."

I laughed. "Exactly. Well, that's the way that Mommy feels about me, right now."

"She thinks *you're* a butt-head?"

"She sure does," I said.

"Did you tease her?" Chandler asked, wide-eyed.

"No," I said. "It's more like, well . . ."

"Daddy," Chandler said, tiring of the conversation, "when we get home, will you give me a ride on your bike?"

"Yeah," I said, gratefully. "We'll go real fast, sweetie."

Karla and I began to slowly strategize how best to be parents apart. It saddened me, but I knew our separation was for the best. The bond of friendship we'd formed over the course of our marriage would last, I was sure of it. Now the important thing was for us to stay close to each other, since we were going to be connected through our children for the rest of our lives.

Life at the shop continued at as hectic a pace as ever. Fenders, once our lifeblood, were now pretty much out of the picture, as we moved into producing our expensive custom choppers full-time. The demand was immense, so I raised my prices precipitously. You couldn't even get in the door without throwing down $60,000 to start. But instead of scaring people off, our high price tags only seemed to attract more interest.

"Dammit," I grumbled, peering at my steadily growing waiting list. "I'll be in my grave before I can make all of these bikes."

"Jesse," Melissa called, "I have a Thom Beers on the line. Will you speak to him?"

"Yeah," I grumbled. "Put him through."

"Hey, Jess!" came Thom's voice. "How's life?"

"Not great. Don't know if you've heard, but my wife and I are splitting up."

"I'm sorry about that," Thom said. "But if it helps, I have some *great* news for you."

"And what's that?"

"Discovery, apparently, is poised to give us a *show*."

"We already had a show," I said flatly.

"No," Thom said, the excitement bubbling up in his voice. "I'm talking about a recurring series, man. Get you up on that screen every single week!"

"That's not where I'm at, dude," I said quietly. "You know me better than that."

"Okay, I worded that awkwardly. What I mean to say is, this show is an opportunity for you to do new and exciting things, and get paid *extremely* well for it."

"Well, now you have me slightly interested," I admitted.

"Can we go out to dinner tonight?" Thom asked. "Have ourselves a little date?"

I laughed. "Yeah. Why not? I'm single now, anyway."

We met in Venice that evening, at a typical West Los Angeles faux-hippie hideaway, where the tablecloths were hemp, and the candles were made out of soy.

"Would you two like to start with something to drink?" asked our waitress.

"I'll have a tofu shake, extra beeswax."

"He's kidding. We'll have a couple of beers, I think," Thom said. "Whatever's local."

"No, no beer for me," I said. "Just water."

Then Thom began his pitch.

"They want to give you a show called *American Chopper*, Jesse," he said. "The network thinks it'd be *very* cool to watch you build your custom bikes."

"No," I said, shaking my head. "I hated having that damn camera crew in my face. And they were only around for a couple of weeks. I can't imagine inviting them into my work for a year."

"Well, they're only offering a four-episode pilot," Thom coughed, politely.

"Even so," I said. "No way."

"Well, then, I don't know," Thom said. He scratched his head. "I sort of thought you'd like that."

"That's not even creative, man," I complained. "Can't we do something a little more interesting? Something a little bit more . . . violent?"

"Discovery's a family channel," Thom pointed out. "In case you forgot."

"I'm not talking violent to *people*," I said. "Just like, a show that has, I don't know, some explosions. If we're gonna build something, then let's build *machines*."

"Tell me more."

"What we *should* do," I suggested, "is push the envelope. Get some of the best mechanics in the world together, and get them to build some Mad-Max, apocalypse-style vehicles."

"War machines," Thom said. "Bikes that spit fire."

"Not bikes," I corrected. "No offense, man, but I've got bikes coming out of my ears. Let's make some cars instead: *mutant* cars."

He nodded. "Sure, sounds great. But what the hell is a mutant car?"

"Like nightmare cars," I said, thinking. "You know, like a Ferrari that can fly."

"Ferraris already fly, pretty much."

"Fine," I said. "A Mustang that shoots missiles."

"At who? The Soviets?" Thom shook his head. "Hate to tell you, the Cold War's over, we won. Our grass was greener."

"All right, then. A Mustang that can mow LAWNS!" I said, grinning as I pictured it. "Can't you just see it? A freakin' Mustang 5.0, mowing the lawn at a hundred miles an hour?"

"That sounds goofy." Thom laughed. "Not to mention *impossible*."

"Well," I said, "if it was easy . . ."

"Then anyone could do it," Thom said, nodding. "I get it. Drama. A bit of a challenge. Maybe we'll even have some good fights among the crew during the build process. Hey, I think you have something there, Jesse."

For the rest of the evening, we shot ideas back and forth. At first, there was talk of situating the show in some kind of Thunderdome, where the mechanics would have to grapple up walls and punch one another in the nose to get the tools they needed to modify the cars, but eventually, that idea was rejected. Soon, the basic premise was born: a crack team of professionals, led by myself, would strip down an ordinary-looking car, bus, van, or limousine to its barest essence. From there, it would be rebuilt from the ground up, until it contained one or more magical secret powers.

"Think about it!" I laughed. "A Mini-Cooper that shovels snow!"

"Oh, wow: NO! I know! A lowrider *Zamboni*!"

"Not bad, but what about slashing a U-Haul, so it splits open to be a wrestling ring!"

"Christ, that's great! We'll have a match in there, with turnbuckles and a referee and everything!"

"You guys sound like you're having fun," our waitress commented, refilling my water glass.

We grinned at each other across the table.

"Yeah," I said finally. "I guess this sounds like a pretty good time. Thom, I'll do it."

———

For our first episode, we decided to go for the speed–lawn mower idea. Discovery presented us with a white 1990 Mustang 5.0, with a V-8 engine. A beautiful little car.

"Let's trash her," I commanded.

My crew, which included Bill Dodge, my buddy who worked in my shop; Mike Contreras, guru of the oil rigs; Carol Hodge, a tough-as-nails chick mechanic; and Bob Cleveland, a lawn mower engineer, stripped the Mustang of all its deadweight. We removed the backseat, unhooked the muffler, heaved it happily into the trash, then tossed the catalytic converter into a deserted corner of our warehouse.

"*That* was easy," I said. "Now for the hard part. Let's figure out how to get a huge goddamn lawn mower attached to the bottom of this car."

I honestly hadn't counted on there being all that much stress or suspense around the build process. But once it got under way, there was almost no end to the bitching and squabbling.

"Listen, we gotta reroute this fuel line, pronto! Otherwise we're gonna have quite an explosion when we try to start this baby up."

"Yeah, sure, but what about the exhaust system. Don't you think we should tackle that first?"

Everyone I'd brought aboard was very talented at what they did, which made it that much worse, because as usual, every fucker thought he was right. In order to heighten the blue-collar drama, Discovery had planned it so we had to complete our task in under a week: typical reality TV bullshit tension, but it seemed to work.

"How are we gonna cut lawns if we can't even get the blade apparatus to mount correctly on the door?"

"Well, we'll put a pivot on it, if you see what I mean . . ."

"No way! Listen, what we *should* do is fabricate a bracket to mount the motor . . ."

After several days of debate, I just lost my patience with the whole game. "Look," I said, "we're going to have to work as a team. Stop fucking talking so much. Start listening to each other." The crew stared at me resentfully, as we sat eating our take-out dinners. "Hey, I'm sorry to have to put it that way. But you guys are screwing around too much. Nothing's getting done."

In the end, we were able to come to a compromise, and the mower got mounted. Tom Prewitt, a pro custom painter, took the car into his shop and made it look cherry, applying coats of ice gold pearl and lime green flake. Signature chopper flames licked up and down the side paneling. We even threw some gold rims on the tires for street props.

For our grand finale, I drove the Mustang out to Indio, where I raced a four-thousand-pound tractor mower driven by a pro lawn mower. I put the pedal to the metal, and it wasn't even close: our Monster actually *worked*! After a week of hellacious work, I was actually cutting grass at a hundred miles an hour.

"Man, that was fun," I said to Thom. "It took a whole bunch of bitching and moaning, but that was actually pretty cool to build this weird thing."

"Well, rest up," Thom advised me. "Because on Monday morning, you gotta do it all over again."

Enthusiastically, we filmed the rest of our four-episode arc. I became absorbed in the bizarre task of creating a Ford Explorer Garbage Collector, a stretch Limo fire truck with a hose powerful enough to put out a ten-story building fire, and a Volkswagen Beetle Swamp Buggy that we took to the Louisiana Bayou, where we floated out among the alligators.

"Cool experiment," I told Thom. "But I'm totally freaking exhausted after all that work."

"Just wait till the show airs," he said, smiling.

"Yeah. It'll feel great to put this crap behind me," I said. "I haven't been by my shop in what seems like *weeks*. The back orders are piling up, and I feel guilty abandoning my ship."

"Just wait until it airs," Thom repeated, knowingly.

He was right: when the four episodes were broadcast, the numbers went through the roof.

"*Madness*, Jesse. Absolute madness," Thom said. "I talked to the boys at Discovery this morning. They want us to do a full season! Twenty-four episodes."

"Twenty-four episodes? Are you *nuts*? When will I sleep? When will I build motorcycles?"

Thom grinned. "So you're going to turn down your own TV show, dude?"

"Of course!" I yelled. "You know why? Because it's freaking *impossible*."

"No, not impossible," Thom argued. "Just difficult. I mean, look, you just churned out four hour-long shows, and you did it like a champ."

"But I'm a walking dead man," I protested weakly. "I'm sorry, Thom. I don't sleep. I can't get to the gym. Dude, I can hardly shove a burrito in my mouth before I'm hit with something else to do."

Thom shrugged. "You got a hit show here, Jesse. You don't say no to that."

I groaned and sank into my seat, defeated. "How did I get myself into this, again?"

———

Suddenly, the main challenge in my life was not simply overseeing what was rapidly becoming a well-known custom motorcycle shop. It was adapting to the crazy phenomenon of "being on TV."

"Did you notice the hordes outside?" Rick asked one morning, when we were working at the shop. Bent over an oxyacetylene torch, he readied himself to heat up a steel pipe that we would in turn bend and form into yet another CFL frame.

"Must have been a car accident," I grumbled.

"I don't think so," Rick said, laughing. "Those fuckers were there for *you*, man."

"Oh my God," I moaned. "Kill me, please."

"The place has become a white-trash landmark!" He chuckled. "Tourists are bringin' their little kids to see you, dude! I seen 'em with Sharpies in hand, dying to meet the man on TV!"

"I'll autograph a few shirts, if they ask real nice."

"Sets a dangerous precedent," Rick warned, flipping down his glasses. "You start with the shirts, then it moves on to the boobs. Before you know it, you got groupies coming out of the woodwork."

"I'll leave the chopper groupies to you, how about that, Rick?" I sighed. "I don't think I can handle them right now."

I had gone out on a few dates since Karla and I split, but they had mostly been a string of extremely well-contained disasters. There was just something soulless about meeting up, going to the Lobster House, and then trying to conjure up some kind of bogus romantic feeling. As much as I hated doing it, I couldn't stop comparing every woman I met to Karla, the original spitfire girl who never knew how to hold her tongue. Stacked up next to her, most of the women I met just came off as boring.

But then one day things changed. Evan Seinfeld, the lead singer for Biohazard, was at my shop doing a photo shoot on a bike I'd built for him. A friend of his, Kristal Summers, an adult film actress, had tagged along and brought a friend.

"Jesse," Kristal said, "I want you to meet someone. This is Janine Lindemulder."

I knew who Janine was. Over the course of the last decade, she had become one of the most famous porn stars of all time, right up there with Jenna Jameson. Janine's trademark, besides her considerable beauty, was that outside of her homemade sex tape with Vince Neil, she'd never performed on camera with a guy.

"Hey there," I coughed. "Pleasure to meet you."

"Hello," Janine said pleasantly. "This is such a great shop!"

If at first I was a little nervous to be around a famous porn star, that feeling dissolved almost immediately. Janine was bright and engaging, but even more, she was somehow conservative: she wore mom jeans and a thigh-length sweater. No question, she was beautiful, but it came through kind of quietly, in her clean, long hair and her striking, high-cheekboned face.

"You do *such* nice work, Jesse," she said, walking around the shop. "I love the colors you use."

"Well, thanks," I said. "Do you like bikes?"

"They're only the coolest machines alive!" she said, laughing. "Man, can't you tell from looking at me I'm a biker chick at heart?"

She pulled up the arm of her sweater to show a full sleeve of tattoos.

"Hard-core." I laughed.

"I can't help it," she said, giggling. "I really love getting these dang tattoos."

"Tell me about it," I said, smiling. I put my own tattoo-covered forearm up next to hers. "It's addictive."

Janine let her arm linger against mine for a second.

"They look pretty good up against each other, don't they?" She gazed up at me, smiling.

"Sure," I agreed. "Not too bad at all."

After Evan was done with his shoot, the four of us went out to grab some food.

"I'm going to be honest," I told the group, laughing. "I'm not really 'familiar' with your work, Janine."

Everyone grinned. "*Wow*," Janine said. "Well, I don't know whether to be happy or offended!"

"Jesse," Kristal scolded. "How could you?"

"Sorry," I said, still laughing, "but I'm kind of behind on my girl-girl porn."

"She's only the *best* of the best," said Kristal. "Cream of the crop, the standard by which all others are measured."

"Thank you, honey," Janine said modestly. "But those days are gone. I haven't done a scene in years. And frankly, I don't want to."

"You don't miss it?" Evan asked, smiling naughtily. "Just the teensiest bit?"

"No," Janine said. She shrugged. "It was wild, and I would never trade it for anything. But it's behind me now. It's the craziest thing, but after all these years, I think I'm finally turning into a grown-up."

"Man," I said, nodding, thinking about my own messed-up past—my years spent busting heads and drinking until I didn't remember who I was. "You said a mouthful."

She smiled across the table at me. "Well, thank you."

She blinked her almond-shaped eyes, and I was captivated. For a moment, the others at our table, charismatic as they were, melted into nothingness. All I could feel was Janine's warm gaze.

———

We were a pair. It was instant.

"I just can't believe how *similar* we are," she marveled.

"Tell me about it," I agreed. "I'm kind of tripping out."

For the first time, I felt very matched, in terms of life experience. My world had changed since the first airing of the documentary, titled *Motorcycle Mania,* and as my local fame gradually transformed into something much bigger, it seemed to change more every day. However, in spite of what I had done thus far, Janine had done far more. She had a name for herself, not to mention her own money and her own source of esteem.

Janine was one of the most beautiful women I had ever seen. She was tan and fit, with a sensual hourglass body and long blond hair. Everything about her seemed equally stunning. And on a purely animal level, she was tireless.

Janine seemed fascinated by me, too. She wanted to know every detail about my life. I had never had anyone ask me about my childhood before, but Janine seemed ready to hear it all.

"What were you like when you were a real *little* kid?" she asked. Her hand toyed across my chest as we lay in bed.

"Kinda nuts," I said, after a second. "A little violent. When I was about five years old, there was this kid down the street who I hated."

"What was his name?" Janine asked, smiling.

"Steven," I said, warming to my story. "We always fought each other. One time, he took off his belt and he smacked me in the head with it."

"Yikes."

"Yeah, right? The buckle tore right into my head and made me bleed," I remembered. "So, I got pissed and went in the house and grabbed this antique bullwhip that my dad had hanging from a hook, and I ran back to Steven. Somehow, I whipped it around his neck. I had him down on the ground, choking him."

"Jesse!" Janine laughed. "You were a *madman*. Nowadays, they'd probably hold some kind of intervention."

"I wish they had," I admitted. "I was kind of unhappy."

"You were lonely."

I looked at her, surprised. "Yeah, I think I really was."

She fixed me with the most serious, concerned look. Right then, I could read the love in her eyes. I could almost hear her saying, *You're not going to be alone anymore.* It was just the craziest thing.

But Janine was more than just curious. She was fun, and she was impulsive. I had never met anyone in my entire life who was as ready to have an adventure at the drop of a hat.

"Man, I am beat. These hundred-hour weeks are driving me crazy."

"Jesse," Janine declared, "you need a vacation."

"I wish. Unfortunately, we're filming on Monday morning, bright and early."

"*And?* It's Saturday."

"And, I haven't been by the shop enough this week. I gotta go in and make sure those idiots haven't burned it down to the ground."

"No way," Janine said, her hands on her hips. "Listen to me for a second. What do you *really* want to be doing right this instant?"

"Well, riding a chopper into Mexico, or something," I said, shrugging. "But . . ."

"And who would you like to *take* there, and have, like, the *best* time ever with?" Janine smiled hugely.

"Well, you, of course," I said, "but the truth is, I really can't . . ."

"I don't want to hear another word *about* it!" she cried. "You know that you want to go! You know we HAVE to go! So get your butt up off that couch and let's go! Come on! Let's go! Let's roll!"

Her enthusiasm was contagious. *Why not?* After all, what good was being a success if you didn't live like one? With Janine laughing delightedly behind me, I throttled my bike through La Jolla, through San Diego, all the way down to northern Mexico, flying through Rosario, into Ensenada, the wind blasting at our faces, her hands gripped tight around my waist and her thighs snug around my hips.

I had to admit, it felt pretty damn good to be with her. I felt free.

———

"Okay, I got it: an ambulance that can pop a wheelie!"

"No . . . how about a Geo Tracker that turns into a helicopter? Wait, I know, a *hot-air balloon*!"

"Listen, what do you think about a hot-dog cart that can go a hundred fifty miles an hour—and still serve relish!"

Thom and I were spilling over with ideas. I had to concede that while *Monster Garage* was an enormous effort, it was still a hell of a lot of fun. And it didn't hurt that, because of the show, I was slowly becoming more prosperous.

The Discovery Channel paid me a nice talent fee for each episode, but the real gain came in terms of my "brand worth." Suddenly, West Coast Choppers was being beamed directly into every living room in America, and because of that, it became an extremely well-known quantity nearly overnight. Truthfully, I could not have engineered a better advertising platform in a million years. *Monster Garage* was a one-hour, uninterrupted commercial for West Coast—and for *me*.

First, Jimmy Kimmel invited me on his show. Then Conan O'Brien made the call. I did the appearances, and with pleasure, but the whole time, I was kind of befuddled: Is this really happening to *me*?

I had to face it: I was getting famous. It was quite a bizarre realization to come to each morning, as I pulled on my T-shirt and beat-up Dickies and considered my face in the mirror. Often, it almost embarrassed me. I was just a *welder*. Why didn't anybody get that?

"You know what?" I said to Bill, as I came into work. "You used to be able to scare people away by being a motorcycle dude. I mean, wasn't that kind of the point?"

"I know, I know," he said, shaking his head. "No one looks very frightened out there, do they?"

Seemingly overnight, West Coast Choppers had turned into Disneyland. Crowds of suburban bikehounds stationed themselves out front, ogling the shop, vying for a glimpse at the crew, their little kids crying and tugging at their hands. To capitalize on the crush of people, we set up a new retail area of the shop, where the fans could blow thirty bucks on a pink West Coast Choppers baby-tee, or a black Maltese cross ball cap. We got them coming *and* going.

"I can't help but hate it," I admitted. "It's lucky I quit drinking, boy, or I'd tell 'em to get lost, real quick."

"Can't do that," Bill said. "These people love you, man."

"That's exactly what I can't stand," I said. "I mean, it would be one thing if they loved me for doing something worthwhile, right? But I'm making mutated *cars*. It's stupid."

"Well then, why don't you do something worthwhile?" he said, reasonably.

I thought about that for a while. When I took a big step back, I realized how lucky I was. I had two kids who I loved more than anything in the world. If I could use some of this new fame I'd accumulated to help a couple of children who'd gotten a raw deal, then at least I wouldn't feel like such a fraud every morning when I saw the crowds.

About a week or so later, I mumbled into my phone, "Uh, is this the Make-A-Wish foundation?"

"Yes, it is. Can I help you?"

"I'm Jesse James," I began, haltingly. "And, well . . . I run a custom motorcycle business in Long Beach, and I'd like to extend the invitation to some kids to come on by and meet us."

Right away, I knew that I had made the right call. I was not much of a do-gooder, but I'd always genuinely dug kids, and kids who were hurting even more so. From the very first child who came by with Make-A-Wish, I was hooked and into doing anything I could for them.

"You think a lowrider that serves ice cream cones would be a good idea?"

"Yeah!"

"I'll tell you what," I said, "we haven't got that one built yet, but if your mom says it's okay, I can take you for a ride in *my* lowrider—how about that, would that be cool?"

"*Yeah!*"

"Better put on your seat belt," I said, grinning. "I drive pretty fast."

After some time of doing volunteer work, a friend of a friend contacted me and told me that her seven-year-old son, Tyler, had leukemia, diagnosed as terminal. The family lived almost across the street from our shop, so right away I made plans to meet him.

"Tyler, I heard that you dug monster cars and trucks."

"I like bikes the most," he said, quietly.

"Well, how about you come take a ride with me sometime?" I asked. "My bikes are right across the street. You can come any time you want."

"Yeah, but my mom says I'm sick, so sometimes I'm too tired to get out of bed."

My heart felt heavy. "Well, I'll tell you what," I said. "Maybe I can bring you some cool remote-control bikes for your room. You can screw with 'em from your bed, and not even have to move an inch."

His eyes brightened a little. "Yeah. That'd be neat."

"I'll stop over tomorrow before work," I told his mom. She nodded at me gratefully.

Doing something positive for the community worked like a salve for my conscience. I knew that I had kind of been a screw-up when I was younger, stealing shit and just being a general menace. Now I was trying to do something helpful. Even if my efforts were probably kind of minuscule in comparison to what some people did, at least I was getting out there.

"I'm proud of you, Jesse," Karla said one day, as I was dropping Jesse Jr. off at her place.

"It's nothing," I said, kissing Jesse good-bye. "Be good for your mom!"

"No," Karla said. "You're changing. I can see it. And you really did quit drinking, huh? I gotta hand it to you, I'm impressed."

I shrugged.

"Almost makes me wish I'd kept you around," she said, laughing. "Not *quite,* but almost."

"Karla . . . I'm sorry I was kind of a loser to you the last couple of years."

"It's okay." She shook her head. "It's odd, but I have the weirdest feeling that we're going to be friends someday, Jesse. In fact, I'm almost sure of it."

"Me, too." I nodded. "Hey, I still got your back."

She sighed. "Same here."

—

Janine and I continued along the frenetic, pleasurable path of our early romance. One evening, she brought two overflowing suitcases over to my house.

"What's all this?" I asked.

"Duh, my *stuff*!" She laughed. "I don't want to be apart from you, okay?"

"Well," I said, choosing my words carefully, "I think alone time can be a healthy part of a relationship, don't you?"

"For what?" She stuck out her tongue at me and unzipped a suitcase. "This house needs a woman's touch something awful. I think I should decorate, don't you?"

Janine had a unique relationship with money: she tried to get her hands on as much of it as possible, but as soon as she did, she would rapidly void it from her system, like a dozen bad oysters.

"Let's go down to the strip," she exclaimed. "I need to pick out some outfits."

"For what?"

"I'm *feature* dancing this weekend! I *told* you that." She hit me on the shoulder affectionately. "You're an intelligent guy, Jesse, but I swear, you need to learn how to listen every now and then."

Janine had long since ceased performing in adult movies, but she continued to cash in on the reputation she'd built over the last decade by dancing at strip clubs. The gigs paid extremely well and involved a lower level of personal investment than performing on film.

"Sweetie," Janine purred, after running up an enormous lingerie and high-heels tab, "could I borrow your credit card? I left my wallet in the car."

I frowned, but opened my wallet and handed it over to her.

"So, how much do you make at one of these clubs, anyway?" I asked, as we walked out to the parking lot.

"I don't know," Janine said, heaving her packages into the backseat of my car. "Honestly, I never take the time to count. It's pretty good for just shaking my ass, though, I'll tell you that."

"But, like, how much?" I persisted.

"Fuck, sweetie," she said, turning to face me, "I *said*, I don't *know*. Five grand? Ten? More?"

"That *is* a lot," I agreed. "So, I mean, excuse me for asking, but where does all that money go?"

"I beg your pardon?"

"Well, all I mean is . . . why can't you pay for your own underwear?"

She shook her head at me sadly. "I can't believe you're being stingy with your own girlfriend. With your own *lover.*"

"I'm not being stingy, I'm merely trying to figure out . . ."

"I'd give you the shirt off my back, Jesse," she said, looking at me sincerely. "I just want you to know that."

"Thanks," I said, beginning to laugh. "Although I don't think your little pink tank top would look very good on me. Look, honey, all I want to know is . . ."

"I have *debts,* okay?" Janine said, looking into the driver's side mirror and adjusting a strand of her hair. "I made some bad business decisions. And I bought a couple of bad cars—really bad deals, you know?"

"What happened?" I asked.

"I didn't like them! They were *lemons,*" Janine said. "So, I just dropped them off at the dealers."

"You can't do that," I pointed out. "Not if payments remain on the car."

"Yes, you can do that," Janine shot back. "I mean, I *did.*"

"How many times?" I asked, frightened.

She shrugged. "Not more than a couple."

"Look," I said. "What else have you done?"

Janine cleared her throat. "Well, gosh, if you *must* know, there are a few levies and liens placed against me by the IRS. But that is for *old* stuff, way back in the early nineties. My sense is that if I just wait long enough, all will be forgiven."

"The IRS doesn't just forgive a lien, Janine."

"Why are you *being* like this?" she cried. "I feel like I don't even know you!"

"I'm not being like anything," I said. "Look, I love you, and I just want to know . . ."

"You what?" she said, brightening. "I'm sorry. What did you just say?"

"Nothing."

"Oh, no," Janine said, sliding closer to me, poking me with her finger. "I heard you. *You* said you loved me."

"You must have misheard me," I said, grinning.

"No, I didn't," she said, kissing me happily on my neck. "Oh, Jesse, you said you loved me!"

"Maybe," I admitted. "It's possible."

"Sweetie!" she cried. "I love you, too! Oh my God, I love you so much. Let's never fight over dumb stuff like this again, okay? Do you promise?"

"Yeah," I said. "I promise."

"Thank *goodness*," Janine sighed, settling back in her seat. She fingered her package of expensive underwear. "Now," she purred, "I think we should go home and, uh, sort through these."

I sped that car home as fast as I could.

———

Day by day, she drew me in. I understood that Janine was a volatile woman, given to making impulsive decisions. But she was extraordinarily bright. She spoke straight from the heart, and it wasn't nonsense that came out of her mouth. She was extremely articulate, and often very funny. Most of all, I loved how she watched me from across the room, totally absorbed in every movement. I felt *seen* by her.

"I love her," I admitted to Tyson Beckford one day when he and I were hanging around the shop after hours, shooting a game of pool. "A lot."

My mom in 1964.

My dad in 1976.

Building cars as a kid.

Family portrait with my mom, dad, and sister, Julie.

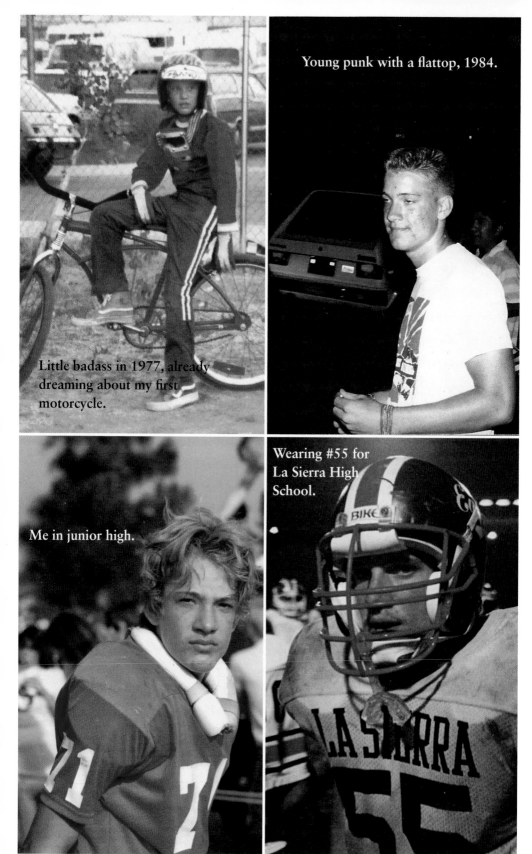

Little badass in 1977, already dreaming about my first motorcycle.

Young punk with a flattop, 1984.

Me in junior high.

Wearing #55 for La Sierra High School.

Rhonda, on the day I surprised her with a customized Volkswagen Beetle.

Laid up from the knee injury that ended my football career.

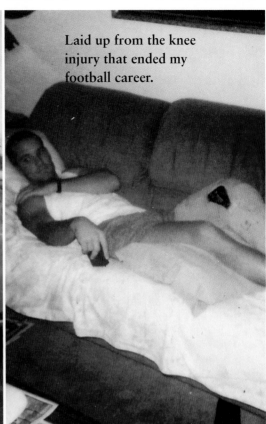

In Scotland with Danzig's Rick Dittamo in 1989.

A little light reading on the tour bus.

Getting my very first tattoo: Karla's name on my leg.

Dressed to impress with Karla, 1993.

The early bike-building days, working in my garage.

New dad with baby Chandler in 1994.

In Long Beach with the 1976
Harley I built myself.

With legendary hot-rodder
Boyd Coddington.

Getting Chandler and Jesse Jr. started early.

From exes to best friends: Karla and me in 2004.

Young love: Janine and me.

Life with Janine
was never boring.

Janine and me on our honeymoon in Mexico, 2002.

Chandler keeping me company while I get inked.

Going for a ride in Daytona Beach with Janine.

In Japan with Chandler in 2003.

In Daytona with Tyson Beckford.

Kid Rock and me in Afghanistan.

Kid Rock, Pamela Anderson, and me.

From welder to reality TV star.

Sandy and Sunny in London.

The happy family: Sandy, Sunny, and me.

The loves of my life: Chandler, Sunny, and Jesse Jr. in 2007.

Father and son in 2009.

Self-portrait in rehab.

Me in 2010, doing what I love.

Tyson and I had kept in touch ever since I'd built him a bike several years before. Whenever he came back into town to film a movie or do a shoot, he called me up. For a black supermodel from New York and a white-trash biker punk from Long Beach, we sure got along good.

"Is that right?" he asked politely.

"Yeah. I almost can't put my finger on it, but she's definitely got me hooked."

"Young lovers," Tyson said, laughing. He slid his cue stick back and forth suggestively.

"Real funny. But hey, dude, you want to hear something kind of crazy?" I said, lowering my voice. "I'm thinking of asking her to marry me."

"Whoa there, buddy," he cautioned. "That was *quick*."

"You don't understand," I said. "Seriously, I have never felt this intense about anyone in my life."

"Fine," Tyson said, "I respect that. But all I'm saying is, do you really *know* this woman?"

"What's that supposed to mean?" I asked.

"Nothing. All I'm saying is, she comes from kind of a funny business . . ."

"I don't care about the porn stuff," I explained. "I really don't. That's behind her. She's done with that."

"Okay," Tyson said. "But didn't you say she had some weird IRS issues, too?"

I shrugged. "Look, if you love someone, then you should be willing to help them out. I have money. I can support both of us."

Tyson held his hands up. "Then, hey, great. That's cool. Who am I to judge, right?"

"Precisely," I mumbled. "Can we get back to shooting pool, now?"

To my annoyance, other friends voiced similar concerns when they heard I was planning to ask Janine to marry me. Chino asked me if I was *sure* I was sure. Other friends just nodded and changed the subject. It pissed me off. It was as if they thought they knew Janine better than I did. After a while, I just stopped talking about it.

Instead, I bought a ring.

"Are you *serious*?" Janine cried. "Are you freakin' serious?"

"I'm one hundred percent serious," I said, laughing. "I want you to be my wife."

"OHMYGOD!!" she yelled. "YES! Yes, I say yes! I love you!"

She jumped into my arms.

"We're going to be so happy, baby," Janine said, her forearms hooking around my neck. "I'm going to be the best wife in the whole world for you."

"I know you are," I said. "We're going to have the best time. I think we should honeymoon somewhere great, like South America."

"I will go absolutely anywhere in the world with you," Janine said. She shook her head. "I . . . I can't believe it. This has got to be the best day of my life."

I didn't tell her about the prenup just then. That came a couple days later.

"Look, don't take it personally," I suggested, embarrassed.

"I'm trying not to," Janine said. She forced a smile, but I could tell she was steaming.

"The thing is," I said, shamefaced, "I talked to my lawyers about it . . ."

"You talked to your *lawyers*. That's just great. That's just *amazing*."

"And they said that it's smarter to keep our finances separate. You owe the government a whole lot of money, babe. And I have a whole lot of money, now. So if we put our money together, they can come take it."

"I *get* that," Janine said. "I'm not dumb, Jesse."

I drew her closer to me. "Do you still love me?"

She sighed. "Yeah, of course I still love you. I'm just . . . a little hurt, that's all."

I said nothing.

"I thought you were going to take *care* of me," she said. "I thought we were going to be a team."

"We are going to be a team," I promised.

"So why this *prenup?*"

"I'm real sorry," I said, again. "I just . . . it's gotta be this way, and I don't know what else to say."

"Oh, fine," she huffed. She folded her arms across her chest, and stuck her tongue out at me. "You meanie."

"I'll make it up to you, okay?" I said. "We'll get married in style."

When Karla and I got married, we were still kind of financially struggling. We'd kept the event real small. This time, however, I wanted to go big. I rented out an immense church and invited everyone we knew. The Discovery Channel decided to record the ceremony for posterity. It was going to be a real California-style fiesta; a coming-out party for the couple made in Biker Heaven: the Porn Star and the Outlaw.

A week before the wedding, Janine and I met with the pastor of the church to discuss the specifics of the ceremony.

"Have you given any consideration to your vows, son?" the pastor asked me pleasantly. He was a gentle-looking old man, with glasses and a well-trimmed white beard.

"I'm gonna make them up as I go along," I confided to him.

"Are you sure?" He looked concerned.

"I'm kidding." I laughed. "I have something written out. It's pretty standard." I squeezed Janine's hand. "I'm just happy to be tying the knot."

"How about you, my dear?" The pastor turned his head toward Janine. "Have you thought about what you might say?"

"I don't know," Janine said, sulking.

"Would you like some suggestions?" the pastor asked. "I've heard many lovely speeches in my days . . ."

"All I want to know," Janine interrupted, "is, what am I getting out of this?"

The pastor stared at her. "How do you mean?"

"Well *he*"—she hooked her thumb at me—"made me sign a prenup."

The pastor turned his head toward me, as if he were watching a tennis match.

I nodded. "It's true."

"So," Janine continued doggedly, "*I* would just like to know what *I'm* supposed to get if this thing doesn't work out."

The pastor looked aghast. Janine tapped her fingers on the table. She looked at him expectantly, waiting for an answer.

"God has a plan, my dear," he managed, finally.

Sitting there that afternoon in the back room of the church, I knew that something was up. A tiny little voice inside of me was pleading, *get out while you still can!* But I was too stubborn to heed the warning.

As usual, I would learn the hard way.

12

———◆◇◆———

We made our preparations to marry. In honor of the occasion, my wife-to-be tattooed a message onto her left shoulder blade: "I Do," in curvy script, surrounded by a large red heart. I responded in kind, inscribing her name in large block letters on the back of my left hand.

You know that expression, "I know it like the back of my hand?" It makes less sense now to most people, because they spend all day staring at computer screens and talking on the telephone. But for people who do manual labor for a living, that phrase still has its full meaning. Because of the kind of work I do, I had to look at it a thousand times a day: *Janine.*

The day of our wedding, we slipped ourselves into our nicest duds and readied to receive all of our friends and family at the chapel. But when I showed up at the church parking lot, a surprise lay in store for me: amazingly, my dad had showed up at my wedding.

"Come by to pay your last respects?" I asked him, in a mildly cold tone.

"You invited me, didn't you?" My dad gave me his hurt face. His beard had gone full white, but it was well-trimmed, and his eyes were vibrant. He looked handsome for an older guy.

"I invited you to my first wedding, too," I said. "But you didn't show up to that."

"Jess," my dad said, "give me a break, why don't you? This is supposed to be a happy occasion. Say, who's this little guy?" he said, turning to Jesse Jr., who was dressed up in a tux.

"Your grandson," I said. "He's five. Nice to meet him after all these years?"

"It certainly is," my dad said, ignoring my tone. He picked up Jesse Jr. and held him in his arms. "Well, hello, young man, hello at last."

My dad didn't fool me for a second. Now that I was a success, he was showing up at my wedding for the same reason he'd come to my football games in high school: he wanted the world to know which tree the apple fell from. Let him preen for the crowd, I wasn't going to fall for it.

"That was real nice," I said, prying my confused son from his grandfather's arms. "But I gotta get married now. Tell you what, we'll see you in five years or so, okay?"

My dad just shook his head. "If you say so," he said. Then he laughed. "I sure hope that wife of yours understands what she's getting into."

An hour later, Janine and I exchanged our vows. It was all easy as pie. We kissed up on stage in front of two hundred cheering people, danced the first dance, real slow and pretty. Just like my dad had done so many years earlier, I'd gotten myself hitched a second time. I'd snagged a new wife, delivered to my kids a brand-new stepmom. We were just another typical, fractured American family: held together with new love, hope, and masking tape.

My kids seemed to like Janine, cautiously. On the occasions when they stayed over at my place, Janine would bake brownies with Chandler and pick out clothes with her, or snuggle up with Jesse Jr. and play pretend, read him bedtime stories.

"Have you ever seen this book, Jesse, *Curious George?*"

He shook his head.

"Well, I *just* found it over at my old house. I used to read this when I was a little girl, just about your age!" Janine smiled. "Would you like me to read it to you? It's about a silly little monkey."

Jesse Jr. nodded, pleased. "Monkeys have *tails.*"

I was certainly happy for any help I could get with the kids. My crazy work schedule continued to wreak havoc on my life. It wasn't enough to have a secretary at West Coast Choppers anymore: I had to hire a personal assistant, Audrey, just to keep up with all my obligations.

"*Men's Fitness* is requesting to do a photo shoot with you."

"Well, tell them no."

"I already did," Audrey said. "They're insistent; they said they'll pay good money. They're even offering discounted ad space on the inside back cover. What do you say?"

"Hell, I don't know," I considered. "What else do I have to do this week?"

"You've got a six-day build for *Monster Garage,* and then you're volunteering at Long Beach Poly on Sunday, doing something called"—she consulted her book—"a backyard build. Plus, you need to complete Kid Rock's bike for his birthday, how far along are you on that?"

"Behind."

"Well, step it up, we can't move his birthday, now can we?" she said. "Oh, and you're committed to do a *GQ* event on Saturday evening."

"Great," I groaned. "Another calm week."

"Exactly," Audrey agreed. "It won't get truly crazy until the holidays."

"Look, do me a favor," I said. "Cancel the GQ thing."

"But why?" she asked.

"I have to do something with my wife."

"Bring her to the GQ party! You're sure to have a good time."

"Can't," I said, regretfully. "Janine works weekends."

My new wife, the retired porn star, was still stripping occasionally. I'd told her there was no need anymore—she didn't need to earn her own money, we were in this together—but she just patted me on the head dismissively. Janine still loved a crowd. She fed off of their attention and acknowledgment; when she was up on stage, working a bunch of starstruck men, she was still the most beautiful woman in the world. Janine had first posed for *Penthouse* at the age of eighteen; the adult business was what she knew. She was going to keep on performing no matter what I had to say. And this weekend, she had a gig at the Spearmint Rhino in Torrance.

When you compared it to other L.A. clubs, the Spearmint Rhino actually came off as kind of a winner. Jumbo's Clown Room hired all the ugly girls. Cheetah's and the Seventh Veil were straight-up Armenian mafia joints. And Bob's Classy Lady in Van Nuys was not so classy. The Rhino, at the very least, lacked a lunch buffet.

"I respect this place," I told Janine, when we'd filed in through the back door and began to make ourselves at home in the dressing room. "It's kind of civilized."

"Huh?" Janine said, distracted, toying with her eyeliner. "What are you talking about?"

"I feel at home here, kind of. I don't feel like, well, killing myself. That's all." Experimentally, I dragged my feet on the synthetic-fibered strip-bar carpeting. A small puff of dust rose up around my ankles, then settled. "Listen, do you need anything?"

"Yes. Be a good boy and get me a glass of vodka, please."

"Vodka martini?" I asked. "Vodka cranberry?"

"A *glass* of *vodka*," Janine repeated, pronouncing every word deliberately. "Be quick. Go, go, go."

A few minutes later, I was back. "Listen, that guy behind the bar gave me one hell of a funny look . . ."

"You're such a sweetheart," Janine interrupted, snatching the drink out of my hand. "Now, leave me alone for a second. I need to get my head together before they call me out on stage."

Just then, though, we heard the club DJ bellow into his microphone.

"*Ladies* and *gentlemen,* let's give it up for our main attraction tonight, a very SEXY lady . . ."

"Oh, fuck me," Janine moaned. "I'm not even goddamn made up all the way!"

"She's a Penthouse Pet and a Vivid Girl . . . a mainstream music video vixen, and a close personal friend of Jenna Jameson . . . and hoo boy, I'm talking *personal*!"

Boorish laughter boomed through the club.

"Time for that vodka," she declared. "Down the hatch."

"People, let's put our hands together and give a warm Rhino welcome to the hottest piece of ass in three states—*JANINE*!!"

"Hold it, honey," I said, "don't you want to wait until . . ."

Shushing me impatiently, Janine brought the glass to her lips, and tipped her head straight back. I stared, horrified, as I watched her throat piston back and forth, until every last drop was swallowed.

"*Ahhh.*" Janine slammed the glass on the table, then wiped her mouth with the back of her hand. She shook her head, shuddering. "That was just what I needed."

My mouth hung open. *What in the hell?*

"What are *you* looking at?" Janine laughed. "Stand back or step aside, dammit! It's time to dance."

Pushing her way past me, Janine clipped briskly out of the dressing room, her slim, exquisite body clad only in spike heels and an expensive bra-and-panty set. Her theme song, Blink 182's

"What's My Age Again?" blared from the speakers, and from the appreciative roar of the crowd, I gathered that she'd made it up on stage. I hung back, not really interested in taking in the spectacle. After all, I'd have her later, at home—this performance was for the schmucks who had to pay for the privilege of watching.

Fifteen minutes later, Janine strode furiously into the dressing room, looking incensed.

"What the FUCK?"

"What are you yelling at me for?" I snapped.

"I just *killed* out there, and you didn't even catch it. Why weren't you *out* there?" she demanded.

"I didn't realize you needed me by your side every instant."

"I don't!" Janine said. "But for some reason, I thought you might want to watch your *wife* dance on stage. Are you ashamed of me, Jesse?"

I didn't say anything. Instead I considered her question. Maybe I *was* ashamed. Part of me had been really into the fact that she'd been a porn star—it sure impressed the average guy on the street. But now I had to deal with the reality of the situation: having a porn star or a stripper for a wife meant the woman you shared a home with got naked in front of other people. And I wasn't really sure I wanted that, to be honest.

"You're a narcissist," Janine said, shaking her head back and forth, furious. "If the spotlight's not on you, then you can't function."

"Don't be crazy," I said, annoyed. "That's not it at all."

"Jesse!" Janine cried in frustration. "Why am I dealing with your bullshit right now?"

"Exactly," I said, exasperated. "After all, isn't this when you're supposed to be giving lap dances to all the johns?"

Janine stared at me balefully. "How *dare* you."

"You know what?" I said, shaking my head. "I don't think I like strip clubs that much anymore. I'm out of here. You can take a taxi home."

I withdrew three twenty-dollar bills from my wallet, and thrust them toward her.

"Keep your money," Janine said quietly. A cool smile appeared on her face. "I'm about to go make my own."

———

She came home very late that night, crawling quietly into bed. The next morning, clad in a conservative bathrobe, her hair pulled back, all traces of makeup gone from her face, she made me a big breakfast.

"I didn't mean to get all upset at you, Jesse," she said carefully, sausage frying in a heavy black skillet. "But I would have really appreciated it if you had come to watch me dance."

"Well, honestly, I would have. I just didn't know it was that important to you."

"Just think about it!" Janine pleaded. "You're good at so many things; I'm only good at *one* thing. Last night, that was my thing! Of course I want the most important person in my life to witness me doing it."

"Man," I said, feeling suddenly guilty. "I'm sorry. I guess I just didn't see it that way at the time."

"Well," Janine said, sliding the sausages onto a plate and placing them before me. "It's my fault, for not explaining it better to you."

I got up and walked over to her. "Will you accept my apology?" I said, sheepishly.

Janine grinned. "Of course, silly." She moved to embrace me. "You are such a sweetie, underneath all that *guff*."

I held her happily for a moment, and kissed her on the side of her temple. "You know what?" I said, suddenly. "You and I should get ourselves a new place to live. A place where we can start over fresh."

"Seriously?" Janine's eyes opened wide. "Are you, like, kidding me?"

"Nope," I said proudly. "Would you like that?"

"Oh, baby!" she cried, leaping into my arms, laughing joyously.

"Let's live by the *beach*! My whole life, I've always wanted to live by the ocean!"

"If that's what you want," I promised, "that's where we're going to live."

Janine's highs were so high, and her exuberance so contagious, that it wasn't merely a figure of speech to say it made me happy to make her happy. Truly, I fed off of her lightheartedness. Her love for me felt like more than just an emotion she expressed. It was a form of sustenance.

Several months later, we went to see a gorgeous house on Seal Beach, about fifteen minutes from downtown Long Beach.

"Oh, I love it, Jesse," Janine said, as we walked across the hardwood of the empty downstairs living room. "I absolutely love it." She smiled at me, her eyes sparkling. "This could be a wonderful house for a *family*."

"Yep. Jesse and Chandler will love it," I agreed.

"That's not exactly what I meant," she said, smiling. "And you know it."

That very day, we signed the papers to purchase the house, and we began to map out the next twenty years together. Flushed by the pleasure of the deal, Janine was expansive, detailing her long-held desire to raise a whole slew of kids, and perhaps someday live on a farm, with livestock and maybe a vineyard. Carefully, I reminded her that I wasn't a farmer . . . I worked on motorcycles for a living. She pooh-poohed me: too rational. Not enough imagination. She ruffled my hair. Stared deeply into my eyes.

The next weekend, I was scheduled to make an appearance at a Walmart in Bentonville, Arkansas, where we were going to introduce a new project, Jesse James West Coast Choppers Industrial Wear, a line of men's work-wear clothing. I was slated to sign autographs and meet some of the company's top brass.

"Feel like coming along?" I asked Janine.

"Of *course*," she said happily. "You know me. I love to meet the people!"

But to her surprise and annoyance, the crowd assembled in the Walmart parking lot took little notice of Janine. In fact, they barely acknowledged her presence. The herd of Southern bikers appeared far more focused on getting an autograph from the man from *Monster Garage* than on approaching his porn-star wife.

"I'm *bored*," she grumbled, after enduring the public snub for almost an hour. "I think I'll head back to the hotel."

"Okay, babe. Catch up with you later," I said, distracted, as I scribbled my Sharpie over yet another bandanna. "And I'm making this out to . . . Jason?"

"Yessiree," said the oldster at the front of the line, gratefully. "My grandson, well, he just *loves* your show."

The line wound on endlessly. I pressed flesh with thousands of fans, accepting their helpful ideas about what might be interesting on the next season of the show. I stood next to pregnant women, my hands around their engorged waists, as I waited for their nervous husbands to figure out just where that flash was on the disposable camera. Slowly, the hours ticked by.

Finally the line subsided, and my handler gave a signal to the event director. "That's it. We're good." He turned to me. "Need a ride back to the hotel?"

"No, I'll drive myself."

"Don't take too long," he advised. "We've got lunch set with the executive vice president of marketing and six of his staff, and they're *extremely* excited to meet you. Hotel lobby, twenty minutes from now. We'll go from there."

Wearily, I trudged to my car and sat down heavily on the hood. I rested there for a moment, rubbing my hand, sore from hours of signing. Then I opened the driver's side door, wedged myself behind the wheel of the rental, and set off for the hotel.

The moment I entered the lobby, several Walmart executives stood up to greet me. Each wore a smile on his face.

"Sir," began the paunchy, excited-looking VP of marketing, his hand extended, "it is *truly* an honor to meet you . . ."

"WHERE THE FUCK HAVE *YOU* BEEN??"

My insides flushed with ice water. Janine was storming out of the elevator, her hair mussed, looking crazed.

"I HAVE CALLED YOU FIFTEEN TIMES, AND YOU HAVEN'T PICKED UP!" She sprinted up to me and jabbed her finger crazily in my face. "DO YOU HAVE ANY *FUCKING* IDEA WHAT I'VE BEEN DOING ALL DAY?"

"Janine," I begged. "Calm down. Please don't do this here. Not in front of everybody."

"In front of who?" She swept her arms wildly, then settled her gaze on the Walmart executives. "Oh, your new best *friends*?"

"Stop it."

"Well, I'm sorry to *embarrass* you, Jesse," Janine continued, "but I think *someone* should know what a *neglectful* and self-centered son of a bitch you really are."

Janine fixed me the dirtiest, most furious glare I'd ever seen. Then she turned on her heel and stomped back toward the elevator.

The silence in the lobby was terrible.

"Excuse me," I said to the executives, finally. "I think I need to go . . . handle this."

No one responded. With my face burning, I walked away.

———

Purposefully, I threw myself into my work, tried to use it as an escape. But burying my thoughts proved more difficult than I had figured.

You may need to walk away from this one, I told myself. *The verdict might still be out, but a few of the jurors are starting to lean toward "crazy."*

A broken driveshaft lay on my table, looking abandoned. "Focus, dammit," I muttered. I had three bikes to build, and twenty more to design. I stared into my toolbox for a few minutes, but was simply unable to concentrate on the job at hand. "Ah, forget it."

I wiped my hands on a rag and threw on my jacket, hustling out to the parking lot, where I hopped on my machine and headed for the highway.

Riding a motorcycle had always been my greatest comfort. It was the only place I could still go to be alone. I threw my bike into high gear. The wind tore into my face as I revved my engine, rocketing past car after car, watching as the industrial wasteland of Long Beach slowly blurred into a seamless track of colors: grays, blues, and browns. After several minutes of stinging pressure and the steady vibration of the powerful, rumbling engine, I began to feel soothed. Even capable of logical thought.

I don't want to get divorced, I told myself. *Above all else, I don't want that to happen.*

I had been through one separation already. The sense of failure had been overwhelming. To me, divorce was like giving up. And this fight didn't seem over yet.

I knew there was someone special inside of Janine, that our connection hadn't all been in my mind. She was a bright, vibrant woman. And there was a deep kindness to her that I felt nourished by.

She's touchy, I thought. *No doubt about that. And her temper is clearly kind of . . . unpredictable. But isn't there some way around that?*

I sunk lower in my seat and throttled the engine, slowly beginning to increase my speed. Shifting my weight subtly, hooking the big machine from one side to the other for no purpose other than to do it, I rode the intricate mass of revolving steel like a surfer rides a wave. Every muscle in my body felt tuned into the cycle's movement, molded to its form.

Janine loved me. I was sure of it. She saw me for who I really *was*—a biker, a punk, a kid from a broken home—and despite all of that, she accepted me without hesitation. Didn't I owe her the same courtesy?

I can bring out the best in her, I thought. *If I'm smart about it, I can save this marriage.*

The highway that I knew so well sped by me, with its dented iron railings and smooth pavement. I gazed over the drop, watching the rocky cliffs blur, all the way down into the vast black waters of Los Angeles.

———

"So what do you think about these new Softail Deuces? Cool, huh?"

"I like them. I like all Harleys, as long as they go fast."

Tyler, the young boy with leukemia whom I had befriended several months before, hunched over a pile of motorcycle magazines I'd brought him. I sat next to him, peering over his small shoulder.

"Yeah, but how about these *Yamahas*?" I asked him, wrinkling my nose. "Pretty bad, huh?"

Tyler grinned. "I hate 'em!"

"What do we call them?" I prompted.

"Crotch rockets," Tyler said.

"That's right," I said, laughing. "But hey, do me a favor, don't say that around your mom. You'll get me in trouble."

I had taken to dropping by Tyler's house about once a week on my way home from work. His family lived so close to the shop, it was simple for me to do. Unfortunately, his condition kept getting worse and worse.

"How's he doing?" I asked his mom one evening after a visit, when we were outside on the lawn alone together.

"Not good," she said, looking upset. "He may only have a few more months. That's what the doctors say."

"He's an amazing kid," I said. "Maybe he'll prove them wrong."

"Mom?" Tyler asked. He pushed open the screen door, joining us out on the lawn. "What are you guys talking about? I thought you were going to leave, Jesse."

"I'm on my way," I told him. "I was just talking to your mom for a second."

"Do you really know Shaq?" Tyler asked, shyly. "My mom said you might know him."

"I built a bike for him once," I said, smiling. "I think that was the biggest bike I ever had to make."

"Can you get me his autograph?" Tyler asked. "He's my favorite basketball player on the Lakers."

"I'll see what I can do," I said. "I better go now. Can I have a hug?"

I knelt down to give a gentle hug to the seven-year-old. As we embraced, I felt the skinniness and fragility of his body through the fabric of his T-shirt. I could feel every rib. Unexpectedly, tears welled up in my eyes.

"Gotta go," I mumbled. "See you soon, Tyler."

Slowly, I drove home in my truck, nearly overwhelmed.

That night over dinner, passing the salad bowl toward me, Janine asked, "How's work going?"

"All right . . . next week, we're going to turn a Chevy Suburban into a wedding chapel," I told her. "We're going to head to Vegas and find a couple to have a real wedding inside of it."

"You guys have the wildest ideas," said Janine. "Who's gonna officiate?"

I grinned proudly. "You're looking at him."

Janine busted up laughing. "*You?* How is that possible, Jesse?"

"The Universal Life Ministry. You can get a license over the Internet. They let anybody be an ordained minister, these days."

"Apparently," Janine said, arching her eyebrows.

Things weren't always tense between us—they were more like . . . schizophrenic. Janine was a personality who thrived on fighting, but like any good fighter, unpredictability was her greatest asset. That week, as we transformed the Suburban into a wedding-chapel-on-wheels, she came to visit me on the set several times, the very picture of a loving wife.

"Well, hey there," I said, pleased to see her. Her face and hair were immaculately made up. "Sweetie," I said, kissing her on the temple, "why is it the only time I see you around my garage is when we're filming?"

"Oh, I don't find the camera," Janine explained, coolly. "The camera finds *me*."

Of course, the guys on the camera crew were always psyched to see a real live porn star there—photographing busted catalytic converters day in and day out can take a toll on any man. So she generally got her wish, a behind-the-scenes interview, even though obviously none of the footage would ever be used for the show.

"Your crew is so *imaginative*," Janine said, wandering around the shop, gazing in at our mobile marriage shack. "Gosh, I wish *we* could have been married in a cool little contraption like this, don't you?"

"Yeah, it would have been a bonding experience. Maybe it would have made you nicer to your husband," I said, tickling her side playfully.

"Jesse!" Janine shouted. "Don't tickle!" She punched me on the shoulder several times, laughing.

"Hey," I said, smiling tightly, "you hit damn hard. Stop, okay?"

"Well, don't *tickle*," Janine said. She shot me a look. "You bring it on yourself, Jesse."

We stared at each other for a moment, on the brink of hostility.

"*So*," she said, sighing, changing the subject, "when are you going to Vegas, to become, like, a minister?"

"Tomorrow." I drew her closer to me, lay my forehead up against hers. "You feel like coming with me?"

"Of course I do," Janine said, looking wistful. "But I can't. I have engagements this whole weekend."

"Well, all right," I said, secretly a bit relieved. "Tell you what. I'll try not to gamble away the farm while I'm there."

"You're funny," Janine said, kissing me lightly on the lips. "Look, I should go. I'm dancing tonight. I won't be home until late."

The crew and I worked until late in the evening, putting the finishing touches on the Suburban. When we were done, we'd installed a set of gull-wing rear doors, a stained-glass roof, and an intricate pipe organ. We were ready to marry in style.

I drove home, dead tired, looking forward to grabbing a couple of hours of much-needed sleep before I rose early in the morning to drive to Las Vegas. I rolled into our driveway, slammed the door of my truck behind me, and trudged wearily upstairs, falling into bed without even showering.

I woke up several hours later to the feeling of my wife straddling my body in bed.

"Fucking bastard," Janine mumbled. Her breath smelled strongly of alcohol. Her eyes squinted heavily.

"Huh?" I asked, still half-asleep.

"You fucking bastard," Janine repeated. Then, cocking back her fist, she punched me right in the eye, hard.

"What the *hell*?" I roared, pushing her off me.

"You took . . ." she mumbled, falling to the side of me.

"Janine!" I cried, leaping to my feet. I clutched my injured eye, my adrenaline racing. "What the fuck is *wrong* with you?"

"You took . . ." Janine said, laughing, once, drunkenly, "my parking spot." Then she shrugged, fell facedown into her pillow, and began snoring lightly.

"*Janine!*" I shouted, furious, my blood racing. "JANINE!"

———

The following day, I drove as planned to Las Vegas to officiate the wedding. A couple from North Carolina had won a sweepstakes from Discovery, securing for them the honor of being married in a car by a dysfunctional welder. Fittingly, my eye had swelled up terrifically where I'd been punched. I had a big ol' shiner.

"Get into some trouble last night, Jesse?" the makeup artist asked me, cheerfully.

"You could say that," I muttered.

"How about you let me cover that up for you?" she proposed. "It might not look so terrific on television."

Humiliated, my mind whirling, I sat in the makeup chair and let her apply pancake and rouge to my swollen eye and cheekbone.

This can't go on, I thought.

With cameras in tow, we set out for downtown Vegas, where we orchestrated a street-side pickup of Chris and Sara, the excited young couple. I let down the automatic doors, and they strutted up regally into the mobile Suburban wedding chapel.

It was showtime. My heart felt unexpectedly heavy as I spoke the words, "Do you take this woman to be your lawfully wedded wife?"

The groom looked at his wife with love and excitement in his eyes. "Yes," he said. "I do."

As I stood there and watched the happy young couple come together, I realized, with a sinking feeling, that this thing I had signed up for might not turn out as I'd hoped.

That evening, I called Janine from my hotel room in Vegas.

"I think we have to face facts. It's not working," I said, flatly. "I mean us. We're not working."

"Jesse, love, I can *explain* . . ."

"You *punched* me last night. Do you even remember that?"

"I recall doing *something* like that," she said, "but if you'd give me a chance to explain, I think you'd understand. It wasn't my fault. I wasn't feeling well . . ."

"I'm frightened to be around you," I said. "Don't you get it?"

"A big, tough guy like you? *Scared?*"

"Janine," I said, exasperated. "I came from a violent family. Okay?"

"I *know* that, but . . ."

"One of my earliest memories is my dad breaking his hand in a fight with my mom," I said. "I *heard* him do it. They were yelling at each other for hours."

"Jesse, please . . ."

"Then I heard him hit something. I heard it through the wall of my bedroom. Do you know what that's like for a kid, Janine? The next day, his hand was broken. They both tried to tell me that he fell off a *ladder*. I was only six, but I was already too old to fall for that one."

Janine waited for a moment. "Well? What does that have to do with me?"

"I can't have that kind of thing in my house," I said. "I just . . . I can't have it."

"I didn't *mean* to," Janine sighed. "I *love* you, honey. Give me another chance."

After some more discussion, we agreed to try again. But my patience was running thin. And then, only a week later, an everyday argument exploded, and I left the house in a huff. Janine followed closely behind me.

"Get back here," she screamed. "Where are you going?"

"I'm out of here," I said, striding past her, toward my vehicle.

Without another word, Janine leaped into her car and gunned the engine. Dumbfounded, I watched as she jerked the car into reverse recklessly, then drove it straight toward me.

"What the FUCK is WRONG with you!" I screamed, leaping out of the way. "You almost hit me, you crazy bitch!"

Janine backed the car up, revved the engine. Again, I leaped out of the way.

"That's it!" I cried. "You are so fucking *out* of here! You're GONE! Now! *Leave*."

"Or what?" she screamed.

"Or I'm going to call the cops and have you arrested for assault, Janine!"

Quickly, she turned off the car, then said she didn't mean it. But by now I'd been through it enough times to recognize things weren't going to change. She had to go.

I watched in silence as she packed a suitcase, and then she left.

For the first time, I had the whole house to myself. I sat down in the kitchen, the weirdly silent kitchen, and poured myself a bowl of cereal. Slowly, I ate, looking out over the beach as I did so. I breathed in deeply, and exhaled a long, relieved breath. I had never felt so tranquil in my own home.

Janine had vacated the premises. But before doing so, she'd left a note: *I hope we can work this out.*

I folded it carefully, then threw it in the trash.

"We were a mess," I confessed to Tyson, the next time he was back in California.

"Bro," he said, smiling, "I *hate* to tell you I told you so. But . . ."

"Why didn't anyone *warn* me?" I moaned.

"We tried to," he said. "But you just weren't ready to hear it."

I sat down at the kitchen table and looked at Tyson gravely. "You knew I came from a pretty messed-up home, right?"

"No," he admitted. "You never really mentioned it to me."

I sighed. "I just . . . I want to do *better* than that. I can't let my kids grow up like I did."

Tyson shook his head. "Jesse," he said, after a second, "no matter how hard it is, what you're doing right now is worth it, man. You have to try to make a new start without this woman."

I tried to make work fill my emotional void. The lineup of customers clamoring for expensive custom bikes was endless, so, digging in, I tried to face the stack of orders with renewed determination.

Soon I lost myself in the rhythmic, soothing tempo of welding. The mask flipped down over my head had never felt so protective. When I was under that metallic hood, shooting sparks and melting steel, I was free from human engagement. There were no stupid conversations. No mindless bullshitting about the NFL or horse racing. No wife who punched me in the fucking face.

Weeks passed, and then months. Gradually I watched myself grow stronger. I spent the weekends alone with my kids, running on the beach with them, laughing, enjoying the process of watching them grow up. They were my saviors.

Still, I couldn't help but feel starved for companionship. I was so used to being in a relationship: Karla and I had been together for the better part of a decade, and I hadn't been alone for very long before I'd found myself head over heels for Janine. For better or for worse, I seemed most comfortable being part of a twosome. I guess I was coming around to the realization that I missed having a woman in my life when, right on cue, Janine finally called.

"I want to see you," she said seductively. "Can you guess why?"

"Janine," I said stiffly. "I really don't think that's a great idea."

"Oh, come on." She laughed. "You're not *still* mad about what happened, are you?"

"Which time?" I asked, angrily.

Janine laughed. "Honestly, honey, I feel *awful* about smacking you. You know I wasn't in the right head space at the time. But I've got things in order now, and I want to make it up to you."

"Well," I said, my resolve weakening. "How exactly do you mean?"

Janine let her voice drop to a whisper. "I'd much rather show you in person than describe it on the phone."

Half an hour later, she was at my doorstep. Five minutes after that, we were in bed together.

We slept together, one last time—my lust had gotten the better of me. But it wouldn't happen again. I had been wrong to believe that I could get closer to her. Janine was too violent, too unpredictable to form a life around. She would never be able to change.

"We should give this another shot," said Janine. "Don't you think?"

I shook my head. "No. This was a mistake."

Janine shrugged and began putting her clothing back on. "Well, you can't say I didn't try," she said, smiling and strangely smug. "I'll see myself out."

13

Several months passed without speaking to Janine. Slowly, I began to form plans for a life beyond our relationship, beyond a marriage that I already considered a regrettable mistake. I knew someday I would find a wiser, more stable person to spend time with. Until then, I would be best off alone.

Then one day, with no warning, Janine appeared at the shop.

"Can I speak with you?" she asked, looking serious.

"You came by on the wrong day," I said stiffly, not looking up from my work. "No filming happening here."

"I'm pregnant."

"Excuse me?"

"You heard me," Janine said, steadily. "I'm pregnant, Jesse. We're going to have a baby."

My mouth hung open, like I'd been sucker punched in the stomach. Immediately, I called bullshit.

"We've been broken up for months."

"The last night we spent together," she said, shaking her head. "It must have been then."

"No *way*," I said, folding my arms stubbornly. "Impossible. I mean, what are the chances?"

"Hey," Janine said, shrugging. "I've done the math, and it *had* to have been then. I haven't been with anyone else."

"Why would I believe *that*?" I snorted. "I don't know who you've been spending time with lately."

"For all I've done wrong, honey, I've never once wanted to be with anyone else," Janine said. "You can believe me or not, but it's yours, Jesse. I promise."

I felt frantic. I had no idea what to say or do. In a single instant, my entire world had just been turned upside down.

"You and I *can't* have a baby," I protested weakly.

"We don't have any choice," Janine said.

"We tried this already. It didn't work. Remember?"

"I'm starting to think that we should give it another chance," Janine said, patiently. "You know, I don't think we've tried hard enough, yet."

"No," I said stubbornly. "I *tried*. I tried damn hard. You know what? I want a paternity test."

"Oh, fine!" Janine said, the frustration finally rising in her voice. "If you want to be difficult about it, then off we go."

That week, we drove together in silence to an expensive doctor's appointment, where a prenatal sampling of Janine's ripening placenta returned the verdict that I had been fearing all along.

"See?" Janine said triumphantly. "I *told* you it was yours. Didn't I?"

I slumped forward, in shock. "What the hell are we going to do now?"

"We'll just have to get along, that's all." Janine kissed me on my neck, and looked into my eyes expectantly. "Because, Jesse, we're going to raise this little baby *together*."

That very evening, she moved back into my house. She marched her clothes back into the closet, marshaled her lipsticks along her side of the bathroom sink.

"I *missed* this," Janine said, kissing me gently. "I missed making a home with you."

I shook my head, still not knowing what to think or how to feel. "Janine . . ."

"Yes, honey?" she asked, turning on the television, settling back onto my bed, as if she had never left.

"This is all happening way too fast for me," I said. "I had sort of gotten used to the idea of . . . well, of us having *separated*."

"We did separate," Janine said patiently. "But," she wagged her index finger at me, "we didn't divorce. And aren't you happy now that we didn't? That would have been a bunch of unnecessary paperwork, huh? I mean, now that we're getting back together."

"What?" I said.

Janine raised herself up on one elbow and looked at me oddly. "Honey, we're having a child together. *Of course* we're getting back together. It may take some work, but I'm willing to do my part. Aren't you?"

"Shit," I stammered, "I don't know. I mean . . . maybe . . . but if I'm going to do this, there's got to be some rules, okay?"

"That's fine," Janine said. "Like what?"

"Like, no more crazy *fighting*. I can't deal with it, Janine!"

"Um, I *hate* to say this," Janine said, calmly, "but *you're* the one who's yelling right now."

I tensed my fists. "Look. I just need this to be different than it was. I don't want to have the same kind of marriage that my folks did. I can't stand battling against you all the time. I can't stand being scared to bring my *kids* around someone who I'm supposed to be in love with . . ."

"So, hey, hey—just take a deep *breath*, baby," Janine said, laughing. "I mean, your blood pressure must be going through the *roof*! Wow, what the hell's got into you since I've been gone?"

"What's got into me?" I whispered.

"You look *frustrated*," she said. Her eyes crinkled sympathetically. "I think you need to lie down next to me. Come on. *Calm* yourself. Take a second to think about this little baby we're having. Don't you want it to come into a sweet and relaxing world?"

I looked at her, shook my head back and forth, pulse racing, words failing me completely.

—

Despite any misgivings I might have had, I knew that the decision was a done deal. She was pregnant with my kid. I had to try again. No matter how bad Janine had screwed with my trust, I was going to have to get over it, and quick.

"My girl's back," I mentioned to Bill, as we began to wrench on a new custom chopper. "She moved all her stuff back into my house."

"Huh," he said noncommittally. "How's that working for you?"

I cranked up the blowtorch and, sighing heavily, dropped my safety goggles over my eyes. "To be honest, I'm kind of relieved."

"Seriously?"

"Yeah," I said. "Gives us both a do-over. We got another chance to make things right."

"Well, remember," Bill advised, "nobody's marriage is perfect. But hell, you're a survivor! I believe in you." He clapped me on the back. "Now go to war."

Janine and I circled around each other uneasily for the first few weeks back, like two lions staking out territory. Out of the corners of my eyes, I studied her, just waiting for her to snap and betray me. But to my surprise, Janine stayed calm and levelheaded, even seeming apologetic for her past indiscretions at certain moments.

Soon, enough trust had returned to where I felt okay bringing my children back into the house while she was there.

"*Janine!*" Chandler said, tossing her backpack onto the living room couch. "When did you get back?"

"Hi, sweetheart," Janine beamed. "It's so nice to see you!"

"Where did you go?" Chandler asked again, hugging her. "Why weren't you *here* for such a long time?"

Janine shot me a glance. "Oh, darling, I was . . . taking a long trip." She pursed her lips, then rubbed my nine-year-old daughter softly on the back. "I won't be going away anymore, okay?"

Chandler smiled, pleased. "Do you want to see the drawing I did?"

"Of course I do!"

Janine had it in her to love a child, that much was obvious. Tentatively, I began to envision us redefining ourselves as a couple, from a dysfunctional duo to a husband and wife who were fit to make a stable home for our baby. The reality of the situation was that there was a new life growing in my wife's belly. In under a year, that life would take shape in Long Beach. She and I were going to spend a great deal of time together learning how to raise it correctly, so we might as well do it together, as a team.

"You know," I said to Janine, as we were driving to the doctor's again a week or so later, "I think we're capable of doing this."

"Well, finally," Janine said, smiling. She reached over and took my hand in hers. "I've been waiting for you to come around."

"I've been watching you," I admitted. "And I can see it in your eyes. You want to be a mom so bad."

"Oh, sweetie, it's true," she said proudly. "I just can't wait."

We arrived at the hospital and went inside. After a short wait, we met our doctor. She was a friendly, goofy-looking little woman who shortly instructed Janine to disrobe and place her legs in the gynecological stirrups for a pelvic exam.

"Do you need me to leave?" I asked.

"No, you can stay," the lady doctor said genially, patting a chair for me to sit on. As she turned away from me, I noticed the doctor's hairstyle. It was business in the front, and nothin' but a party in the back: a *mullet*. On a female doctor, no less. How funny was that?

"Now then, have you two decided on a name?"

"Oh, we'll probably have to mull it over for a while," I said, winking at Janine.

Janine shot me a dirty look. As she struggled uncomfortably to place her legs in the stirrups, she appeared to be sweating. "My husband's just trying to be funny," she said.

The doctor looked confused. "Oh?" she asked.

"Don't mind me," I said. "It's a very important decision. I'm just trying to *mull it* over in my head."

We completed the exam without further incident. Then, as we walked out to the car, Janine turned to me and said, "I can't *believe* you!"

"What's the big deal?"

"That whole 'mull it' thing? What the *fuck* were you going on about?"

"She had a sweet hairstyle," I said, laughing. "Look, I was just having some fun, okay?"

"I was down there *naked,*" she hissed at me. "That was not the time or the place!"

We reached our car. "Give me a break, all right?" I said. "It's not that big a deal . . ."

"You don't *know* what a big deal *is*!" Janine cried, digging in her purse. "That's always been your biggest FUCKING PROBLEM!"

She found her big ring of keys, gripped them in her fist, and threw them directly in my face as hard as she could.

"*OWW!*" I yelled, dropping to my knees in the parking lot. "*Janine!* What the hell was that for?"

"*You think this is all a joke?*" Janine screeched, standing over me. "I'm going to have your baby! And you want to treat me like some *fucking joke?*"

Slowly, my breath heaving, I picked up Janine's keys from the ground and handed them to her.

"Drive yourself," I said. "I'm walking."

———

I slept at the shop that night.

I can't go on with this woman, I thought to myself, rolling uncomfortably on the futon I kept in my office, trying to steal an hour or so of sleep. *There's just no way.*

But I seemed to have little choice in the matter. I was boxed in with nowhere to go. *She's going to have my kid!* I thought, desperately. *And yet . . .*

And yet I'm afraid she could run me over.

I rolled off the futon at six o'clock sharp the following morning, having gotten about forty-five minutes of rotten, dreamless shut-eye.

"Hey, Jesse. Good morning!" My custodian, Dennis, was a mentally challenged guy about my own age—like Boyd, I'd kept up the tradition of employing developmentally disadvantaged adults. Dennis never failed to raise my spirits and keep me humble at the same time.

But this morning, I didn't want to hear anything from anyone.

"Hey," I said shortly, brushing past him to go wash my face in the restroom.

"Did you *sleep* here?" Dennis asked, giggling.

I didn't answer, just slammed the bathroom door hard behind me and looked at myself in the mirror. My eyes were bloodshot and underscored with dark rings. *Fuck,* I thought. *I've aged ten years the last ten months.*

I splashed cold water on my face and tried to come back to reality. There was business to take care of. Soon everyone would be arriving. As always, I had to be ready to take the wheel of the ship. Pretend like I knew what I was doing.

"Jesse," my assistant began, as soon as she settled in. "Season two of *Monster Garage* is going to start filming in three weeks. Thom Beers called. He wants to get together ASAP, to bat around ideas."

"Yo, Jess," Bill Dodge yelled, "we got two CFL frames to get chromed by next Tuesday—are we ready to send them over to the shop in Riverside?"

"Jesse," apologized Melissa, my secretary, "I don't want to alarm you, but retail's been experiencing a *ton* of shoplifting lately. Are we going to go forward with installing those electronic scanners by the door, or what?"

Leave me alone, guys. Please, fucking leave me alone . . .

"Jesse, we've got a big show set up in Japan for you to make an appearance at this November. They're still waiting on your decision. Do you want me to tell them yea or nay?"

"Jesse! Walmart's looking for a quarterly update on the menswear line. Do we have anything new?"

I hid behind my desk, feeling completely overwhelmed.

———

When I got home, the house was empty. Exhausted beyond belief, I sank into my couch and switched on the television. I watched fifteen seconds of a basketball game, then fifteen seconds of cable news. Then some cheesy murder mystery. And on and on. My stuttering mind wove the random TV snippets into a singular saga, a story bearing a nonsensical plotline that nevertheless seemed to make more sense than my own life.

I waited for Janine to show up, but she never did. I went to sleep uneasily, and woke up alone.

Her absence continued the following day. Janine was nowhere to be seen.

When, on the third day, she still failed to appear, I began to relax. *Maybe it's over,* I thought to myself with some relief.

The following week, I was scheduled to have surgery on my shoulder. Over the years, the accumulation of injuries sustained through football and as a bodyguard, including my stage dive at the White Zombie show, had just gotten too painful to deal with on a daily basis. After consulting the X-rays and running me through a battery of tests, my doctor advised me to go through with the surgery.

"How long will the rehab be?" I asked.

"You'll be in a sling for six to eight weeks. Then you can start physical therapy," he said, smiling. "By my estimation, you should have a pain-free shoulder in under a year's time."

I sighed. "Well, that sucks. Timing's not good. We're going to start filming the next season of my show soon."

"Timing's never good for going under the knife, is it?" he said. "I strongly advise this surgery."

Bill Dodge drove me to the hospital.

"Are you nervous?"

"I hate hospitals."

"You'll be just fine, man. I'll pick you up when you're done."

The doctors put me out and began the long process of removing old scar tissue that had collected around the head of my humerus. When I awoke, I was alone.

Bill took me home. I slept for what seemed like days. It wasn't quite like coming back from my knee surgery when I was twenty; this time I felt almost unnaturally tired, older, and weary in my bones.

Finally, after about a week of lying around, sluglike and depressed, I pushed myself back into gear. The kids were staying with me for the weekend, and it was up to me to step it up and act like a parent.

"Daddy, what *happened* to you?" Jesse Jr. asked me. He was

five years old, and at the stage where every word out of his mouth seemed to be a question. His hands played against the blue sling that covered my left arm and shoulder.

"I hurt myself playing around too much," I said, hugging him to me with my good arm.

"But is it ever going to get better?" he asked, looking concerned.

"Of course it is," I said, laughing. "Very soon. Right now, Daddy just has to be patient and let it heal, okay?"

Being on my feet energized my spirit. I looked at the house around me: it had been several weeks since Janine had disappeared. She'd never bothered to call, so I just figured she had no intention of coming back.

I called Bill Dodge.

"Bill," I said. "Look, can you help me out with something?"

"No problem, man. What is it?"

"I need you to rent a moving van for me, and then come on over here. Get a couple of guys from the shop to help. We're going to get rid of Janine's stuff."

It was time. I needed to clear my home of her.

Bill showed up soon thereafter with the van and the extra sets of hands, and we got down to work. My kids watched us curiously as we carefully loaded all of Janine's possessions up into the van.

"Feels good, doesn't it?" asked Bill, grinning.

"It's just time," I said.

We were about three-quarters of the way done with the job when Janine showed up.

"What the hell are you *doing*?" she cried.

"I didn't think you were coming back," I said calmly. "So we're moving you out."

"How could you do this to me? We're in a partnership!" Janine cried. "We are there for each other, can't you understand that . . ."

"You haven't exactly been THERE for me this whole time," I said. "Fuck, Janine, living with you is like living with a crazy person.

I never know who's going to be there for me: the wife who's normal, or some psycho bitch who's ready to throw her keys in my face . . ."

"Daddy?" Jesse Jr. said, appearing at the door. He looked ready to cry. "What are you yelling for?"

"Go back inside," I said to him. "Go on, Jesse. Back inside, this very instant."

Jesse looked at me, confused and scared, then turned around and padded back to his room.

"You see," I whispered angrily to Janine. "See what you made me do?"

"That's fucking nonsense," she said. "I didn't *make* you yell at me—*you* yelled at me! You have an anger issue, and a control issue, Jesse, and I think it's time to face it!"

"I am so *tired* of this endless mind-fuck," I said. "So over it. So over you."

"You gutless man," Janine said, spitefully, pushing past me into the house. "There's nothing good about you when you're like this, do you know that?"

"Keep your voice down," I warned, following her. "I don't want the kids to hear you like this."

"You GUTLESS FUCK!" she screamed. "How's *that,* Jesse? Is *that* what you mean?"

"Stop it," I warned, stepping closer to her. We edged into the kitchen. "I am goddamn serious, Janine. You better shut up, right now, and get out of my house."

Bill appeared next to me. "Hey man, I think we better call the cops, okay?"

"Yeah, call the cops," taunted Janine. "Or what? You gonna punch me, you fucking COWARD? You gonna punch me?"

"Daddy!" cried Jesse Jr., appearing at the top of the stairs. He was sobbing, tears running down his face.

"Janine, STOP IT!" I screamed, stepping closer to her.

She whirled and picked up a large stainless-steel knife from our cutting board. "Don't FUCKING TOUCH ME!" she screamed. "I will cut you wide open!"

I was stunned. Holding my hand up, I backed away from her.

She jabbed the knife toward me threateningly. "Move!"

Slowly, I backed my way up the stairs. When I reached the top of the landing, I picked up my son with my one good arm.

"Daddy's so sorry," I whispered to him. "I'm so, so sorry. I never meant for this."

He cried into my chest. I placed him gently into his bed, walked out into the hallway, and shut the door firmly behind me.

"I called the cops, man," said Bill. "They'll be here any minute."

"You understand what's going on, Janine?" I said.

She sneered. "I can't wait until the police come. I'll tell them how you mentally abuse me, day in and day out, every day," Janine said, laughing loudly. "I can't fucking *believe* it. You are so out of control, you know that, right?"

"Janine, I swear to God, keep your fucking voice down. You just scared my son half to death."

"Because you MADE me!" Janine cried. "Oh my God, it is SO hard being your wife! This is the hardest thing I've ever had to do!"

"I'm going downstairs," I said. "To wait for the cops. You are staying up here in the bedroom. Is that understood?"

"Oh, so you can give them your story first, and make me out to be the bad guy, as usual? Thanks, but no thanks!"

I went down the staircase, with Janine following on my heels, only inches behind me.

"You big, fucking bully," she taunted me. "Calling the cops on your WIFE? That's a new low. Messing with your *pregnant* wife! I can't wait till these cops get here, I'm going to give them an earful!"

"Please, be quiet, Janine," I breathed, unlocking the front door, looking both ways down the street, in hopes of seeing an approaching squad car. "Just shut your mouth. I can't take it anymore."

"Really?" Janine said. "Why don't you make me shut up, then?"

"The police will be here any second, Janine," I said, walking as far away from her as I could, back toward the living room, "so honestly, if you know what's good for you, you'll calm down . . ."

Janine tackled me, clawing at me. The force of her attack made me fall against the couch. She punched me hard in the face, and then I rolled on top of her and used my knees to pin her underneath my body.

"*Do* not *hit me again*," I said. "Dammit, Janine! Stop moving!"

She squirmed under me. With all the strength in my body, I struggled to keep her pinned down. Using my good arm, I forced her writhing shoulders down.

"What's going on here!" said the police, as they burst through the open front door.

Reflexively, I held my good arm up in a gesture of surrender. Janine, seizing upon the opportunity, reached across me to the side table next to the couch. With her right hand, she picked up a ceramic vase, and with all her might, smashed it against the side of my head. The vase shattered on my temple, and I went down.

—

Janine was taken to jail that night, and I had her charged for spousal abuse. Jesse James: bodyguard, motorcycle outlaw, domestic abuse victim.

The next day, I had the locks changed. I was completely, finally done.

14

My skull ached for days from the impact of the blow. But a huge weight had been lifted from my shoulders.

I couldn't avoid the truth anymore. Conclusive separation from Janine wasn't just a potential scenario. It was the only responsible move I could make for myself and my kids. My second marriage was ending for real, with no more chances. And that definitely filled me with grief. But I knew that I no longer had any choice in the matter.

Once, I'd loved Janine and the way that she made me feel. The chaos we created together was almost transcendent. But our vicious fighting made me feel outraged. I felt like I was going crazy. There was just no way that I could allow my children to be around her and still believe that I was actually being a good parent. I felt desperately guilty for what Jesse Jr. had seen, knowing that, even though I hadn't intended for it to happen, I'd played a part in repeating the cycle of abuse that I'd grown up with.

She was pregnant with my baby. But Janine and I were never going to be partners. We were never again going to live under the same roof. It was time for me to face it, and to move on with my life.

"You're actually not *too* bad at welding, I guess," Rick said, with his hands on his hips, watching me work. "I mean, for a one-armed dude."

"Light of heart," I explained. Tentatively, I wiggled my healing arm around in its sling. "Been to hell and back."

I'd returned to the shop bruised and bandaged, but with renewed optimism. What I really needed, I thought, was a week or so of hard labor to lift my spirits. Life would get back to normal soon enough if I just kept on wrenching, sweating, and cussing over broken gears, listening to heavy metal, and leading my team. As long as I could immerse myself in tools, dirt, and grease, I was going to be all right.

"Got any new chicks in the wings?"

I laughed, but with some difficulty. "Are you fucking kidding me?" I asked. "Dude, I'll say it once, and you can *quote* me on this: I'm going to be a fifty-five-year-old bachelor. *Bet on it.*"

My assistant returned to my side, explaining to me that the show in Japan was still on for Thanksgiving, and would I be attending?

"Yeah," I decided. "I'm gonna go. And I'm going to bring my daughter."

I loved traveling, and my kids were getting to the age where they made the trips just that much more fun. Jesse Jr. was still a little too young to handle a long flight comfortably and then do a week in a strange country, but my nine-year-old daughter would be just fine. So I proposed the idea to her.

"Hey, Chandler, you want to taste the best sushi in the whole world?"

"What's sushi?"

"It's raw fish."

"Yuck!" Chandler said. "I can't eat that!"

"Okay, I'll find you a hot dog," I promised, laughing. "Don't worry. Japan is gonna be a blast."

I set about packing for the trip, really feeling lighter and happier than I had been in almost a year. When it came down to it, the most important thing in my life, no question about it, was being a dad. I couldn't believe that I had almost endangered my children's safety by allowing them to be around someone so unstable. My priorities had been jumbled. As I'd gotten caught up in the seductiveness of Janine's high-wire drama, I'd nearly forgotten what mattered most in my life.

About one week before Chandler and I were set to fly to Japan, I made a quick stop after work to check in on Tyler, the young boy with leukemia.

"I'm sorry I haven't been by in a while," I said, when his mother answered the door. "How's he doing?"

"Oh, Jesse," she said, looking distraught. "It's so nice of you to come by, but Tyler's health has declined."

From the tone of her voice and the look on her face, I realized how grave the situation was. "Can I see him?"

"No, I'm sorry," Tyler's mother said. "He's so weak now. He's sleeping. Could you come back another time?"

"Yes," I said. "Although, my daughter and I are going away for a while, to Japan . . ."

Suddenly, I cut myself off, feeling guilty for having a daughter who had her health. Who could board a plane without any problem.

"Well, you just give us a call when you get back," Tyler's mother said, nodding woodenly. "I'll be sure to tell him you stopped by."

Chandler and I went to Japan as planned, both of us excited: her to be alone with her dad on an adventure, and me to experience a new culture in the best way possible, through the eyes of my nine-year-old daughter. But just as our trip began, I received a voice mail from Tyler's mother. He had died. I spent the holiday saddened inside, yet at the same time more grateful than ever for the blessing of my kids.

When we returned home a week later, another message awaited me: it was Janine, who had been living on her own for months. She was nearly due to give birth, she said, and she wanted badly to be with me when it happened.

"I want to do this as a couple," she pleaded. "You and me. One last time."

I weighed her proposal in my mind. After all, this was a life that we had created together. In that respect, it made perfect sense that Janine wanted me there when the baby was born. But she had hurt me so badly, I was reluctant to form another bond with her.

"Call me when you go into labor," I said, finally. "I'll be at the hospital. But that's all I can promise."

Tyler's funeral was announced in the papers. It would be held on the day of his eighth birthday. As much as it would have been easier to sit it out, I went to the ceremony. When I arrived, I saw Tyler's entire third-grade class gathered at his grave, looking sad and confused.

Their teacher hushed them all, then gave a signal for them to begin.

"Happy birthday, dear Tyler," the children sang. *"Happy birthday to you."*

I just lost it. The force of the emotional storm that had been my life for the past year hit me full on. I began to weep, and I couldn't stop. My whole body was wracked with sobs.

Leaving the young boy's grave site, I realized more fully than ever that life was unfair. More than anything, it was *brief*. We were here for a limited time, and I could not keep giving my love to someone who would never truly know how to accept it. My separation from Janine was going to have to be complete. It was going to have to be real.

She called me on the day she went into labor. As I'd promised, I came to the hospital. But I didn't go inside the room when she gave birth, choosing instead to stay outside. Hours later, when my child had been born and had been moved to the newborn wing, I requested to hold her.

"Mr. James?" the nurse said. "It's time. You may see your baby now."

Gently, I picked up my child, and held her tiny body in my arms, awed by her exquisitely small, puckered features. I felt her tiny heart beat against my chest. Looking around to make sure no one was watching, I took a pocketknife from the back pocket of my jeans, and carefully cut the baby bracelet off her wrist, so someday, years later, I could prove to her that I had been with her and held her in my arms on the first day of her life.

Sunny. Her name was Sunny.

———

My life moved on, and I adjusted to being a single man. Kid Rock had watched the whole Janine thing happen, and he was a good friend to me during my time of need. Tyson Beckford also came over often, and he talked sense to me. Karla was a sympathetic and wise conversation partner, too. All of them made a huge difference. I felt embarrassed by having fucked up in front of all my friends, but emotionally, I definitely felt like I was on the mend.

Time has a way of putting things in greater perspective, and eventually, I started to understand why I'd put up with Janine for so long, why I'd kept on taking her back every time she'd hurt me. The truth was, Janine fit handily with my childhood sense of myself. I'd grown up in a home with zero stability, where the only common threads were violence, chaos, and my never-fulfilled need to be valued and acknowledged. Janine was a perverse consolidation of all the pissed-off, tweaked-out stepmoms I'd ever had. It was almost stunning how craftily I'd managed to create this psychodrama that wasn't good for me, but that had satisfied me in some deep way, maybe because it felt so *familiar.*

But I was finally outside of the eye of the storm, and the relief was enormous. At last, I had the solitude necessary to be able to think clearly and begin to gain my bearings. Of course, there was an incredibly painful side to the separation, which was that for a time, I wouldn't be with my own child.

"I want to be a dad to her," I told Karla. "Of course I do. But I know that the moment I step in, Janine will tangle herself up in my life again. And then I'll end up involving Jesse Jr. and Chandler, too. Soon we'll be right back where we started."

"None of this is easy, is it?" Karla asked.

"It sucks," I agreed.

It left a huge, guilty hole in my heart to entrust my own child to a woman I considered unstable. But I swore to myself that it would only be temporary. Someday soon, I would be in my child's life again.

During this rebuilding period of my life, *Monster Garage* continued to chug onward. By now it had become a reality TV juggernaut in its own right. Our ratings were terrific. The fame still felt strange to me, but I felt kind of gratified that we were making mechanics and hot rodders cool again. Blue-collar dudes, messing around in their own garages at home, hopefully felt at least a little bit proud.

I yearned to do more, though. Now that I had a little showbiz capital to throw around, I wanted to do something useful. Since I had the power to do it, I figured, why not do something that would actually make a small difference in people's lives?

In early 2004, I told the guys in my shop, "I want to go to Iraq."

They all looked at me like I was crazy. "What for?"

"For the kids fighting over there," I said. "To remind them that there are people stateside who support them."

I didn't envision doing anything all that complicated: instead of some massive USO tour, I just wanted to take a team of soldier mechanics and transform a standard Humvee into a badass custom truck with a giant engine and some gold rims. It would be like an episode of *Monster Garage,* I reasoned. Just set in the desert. You know, in the middle of a war.

I'd befriended a producer on *Monster Garage* during the third season named Hildie Katibah, and I started to bend her ear with the Iraq idea every time I saw her.

"Do you get where I'm going with this? It would just be a real simple build, but something the kids involved would remember for a real long time."

"It's a great idea, Jesse," Hildie said. "I think there's a show there. But you know that Iraq's probably not the safest place to go right now, right?"

"Yeah, and?"

"Well, hey, if you want to brave it, I'm behind you. All I'm saying is, it might be a hard pill for Discovery to swallow."

Hildie was right: we put out feelers at the network, and most of the people making decisions felt the mission was unnecessarily dangerous, with no real upside. Disappointed, I agreed to shelve the idea temporarily.

Instead, we continued to film *Monster Garage* right there in Southern California, where we had our silly fun. We took a 1964 Peel Trident, said to be the world's smallest car, and gave it a face-lift using an all-midget crew. A cool '69 Rolls-Royce Silver Shadow got transformed into a Porta-Potty pumper. We even turned a fire truck into a professional-grade brewery. I had a stellar time using my brain to dream up the outlandish vehicles, and it was always an immense, fulfilling challenge to get the crew to transform them into realities. But despite all this, I couldn't help but notice the show was beginning to outlive its usefulness in my life.

Quietly, without even realizing it, I was becoming more serious, and more inward. The fucked-up events of recent years had quenched my thirst for chaos and thrills. More and more, I found myself wanting to focus on what was really important in life: my children, meaningful work, and people who had some kind of substance to them.

So, it was while in this general state of mind that I met Sandra Bullock for the first time. And my life would be forever changed.

Her godson wanted to see West Coast Choppers. That's how it started.

It was Christmastime, 2004, when I received a call at the shop.

"Jesse, my name's Terri. I'm calling on behalf of Sandra Bullock. I'm her assistant."

"Hi, Terri," I said. "What's going on?"

"Well, we have a favor to ask you. Sandra's godson is a *huge* fan of *Monster Garage*—just huge."

"Okay."

"And well, Sandy would like to do something special for him for Christmas. So we wanted to ask you if perhaps you'd take some time out of your day sometime this month to give Bryan a little tour."

I sighed. "It's a real busy time, Terri."

"Of course," she said. "I understand. But it would mean the *world* to Bryan. He's such a big fan!"

"Well, all right," I relented. "Just an hour, though, okay?"

"An hour would be *amazing,*" Terri said. "Oh, Sandra's going to be so thrilled. Thank you, Jesse."

They arranged to stop over at the shop later that week, and I cleared a spot in my schedule to give the movie star and her godson the grand tour. I certainly wasn't expecting anything romantic—while I knew who Sandra Bullock was, I wasn't a fan. The only time I could remember seeing any of her movies, I'd been half-asleep on a plane.

"Excited to meet America's sweetheart?" Bill Dodge kidded me.

"Huh?" I asked. "No, man. I don't really dig movie stars. She's probably kind of stuck-up, don't you think?"

But when she showed up at the shop, I was immediately impressed by the big star's warmth and friendliness.

"Hi!" she beamed at me brightly. "I'm Sandy. And this is my

godson, Bryan! He's really excited to be here. We both want to thank you so much for taking the time to show us around."

"It's no problem," I said. "So, what do you think, Bryan? You want to take a look around?"

Bryan nodded quietly. He looked really nervous, and as I led him from room to room, detailing what went on in each section of the shop, he barely said a word.

"This is our paint booth," I said, my hand on his shoulder. "That's where all the finishing touches happen. Some of this paint costs like five hundred bucks a gallon—kinda pricey, huh?"

He just nodded.

"Over here's our newest chopper. It's still got a ton of work to go, or else I'd let you hop up there and see what it's like to ride it. Do you like motorcycles?"

Bryan just blushed and toed at the ground.

"He's pretty nervous, huh?" I whispered to Sandy.

"He'll be fine," she said, putting her arm around her godson. "Your shop's really great, Jesse. It's so intricate. And you're in such a beautiful building, too. When was it built, do you know?"

"Actually," I said, happy to supply her with the trivia, "this building was constructed in 1921. It's an old laundry facility for the port of Long Beach."

"Oh my gosh," Sandy said. "That's fascinating. You're a part of history, over here."

"We're trying to be," I said, smiling.

I had sort of figured that I'd feel like an indigent welder or something, talking to a big movie star, but Sandy made me feel very at home with myself. We continued to walk around the shop with Bryan, making easy conversation about Long Beach and the responsibilities that came with having a custom motorcycle business.

"And of course you have your television show to take care of, too."

"Yeah, I'm getting kind of sick of that, though," I admitted.

"Really? I can't imagine why. It's such an inventive, fun show. When Bryan told me he wanted to come visit you, I watched a few episodes—it's really addictive."

The more we spoke, the more under her spell I fell. Sandy was gorgeous, but in a natural, real way. And she was so authentic and easy to talk to that I found myself completely unintimidated. In fact, I was having the time of my life gabbing with her. By the time I looked up, the hour had passed without my realizing it.

"Well, okay, Bryan," I said, somewhat regretfully. "This concludes our tour. I sure hope you had fun."

The little boy just looked up at me and nodded.

"He had a *great* time," Sandy said, smiling, poking her godson playfully in the side. "We both did."

The minute Sandy and Bryan left, I went into my office and sat behind my desk, grinning like an idiot. I just couldn't wipe that smile off my face.

"Terri?"

"Yes, may I ask who's speaking?"

"This is Jesse James."

"Oh, Jesse, *hi*! How did everything go with Sandra?"

"Really great," I said. "Listen, can I ask you something?"

"Of course," she said.

"Is Sandra . . . well, is she dating anyone right now?"

"Not really."

"Well," I said, "I'd like to ask her out."

"Fine," Terri said. "I'll let her know, okay? And I'll give you a call when she makes up her mind, Jesse."

"No," I said, laughing a little bit. So *this* was how you did it in A-List Hollywood, huh? "With all due respect, I'd rather not ask her *assistant* to ask her out for me. I'd like to call her up myself. Do it properly."

Terri sighed. "Jesse, you seem like such a nice guy, but I can't give out Sandra's number. It's part of my job."

"Well, how about a good old e-mail—that's not too invasive, is it?"

"Okay," she said, considering. "I can give you that. Got a pen handy?"

"Right here," I said, my ballpoint poised over a fresh, clean sheet of paper. "Give it to me."

I sent Sandy a short message that evening, telling her what a pleasure it was to meet her, and how much fun I'd had spending the afternoon with her. I mentioned, casually, that I'd love to show her around Long Beach again—and would she care to have dinner with me, sometime?

Sandy got back to me right away: she was really flattered by my invitation, she said, and absolutely, she would love to have dinner with me at some point. Right now, though, she was extremely busy and simply didn't have much time on her hands. She asked me to please stay in touch, and we would make a date to get together at some point down the line.

I got the point. She'd said yes, in so many words, but what she was really saying was, *eh . . . not that interested.*

I kind of shrugged it off, knowing that at least I'd tried. It was probably *good,* actually, that she wasn't that into me—after all, wasn't my goal nowadays to be the fifty-five-year-old bachelor? I'd been through hell and back with Janine. The last thing I needed was a new heartthrob.

But something wouldn't let me forget Sandra Bullock. Simply put, she was captivating. Everything about her was attractive: her spirit, her energy, her laugh. I loved the sensation of having walked around the shop with her and feeling like we were instant friends. There was something about this woman that made me want to know more.

So I set out to woo Sandy, over e-mail. It was funny, because most of the people who saw me on *Monster Garage* probably imagined I didn't even know how to turn on a computer. But e-mail was the only tool I had in my belt, so that's what I went for.

I started out sending her short, funny messages, recounting random weird events from my life, once in a while politely asking her opinion on inconsequential matters. She always responded the same day, polite and measured, seemingly always a bit surprised to hear from me again. I kept the charm coming, though, and gradually, I upped the ante to two messages a day, then to three. Soon, we were e-mailing each other all the time. It was actually lots of fun, like a secret buddy. Finally, the day came when Sandy relented and let me graduate to the phone.

"Boy," I said, when we first spoke. "I'm moving up here!"

"I work slow," she said, laughing. "Friends first."

"That's cool," I agreed. "I like friends."

What began as just a spark of interest evolved into a real courtship. The great thing about talking and e-mailing with Sandy is that I actually *was* interested in what she had to say. We actually *were* friends first. She was such a sweetheart, and such a real person, that I rarely felt the need to try to impress her, to be someone I wasn't. We were just there for each other, a sympathetic ear willing to listen to whatever problems the other person was having.

Sandy wasn't actively filming during this time. Instead, she was spending most of her time in Austin, Texas, where several years before she'd begun to have a home constructed. Her builder had done a terrible job on the construction, though, and now she was embroiled in a convoluted legal dispute with him.

"It's a nightmare," she confided to me. "And I hate that I am so caught up in this case! But I can't help it. I'm losing sleep over it."

"I think you should move back to L.A.," I said. "Who wants to live all the way over there in Austin, anyway?"

She laughed. "Ulterior motive?"

"Oh, maybe just a little," I said. "So, hey, seriously, when are you visiting next?"

"In about two weeks," Sandy said. "I have business I need to take care of—rewritten scripts to read, meetings with overbearing producers . . . you know. All that glitz and glamour."

"Will you go out to dinner with me, then?"

"Oh, I *suppose*." She laughed. "You've been the perfect gentleman to this point. I think you should be rewarded."

"Hey, all *right*!" I whooped, overjoyed.

"Okay, calm down, calm down." Sandy laughed. "Actually, the truth is, I'd love to see you."

As promised, she flew into Los Angeles precisely two weeks later. We made our plans to go out. The night of our date, I drove my brand-new black Porsche 996 Twin Turbo to her house to pick her up. Kind of cheeseball, I know. But I was trying hard to be classy.

"I thought we might go to Balboa's," I stammered nervously. "Do you like steak?"

"Yes," Sandy said. "That'd be great." She patted my hand. "Calm down. It's good to see you."

I mostly relaxed after that, and enjoyed being in the same space as she was. At the restaurant, I noticed how nice Sandy was to the hostess, to the waitress, to the guy who took our car—to everyone.

"You kind of have to do that, huh?"

"Kind of," she admitted. "But it's not hard. I tend to like most people."

"Don't you ever wish you could just stop being famous?" I asked.

She thought about it and laughed. "Oh, I don't know . . . only every single day, that's all."

I grinned. "What's the worst thing about it?"

"Hmm," Sandy said. "There's so much to choose from. There was a stalker for a while. That's a pretty big downer."

"I just don't comprehend stalkers," I said. "It's dumb."

"You mean, you wouldn't wait outside for twenty-four hours to steal my trash? My *goodness,* what's wrong with you?"

"I might have tried to steal your trash," I said, smiling. "That is, if you hadn't agreed to go out with me."

"Well, good thing I agreed," Sandy said, sweetly. "Anyway, I had to see."

"See what?" I asked.

"Well, I just wanted to know if . . ." She turned her head to look up at me. "I wanted to know if the feeling that I'd been having on the phone with you would be the same in person."

I grinned. "And?"

"And . . . yes," she said, laughing softly. "It's exciting. I really like how I feel around you."

I drove her home at the end of the night. We stopped in her driveway.

"Well, I had a lovely time," Sandy said. "Do you think we should do this again sometime?"

"Yes," I said instantly.

She laughed. "And when would you like that to be?"

"Tomorrow."

We both burst out laughing.

———

Our romance grew from there, although in a much more deliberate way than I was accustomed to. I came down with the flu the next day, and I couldn't go out. I half expected Sandy to zoom over and nurse me back to health; but no, she left town as she had planned. It became clear that Sandy wasn't going to give her heart up easily. That wasn't because she didn't like me, she just wasn't simple to win over like that. All that was cool with me, I decided. Recent experience had shown me that the chaotic, head-over-heels sensation of wild infatuation might not be the best way to begin a relationship.

Anyway, I'd always enjoyed a challenge. So I continued to court her from afar, trying to win her trust and her approval. My steadfast efforts were rewarded when, several weeks later, Sandy invited me down to Georgia, where she was working on a project.

"How about you come down and keep me company? It can get awfully lonely, way down south," she said, laughing. "Even though I'm a Southern girl at heart." Sandy had spent part of her childhood in Virginia and had gone to college at East Carolina University.

"Hey, my bags are packed," I said. "You don't have to ask me twice."

I flew down to see her, and drove a rental car out to where she was staying.

"Pretty rural," I remarked. "What do you guys do for fun out here?"

"I've been running to stay in shape," Sandy said. "These roads are really beautiful. Perhaps you'd care to join?"

We went jogging the next morning, and I couldn't help but agree that the winding roads really were kind of pretty.

"I never do this," I admitted. "But I have to say, it feels pretty good."

"Gets the blood going," Sandy gasped. "In half an hour, we'll be ready to collapse and face the day."

My T-shirt was soaked, and I was feeling pretty disheveled by the time we'd made our turn and headed back to Sandy's place.

"Oh, shoot," she remarked. "Just keep on running, okay?"

"What's up?"

"It's nothing," Sandy said. "Just some photographers. They've been lurking around for the whole week, but I'm afraid I've been such a boring subject, I don't think I've given them anything good. Now that I've got a gentleman jogging partner, they're sure to be interested . . ."

"Are we talking about paparazzi here?" I asked, mildly amused.

"Yes, indeed," Sandy said apologetically. "It'll be fine. They're minor annoyances. Just jog on by."

When we made the last leg of our journey into Sandy's house, I saw the small clutch of paparazzi pull out their cameras to record our entrance enthusiastically.

"I feel like I'm at the Kentucky Derby." I laughed, as we stumbled into the house. "Photo finish."

"It's so stupid, isn't it?" Sandy said. She tossed me a towel. "I'm this normal person who does acting for a living, and for some reason, these guys can make thousands of dollars selling a picture of me, I don't know, picking my nose or something."

"Do you really pick your nose?" I asked, raising my eyebrows.

"Wouldn't you like to know," she said, hugging me. "Ooh. I'm so sweaty. We should shower."

"Yeah," I agreed. "We should."

It was just the best time. New romance always feels good, but there was something so wholesome and so incredibly positive about Sandy. She didn't waste much of her time complaining, and I noticed that she seemed averse to voicing criticism, unless it was really called for. And contrary to the typical actor stereotype, I didn't find her self-centered in the slightest. Our conversations didn't tend to be about her, or me; instead, they were about art and film and ideas she found engrossing. Gradually, I got the sense that I was hanging out with an evolved human being. Or, perhaps a little more simply put, a grown-up.

It was kind of a laugh, because it showed me in such vivid detail how much of my life I'd been lurking around in the shadows, waiting for someone to invite me into this kind of conversation. Maybe it sounds like a load of crap, but the truth is, from the start, being around Sandy made me want to be a better guy. Whereas with Janine I was always riding that wave of her attention, watching myself reflected in her eyes, with Sandy, I saw her watching the world, and wondering how she could contribute. The better I got to know her, the more I wanted to be by her side, doing the same thing.

"Daddy, you're in the *magazine*!" Chandler said one evening as we wheeled through an Albertson's supermarket in Long Beach. Happily, she held open a glossy gossip magazine. "See?"

Sure enough, there I was, jogging through Georgia, alongside none other than Ms. Sandra Bullock. I scanned the caption, my eyes falling on the words "heavily tattooed biker boy toy."

"Awesome," I mumbled.

"Should we buy it?" Chandler giggled. "Look, you're *sweaty*."

"Uh, nope, that's okay, sweetie," I sighed. "There'll be more where that came from."

Sandy and I continued to see each other when our busy schedules would allow for it. She worked very long hours, both as an actress and as a producer, and *Monster Garage* continued to keep me busy and sleep deprived. For years now, I had been shooting three weeks on, one week off. It was really starting to grind on me.

"This is just *stupid*," I remarked, after six straight days of trying to convert an armored car into a festival dunk tank.

"Huh?" said one of the cameramen.

"It's pointless," I said, motioning to our almost-complete car. "I mean, it's funny, it's a challenge and all that . . . but would the world be a single bit worse off if we never even thought of this garbage?"

The kid just looked at me, a bit at a loss for words. "It's . . . entertainment."

"So's a fucking cartoon." I reached for my keys, walked off the set, and headed home.

For the first time in my life, I felt like I'd found myself in a relationship that was enlightening. It couldn't help but illuminate the parts of my life where I'd been content to stagnate. I wasn't a soap opera addict or anything like that, didn't sit on the couch eating bonbons—far from it—but really, when was the last time that I'd tried to expand my horizons? Make myself into a well-rounded and, well, cultural dude?

"I want to confess something to you," I said.

"Oh?"

"I've never been to a Broadway show."

"Oh, that's okay," Sandy said. "Lots of people haven't been."

"No, it's not okay," I said. "I'm hanging out with one of the greatest actresses in the world. I'd like to go to the theater with you."

"This could be arranged," Sandy said, grandly. "Now, what play would you like to see, Mr. James?"

"Something with Slayer," I said.

Sandy grinned. "Uh . . ."

"Come on," I said. "I'm kidding. Anything. Just bring me to something that I might actually *like*."

One week later, we flew to New York, where Sandy scored us front-row tickets to *Spamalot,* the Monty Python musical. It was totally hysterical. I loved it.

"Well?" Sandy asked, grinning happily. "What do you think?"

"Dude, I've done Broadway!" I exulted. "Hey, did you realize there's a whole *band* down in that pit? For the whole first act, I thought all that music was piped in."

I broadened her horizons, too. Before she met me, Sandy had never been in a car going a hundred miles an hour.

"Are you *serious*?" I yelled, as we gained velocity, the wind from the open windows whipping at our faces.

"*Why would I kid?*" Sandy screamed, her hair flying behind her.

"If I don't go a hundred every single day," I yelled, "there's something wrong with my car!"

Sandy's eyes widened as the scenery outside began to blur, and she gripped the sides of her seat with clenched hands. "Are you absolutely *sure* this is a good idea?"

"Come on," I laughed. "You were in *Speed,* weren't you?"

"*THAT WAS A MOVIE!*" she screamed.

We were coming together. Not out of weakness or need, but as two people who genuinely liked and respected the other.

"I like the way this feels," I confessed, during another one of our weekend getaways together.

"Me, too. When I'm alone, I laugh sometimes, thinking about us," Sandy said. "We're kind of like Felix and Oscar."

"I'm Felix, right?" I said.

"Oscar."

I caught myself looking at her hopefully. An excessive sense of wonder and deep appreciation filled me as I observed her doing small tasks, like washing dishes or typing an e-mail. Clearly, I was falling in love.

"I don't want to promise too much," I cautioned. "I want to warn you, I don't like shopping. And I don't much care for chick flicks."

"Don't worry about it. I'll probably never pop a wheelie. Is that going to be an issue?"

"For you?" I said. "I'll make an exception."

Obviously, my guard was still up; it had to be. I had been hurt so badly and so recently. But Sandy was everything she appeared to be on the outside. She was a sensitive listener and a good conversationalist who was also willing to engage at a deeper level. As we slowly got to know each other more authentically, I was gradually able to admit that there were some very old hurts that I was carrying around.

"It's been a rocky couple of years," I admitted, laughing, late one night when we were lounging around in my living room.

"I can only imagine."

"Janine, that whole thing . . . it was just a tornado." I squinted, embarrassed. "The truth is, I felt like I *deserved* it. Do you understand what I mean?"

Sandy nodded. "I do."

"I . . . I grew up in a really hard situation," I said. "I don't tell people about it very often."

Sandy looked at me deeply, with real sympathy in her eyes. "I promise you, if you want to confide in me, I will never judge you for it, Jesse."

I took a deep breath. "Well, I used to get smacked around."

Sandy said nothing. She just watched me.

"I grew up scared shitless of my dad," I continued. "He punched me and blacked my eye. When I was fifteen years old, he accused me of burning down our house and I got into such a big fight with him that we would literally have killed each other if we hadn't been pulled apart."

"Oh, Jesse." Tears were starting to well up in Sandy's eyes. "I had no idea."

I was starting to cry, too. "When I was six, I was so afraid of him," I said, my voice cracking. "He was yelling at me and I ran away from him into the pitch-black night. I've never been so scared. I don't know why anyone would do that to a kid. You know?"

"Jesse, you don't have to . . . What happened?" Sandy asked softly.

"I tripped over a low fence. And I broke my arm."

Sandy rose and slowly walked over to me. She embraced me in her arms, and rocked me, saying nothing.

"He *laughed* at me," I choked, bitterly. "He heard me crying, wailing with pain, and he just laughed. 'Why'd you trip, dummy?' I thought he was going to kill me. But he just stood over me and he laughed."

It was a secret I'd been carrying with me for thirty years. I wept, ashamed. I sobbed like a kid, crying into her shoulder.

——

By the summer of 2005, Sandy and I had been dating for almost six months. She was still caught up in the lawsuit surrounding her disappointing house in Austin. She was emotionally wrapped up in the case, and it was stressing her out pretty badly.

"Hey," I said to her, "I'd like to talk to you. Do you have a second?"

We'd been getting along great. But I honestly wasn't sure how she'd react to what I had in store for her.

"Sure. What's up?"

"Well, I . . . I just wanted to . . . I wanted to know if you'd marry me."

She looked at me, amazed. "Are you . . . serious?"

"Yeah," I said. "I'm serious. I want you to marry me."

I had promised myself I would never get married again. But that was before I'd met Sandy. She had turned my plan upside down. She was such an impressive person from every angle—calm, stable, intelligent, beautiful, fun, articulate, compassionate. I almost couldn't believe that one person had so many great attributes, and even more, that this person found me compelling enough to keep around. I guess part of me looked at her and clearly envisioned just how much better she could make my life.

"Oh my God," she said. "I . . . wow. This is a surprise." Sandy looked like she was trying to catch her breath. "Yes."

"Yes, as in, you'll marry me?" I asked, nervously.

"Yes, as in *yes*!" She laughed. "Yes, I will marry you. I love you."

I exhaled, relieved. "Oh, man. Thank God." I laughed. "I mean . . . I love you, too."

We didn't even tell Sandy's closest friends that we were getting hitched. Instead, we pretended we were throwing her a big birthday bash. We treated it like a full-on military operation, with vows of total secrecy. It just felt more special that way. Because Sandy was so well known, news of her engagement would have gone public in mere seconds. We didn't want to share our happiness with anyone. Least of all the supermarket tabloids.

We hatched a plan to hold the ceremony at the Santa Ynez Ranch, near Santa Barbara. Together, late at night, we dreamed up intricate strategies and complicated deceptions, winking at each other, excited and proud that we were going to throw a secret, million-dollar wedding. For me, it was like getting paired up to do a project with the prettiest, most popular girl in school. I had never felt so lucky in my whole life.

Finally the day came. I found myself face-to-face with the most gorgeous woman in the world, surrounded by loving friends of hers and mine. This time, the video cameras were conspicuously absent. So was my father. I felt more at ease with myself, less motivated to impress anyone. With calmness and pride, I prepared to let Sandy into my life.

15

One of the biggest injustices of life? Kids don't get to choose their stepparents. I still felt guilty about exposing Chandler and Jesse Jr. to Janine. Nevertheless, I felt confident delivering Sandy onto their doorstep.

After the wedding, Sandy moved into the house on Sunset Beach, the one I'd purchased to live in with Janine. My kids had been living with me full-time throughout the divorce, but suddenly there was a new addition to the family.

Sandy was calm and responsible—probably more responsible than I was. And she had always gotten along well with my kids when she'd spent time with them before. Granted, that wasn't the same as living in the same house, but as it turned out, I was right. Sandy took to being a mom like a fish to water.

"So, what are you studying in school this week?"

"Division," Jesse Jr. said.

"What do you think of it so far?" Sandy asked with a smile.

"Oh, I hate it."

"I used to be pretty good at math when I was your age. Would you like some help?"

"Nah, that's okay," Jesse Jr. said, unzipping his book bag. "It's really dumb."

"Math can be pretty boring," Sandy agreed. "But tell you what, let's see if we can make it a little more fun, okay?"

I liked watching her with my kids. She spoke to them with respect and interest: not like they were tiny adults, but as if they were simply people younger than her, whose opinions were as valid and interesting as anyone else's. And Sandy just breathed organization and structure. By this point, I was one hundred percent dedicated to being a dad, but my dedication manifested itself in a formless kind of devotion and love. I didn't really know exactly how to do things like find them the best schools or after-school programs. Sandy was the polar opposite: she studied the school districts, and took it upon herself to see what opportunities were available for Chandler and Jesse Jr. Before long, my kids were very fond of her. They trusted her.

During this period, my only real contact with Janine was financial. I was sending her $15,000 each month for child support.

"That's quite a sum," Sandy remarked.

"I'm okay with it," I told her. "This way, at least I know my daughter's needs are paid for."

But before too many months had elapsed, I realized this wasn't necessarily so. One morning, I received a phone call from one of Janine's old boyfriends, a guy I'd become friends with after the breakup. We sympathized with each other and traded war stories. He'd maintained communication and a kind of friendship with Janine, and now, he informed me, all was not well in my ex-wife's world.

"She's living in Oregon nowadays, man."

"I know," I said. "Kinda weird. I didn't even know she knew anyone up there."

"I'm not sure she's being real social, exactly," he said. "From what I can tell, she's always holed up in this house she just bought, man. She never leaves, like, ever. I'm pretty sure she's doing drugs."

I felt sick inside.

"She's been in a bad space," he continued. "That's why I called. She's not doing the mom thing right, I can tell you that much."

After hanging up the phone, I let the news sink in for a moment. It had been pretty ridiculous of me to think she was capable of being a responsible parent to my daughter. I'd hoped that I could somehow ensure my child's safety by simply sending a big check every month, but that had just been a pipe dream. I made up my mind: I wanted custody of Sunny.

Like everything legal, our custody battle was long, tedious, difficult, expensive, and frustrating. Sandy was totally supportive of me in the process. She realized that it was my child and in the end, my decision, but there was no question about it, she wanted Sunny in our household as much as I did.

"This blows," I told her, discouraged, during one of the more difficult moments, when it felt like the case would never unfold or change. "Sometimes I just want to fucking give up, you know?"

"I understand," Sandy said. "But it sounds like your daughter's not growing up in a safe home. I can't think of anything more important to focus your energy on."

It was almost like Sandy understood me more than she let on. I know that when she looked at me, she could see the neglect and abuse that I'd gone through. I don't know whether she realized that, in a certain way, me having been through all that pain made me believe it was inevitable that my own offspring would go through the same hurt.

But I do know she realized that, deep down, I wanted more than anything to save Sunny from the pain of a truly unstable environment. In the months that followed, she kept me focused on the goal, and tried to help me stay upbeat in the process of the slow, plodding case.

Eventually, we settled into a normal kind of life in Orange County, or at least as normal as was possible for a famous movie star and her "heavily tattooed biker boy toy" husband.

"What should we have for dinner?"

"I don't know." I shrugged. "Hell, let's just go to the supermarket and see what hits us."

If we'd lived in Hollywood, it would have been more difficult to go to a Safeway and push around a shopping cart, but in Huntington Beach, things were often kind of laid-back. People seemed to understand that Sandy and I were in our home zone, and they mostly left us alone. I appreciated that, especially since Sandy was so nice that she'd inevitably humor whoever it was that managed to lure her into a conversation. I felt like it was important we were allowed to roam free in at least one little corner of the world. I didn't really feel like ceding the privilege of buying a carton of eggs for the rest of my married life.

"How about the gym?" Sandy asked me, after our successful foray to the supermarket.

"I go to Gold's."

"Lead on."

And we did. Sandy and I worked out at odd hours, when the gym was less likely to be full of people, but the point is, we *went*. We packed an old gym bag, wore sweatpants, and hung out with each other by the machines. We really tried our best to be a normal couple. And to an extent, there in the beginning, it worked. I know that I myself had never taken my own celebrity seriously. I was a metalworker, for Christ's sake, and I was still putting in fifteen-hour days. There was nothing glamorous about that.

And Sandy, for her part, was about as down-to-earth as you could get. That was her whole appeal. She was an uncommonly pretty woman, but nonetheless, hers was the type of beauty that seemed almost attainable by most of the attractive women in America. She wasn't an intense, bitchy, ruthless megastar; nor was she ultra-chic, irresponsible, and moody. Sandy was grounded. Normal, even. She was the superhot version of *regular*. That's why America loved her.

As our marriage developed, I felt surprisingly pleased with the way my life seemed to be playing out. I'd struggled for such a long time, willingly placing myself into the oddest of configurations possible: head breaker, football nut, porn-star hubby. Finally, it seemed that I was on a sane path. More and more, I found myself wanting to take advantage of my stable foothold to do something half worthwhile, something that might help other people.

"I can't stop thinking about going to Iraq," I told Hildie Katibah, the producer with whom I'd discussed the project several months before.

"Jesse, you know I think it's a great idea to do a show over there. But we already talked to Discovery. It's not popular with the network."

"Fuck them," I said. "I'll put up my own money."

She cleared her throat. "You may have to form your own production company."

Though it seemed a daunting task, I was stubborn. I just really wanted to do something positive. I realized I wouldn't be stopping the war, but that wasn't my intention. I knew that kids who'd enlisted in the army were my kind of people. They were blue collar; they understood how machines could be your allies when nothing else made much sense.

"Then I'll form a production company," I said. "Just tell me what needs to get done. I'll do whatever it takes."

I don't know why I was on such a mission. Maybe it was because people were telling me that I *couldn't*—opposition always added fuel to my fire. With Hildie guiding me, I formed Pay Up Sucker Productions, a company that would bear the cost of getting us over to Iraq, filming there, and procuring the necessary permits from the U.S. government.

"Boy, I sure hope we can *sell* this," Hildie said, smiling. "Or else you're going to be out a good deal of money."

"We'll sell it," I said, already excited at the prospect of going overseas. "People are going to love it."

Of course, not everybody loved it. As permits started to come in for me and the film crew, and things started to fall more and more in line, certain powers at the Discovery Channel voiced their strong disapproval for the project. It was even insinuated that I could be fired if I went over there, for being in violation of my *Monster Garage* contract.

"How am I in violation of my contract?" I asked Sandy, that night.

"Because you're endangering a company product, sweetie." She patted me on the chest. "In other words, their star."

"I'll be fine," I assured her. "Come on."

"Well, I understand their objections—they're still bombing over there. It's not that safe."

"Well, what's the point of doing *anything* if it's safe?" I said. "I mean, where's the prime-time drama in that?"

Sandy understood why I was so hyped up to go over there. She might even have gathered that part of the reason I wanted to visit the troops and participate with them was to live up to the standard she was setting. But she was still worried about me. Nonetheless, I never felt like I didn't have her permission to head over to a war zone. In the end, it was going to be my decision, and she wouldn't lay too much of a guilt trip on me because of it.

"Just come back," she whispered. "Okay?"

"I promise," I said.

I had been to Iraq with Kid Rock several years before, during 2003, on a USO stop. That had been a really fulfilling experience for me—the enthusiasm of the soldiers who'd shown up to see us had blown me away. Things were different, now, though, and Iraq in 2005 was a hectic scene. Public support for the war in the Middle East had really waned, and that made me all the more determined to come over and make it clear that I was supportive of the kids who were putting themselves in harm's way.

And they really were *kids*. That's what impacted me the most. Some of these guys could barely grow whiskers on their chins, and yet here they were, wielding these crazy sniper rifles. It brought back memories of how, fifteen years earlier, during my early twenties, I'd moved to Seattle. I'd been a confused, overgrown kid who'd thought he was going to be a football hero, but instead found himself in the freezing Pacific Northwest, trying to figure out what life was all about. It was kind of compelling to observe these young men and women, still trying to get a grip on who they were, who, against all odds, now found themselves in Iraq.

We had only seven days to pull off our *Monster Garage*–style build, which, as we'd planned all along, was to transform a standard-issue Humvee into a souped-up, desert pimpmobile with giant tires and spinning rims.

"Think we'll pull it off?" I asked Command Sergeant Major Cynthia Graham, a woman with a ton of grit.

"It'll be a damn sight to see if we do!" she said, laughing, the lines of her face creasing appealingly. This was a woman who'd been out in the desert for a good long time. "These guys are really excited for you to be out here, Jesse. I'll say that much."

The whole week I was there, I was filled with a sense of purpose. We weren't pulling off the most creative build we'd ever done; there was no beer being distilled inside of a fire truck, no PT Cruiser turning into a wood chipper. But the soldier-mechanics doing the grunt work loved the challenge. They liked the cameras, too—I'm pretty sure it was sort of appealing to think about becoming a star, if only for the briefest of moments. But most of all, I sensed that the troops involved with the build dug doing something *different*:

a mechanical project that, for once, wasn't centered around the depressing subject of battle and death. Every day, these guys repaired jeeps that had been crushed by improvised explosive devices. To them, a week with me was a lark, a much-needed vacation.

We were having so much fun, and the work felt so good, that I almost forgot we were in a war zone. I was reminded of that fact, however, when, one evening, our peace was interrupted by a wailing siren.

"What the fuck is *that*?" I asked.

"Air raid, man. Come on, we gotta get inside. Bombs are dropping somewhere out there."

We were fine, of course. We even joked around in the bomb shelter, just to pass the time. But later that night, I quit joking. Three soldiers had died in the mortar attack, and nine more had been injured.

In the back of my mind, I couldn't help thinking: that's what these guys live with every single day. Every time they went out on a mission, they were faced with the possibility that they weren't coming back. And it kind of made me feel awed and sad at the same time, to know that such young men had made peace with death.

After working all week, we finally completed the Humvee to our lowrider-in-the-desert specifications, but, because of a faulty transmission and our inability to obtain a new one inside of a war zone, the car wouldn't fire up. Disappointment came, because that was inevitable, but it was short-lived. The mission had so clearly been a success for all of us.

"These guys won't forget you, Jesse," Sergeant Major Graham said. "This was one of the best weeks we've had here. It really was."

During their closing ceremony, I was presented with the American flag that had flown over their base during the week I'd spent there. Emotion overcame me, and I had to choke back tears. I'd never felt prouder to be a part of something.

My life felt blessed. There was purpose in my work, and family all around me. More and more, I pictured just exactly how great it would be to have Sunny join us. She would have Chandler as a sister, Jesse Jr. as a brother, and me and Sandy as parents who loved her, as well as one another. The custody battle in the courts was taking its own sweet time, however, so I battled constantly with myself, trying to be patient, yet often failing.

As the months passed during our first year of marriage, Sandy and I passed out of our honeymoon period, but without much of a hitch. I think sometimes we both felt the other was a bit too busy, but there was no getting around it, because work was so important to both of us.

"You're going into the shop on a Sunday?" Sandy asked me sleepily.

"Sunday's my favorite day of the week to work," I told her, happily. "No one in there to bug me!"

My workaholic ways hadn't changed much over the years. I just felt my most fulfilled when I was cutting metal, sweating into my shirt. It wasn't anything that I could share. That morning, as I drove to the West Coast Choppers shop, I noticed a small church I'd seen many times before. On a whim, I decided to stop by.

The church was a regular-looking house of worship that had likely gone through several incarnations across the years, housing various ethnicities and Christian sects, from Cambodian Evangelicals to Mexican Catholics to Seventh-Day Adventists. Now it was an African-American church. I grinned as I approached the door and heard the pastor firing up his sermon with a vengeance.

"*None of us are perfect!*" he yelled. "Even at our BEST, we have committed major indiscretions against the LORD!"

"Amen," came the pleased rumbling of the congregation. "Amen." The women wore floppy hats and fanned themselves, and the men clapped and nodded. The church was small, but no one was stingy with their applause or affirmations. There was a buzz in there, a vital life energy.

Feeling more curious, I slipped inside the doorway and found myself a corner in the back, where I could observe unnoticed.

"Don't you ever get so holy you develop AMNESIA!" the pastor cried. He strutted back and forth across the small stage. "Don't you EVER get so holy, you can no longer remember there was a season in your life when you made colossal mistakes!"

I nodded, digging the guy's electric enthusiasm.

"I'm talking *womanizing*! I'm talking *stealing*! I'm talking living without *purpose*!"

"Amen, brother," I said under my breath, laughing. This guy was pretty good. In fact, he seemed like he was speaking directly to me.

"There's been time when I've taken some wrong turns!" the preacher boomed, sweat dripping from his brow, as he paced back and forth. "When I've messed up something bad! It was NIGHT for a very LONG TIME! But we all have the chance to turn it around— brothers and sisters, MORNING IS COMING!!"

"Amen!" cheered the congregation, growing in ardor. *"Amen!"*

"MORNING IS COMING!"

"A-men!"

The cords of the pastor's neck stood out against his shiny skin. He clenched one fist, and his voice crescendoed mightily:

"WILL YOU PRAY WITH ME?"

—

I drove away from that church whistling, feeling cheerier and more hopeful than I could ever remember feeling. I had so much. And I was profoundly grateful.

On days like these, it felt like my life just couldn't get much better. But on other mornings, I had to admit there were downsides to the path I'd chosen for myself, ones that I had never counted on experiencing. Most prominent was the fact that ever since I'd gotten married, I'd seemed to have outgrown a lot of my old friends.

Paul, one of my old carousing friends from the neighborhood, was a perfect example. He was a guy I'd known since before I'd even met Karla, and throughout the past decade, I could always count on a phone call from him at the shop around happy hour.

"Yo, Jesse," he cried. "How about coming out with us and getting your drink on?"

"Come on, you know I haven't had a drink in five years," I said.

"Well, fine—how about hitting the strip clubs all the same? We haven't seen you in months, man!"

"Nah. I don't really do that anymore," I explained.

"What, because you're not *allowed* to?"

"No," I said, mildly annoyed. "I can do whatever the fuck I want. But that stuff kind of lost its thrill for me a long time ago."

There was silence on the other end of the line. "Boy," Paul said, "you were the last dude I ever expected to go Hollywood on us. I guess I was wrong. See ya around."

I felt like what he was saying was total bullshit, of course. I mean, what did it really mean, anyway, to go Hollywood? I'd had one show or another on television for more than six years. Hadn't I been famous for a pretty long while? But I guess I was starting to realize that there was a difference between being pretty well known, and being REALLY well known. Like, Sandra-Bullock-well-known.

"People don't get it," I told her. "They think I'm stuck on myself, or something like that."

"It's difficult," Sandy said. "Sometimes I think it's a pretty lonely path, being this recognizable. You have to work at maintaining some of your friendships."

But I didn't exactly feel like doing maintenance on my old school buddies. To me, it felt like a betrayal. If they didn't take me as I was in this moment, well, fuck them. I could make new friends.

Except it wasn't really as simple as that. Sandy was incredibly welcoming, in terms of trying to bring me into "her world," but when it came down to it, I was really a kid from the streets. That's just who I was. I knew that I was smart, and that I could hold my own in a conversation, but I just didn't seem to have much in *common* with her friends, some of whom happened to be the movie-producing elite of the world. Some of my hardest moments were going with Sandy to her premieres and award shows. I was incredibly proud of who she was, and it felt absolutely right to support her. But sometimes I just wished she was a teacher or something. That I could go to PTA night at the school, and support her that way.

"You look handsome," Sandy remarked to me, as we readied ourselves for a red-carpet entrance.

"I feel, uh, a bit out of my element," I admitted, from the backseat of our hired car.

"You're fantastic," Sandy said, looking me deep in my eyes. "Thank you for coming with me."

Sandy always saw the good in me, the promise I had. But all the love and support in the world still wouldn't have been enough to make me comfortable up on the red carpet with her. Sometimes I look back at the pictures we took together, and I can read the discomfort all over me: the clench of my jaw, the way I'm holding myself. I never could seem to shake the feeling that it was all a huge farce, one big mistake. How in the hell did I end up in front of ten million flashbulbs? Wasn't I supposed to be selling refurbished furniture at the Long Beach swap meet with my dad?

The after-parties were even more painful. No matter how much I tried otherwise, I still felt like Jed Clampett there, stuffed into a suit, hoping no one would unmask the fraud that was me. If there was an unoccupied corner in the room, I'd quickly wedge myself into it, smiling weakly, waiting for the night to extinguish itself.

"Jesse James!" cried a drunk producer at one of these many shindigs. He looked nearly ecstatic to have found me. "How the *hell* are you?"

"Awesome," I said guardedly.

"Boy, I've been thinking about you a *lot*! I've been talking with my wife about restoring this vintage motorcycle—you might not know it from looking at me, but I'm a *total* bike freak, man!"

I tried not to express my total lack of enthusiasm for Sandy's scene, because it was always her night, and the last thing I wanted to do was throw a damper on her mood. But she was a pretty perceptive person. She could always see right through me.

"You hated it."

"What?" I said, on the drive home. "That's not true. I had a pretty good time."

Sandy laughed. "Come on, be honest: you were miserable."

"Miserable's a strong word. More like . . . I hoped I would die?"

"I know those events can be a bit stuffy," Sandy said, patting my leg. "I'm sorry, Jesse."

"I just feel like . . . well, everyone's looking at me. I'm completely out of place there."

We looked at each other for a second, then both grinned.

"We're such an unlikely pair," I said.

"I love it," Sandy said. "Wouldn't have it any other way."

Sometimes I wondered if she truly felt that way, though.

I mean, if *I* had been her, and I'd married some welder dude, I would have hoped to transform me, at least a tiny bit. My idea of a good time was to shoot guns, watch NASCAR, and babble about custom bikes. Truly, that's what made me happy. It couldn't have pleased Sandy all the time.

"Let's get away together," she proposed. "Just the two of us. I have a friend who'll let us stay at her villa in Cabo San Lucas."

Lounging around in a private villa in Mexico with a hot movie star wife probably sounds pretty good to the average guy on the street. And hell, I wasn't complaining. But every flight we took had to be a total military operation, because of Sandy's fame and the security it demanded. And then, once we'd successfully made it to our vacation house unobserved, it was hard to leave. There was peace in that villa, but sometimes I felt caged.

"Where are you headed?"

"I think I'll go take a drive. Explore Cabo."

"Are you going to take a map?"

"I'll live dangerously."

"Okay," said Sandy, laughing. "You know what? I'll come with you."

We showered, changed, then headed out to our rental jeep.

"I'm just going to get my cell phone," she said apologetically. "Just in case we get lost."

I sat in the car, jaw clenched, trying not to be frustrated. Next she'd be telling me to wear my seat belt.

As I waited for Sandy, I popped one of the CDs I'd brought into the car stereo. Circle Jerks blasted out at full volume, abrasive and mean.

"All set," Sandy said, opening the passenger-side door and slipping into her seat. "Hey, wow. That's a bit much for these eardrums. Can you lower the volume, please?"

I lowered it. Of course I did. That's what any husband would do for his high-class wife. She wasn't some whore in the back of a Daytona nightclub: she was a lady, with gentler tastes. But in the back of my mind, I couldn't help but feel kind of cheated. It was like I was Huckleberry Finn or something, when Widow Douglas decides to adopt him. They were "sivilizing" me, and I didn't know how to make them stop.

In the space of a few scant years, I'd gone from the hellacious pandemonium of an ex-porn star who didn't even know herself what her next move would be, to a calm, steady, and predictable wife, for whom a night at home watching a new-release DVD constituted a thoroughly stimulating evening of entertainment. Simply put, it was an adjustment.

It wasn't like I regretted my decision: I was in love with Sandy.

I really was. It's just that our marriage wasn't quite as simple and easy as I had hoped it would be. But then, I suppose nothing ever is.

———

The custody battle with Janine raged on. Finally, the courts threw me a bone, and I was allowed to visit Sunny in Oregon when she was three. The visit wasn't long, but it upset me.

"Sweetie," I said, hugging my daughter to me, embracing her skinny bones. She felt light in my grip. Her skin was incredibly pale.

"Boy, does she ever get outside?" I asked Janine.

"Of course she gets outside," Janine snapped. "I know what I'm doing."

But things seemed kind of strange with my daughter. Sandy and I took her out for the day, hoping to get to know her and sort of introduce our presence to her life. We took her to a playground, and she seemed disoriented.

"Look at her running up to the other little kids," I said. "She doesn't even know how to interact with them."

"She's not saying much," Sandy observed.

It was true. My daughter wasn't talking. She was running up to the other children, looking fascinated, as if she'd never seen another little person her own size, but didn't seem to know where to go from there.

"This isn't right," I said, frustrated. "Janine is keeping her isolated in the house all day. It's not the way a kid should grow up."

We played with Sunny all day, and I had never felt quite so sad being around one of my kids.

"Someday real soon, she's going to live with us," I told Sandy. "I swear." My determination to get my daughter had never waned, even in the face of the slow-moving justice system. But now when I saw just how pale and fragile she was, it was renewed a thousand percent.

"I believe in you," Sandy said. "We'll keep at it. Come on. We better bring her back."

It was huge to me that Sandy was so firmly in my corner. I knew that she could be a great mom to Sunny, and, if given the chance, could make a momentous difference in her life. But it wasn't just that she was capable of doing the job: I could tell that she *wanted* to do it. Sandy wanted to support me, but even more, I think she wanted to change things for this little girl whom she'd just met and already loved.

As always, the events of my life influenced how I approached my creative process, and one morning, I felt ready to announce to Sandy that I had news.

"I've come to an important decision," I told Sandy. "I'm through with *Monster Garage.*"

"Really?" she asked. "But why?"

"You know, I haven't felt that excited about the show in years. I don't want to milk it for all it's worth. I'd rather cut it off while there's still some interest there."

I'd been wanting to shift more of my energy to the home front, anyway, to getting custody of Sunny and running my motorcycle shop with a more careful eye. But the real straw that had broken the camel's back, I told Sandy, was the way the network had dealt with my journey to Iraq.

"I just didn't feel supported by them. I went overseas on my own dime, pretty much against their wishes. I don't know, I just felt like I was trying to do something good, and they fought me every inch of the way. It left a bad taste in my mouth."

Unsurprisingly, Discovery accepted my resignation.

"We'll miss you, Jesse," a network executive told me.

But I didn't think they would miss me *too* much. I hadn't always been the easiest guy to work with. In any case, it was possible that they, too, felt *Monster Garage* had run its course. After all, we had done five full seasons, and there's only so many mutant vehicles a man can build. We didn't part on bitter terms, though. They ended up running the footage we shot with the troops as a two-hour special, *Iraq Confidential*. In the end, I think we all felt the final chapter of our collaboration was a success.

But with the show gone, there was an immediate gaping hole in my life. For five years, I had worked around the clock, leading crews, doing demolition, design, and reconstruction. Now, suddenly, I had a lot of time on my hands. It felt strange and very unlike me to be twiddling my thumbs.

What the hell do I do now? I wondered.

At first, I figured the easy solution would be to spend all my time at West Coast; after all, we still had plenty of business to attend to. But dealing with the constant daily pressures of customers, crowds, and payroll stressed me out.

"I don't know how I did this for so many years," I admitted to Bill. "What the hell, man? We got thirty customers lined up to get their choppers, and every single one of them wants it *now*."

I had never considered myself an artist, exactly, but I had to be in a certain mood to get my work done correctly. I had to have a certain clarity and focus, or the products I produced were going to be subpar and unremarkable. Simply put, I had to *want* to do it. And I felt that desire slackening.

"I used to really need to prove myself to everyone," I explained to Sandy. "That's what motivated me. But now I feel like I've proved myself. Making bikes is just not making me happy anymore."

Sandy hugged me. As perceptive as she was, I'm sure she realized that my divorce from *Monster Garage* had left me feeling somewhat adrift. I also think she felt some mild guilt over her own stupendous career success. She was a sensitive, clued-in person, and she probably understood that no guy, no matter how generous he is, wants to be overshadowed by the woman he's with. She wanted me to feel as confident about what I did as she felt about her acting, where she'd achieved so much.

"Well?" Sandy said, sympathetically. "What do you think we can do to make you feel alive again?"

I thought about it for a long time, but answers that important don't just appear out of nowhere. I was looking around for passion, but couldn't quite seem to find it.

Racing, however, had always been a kind of hobby of mine. Ever since I was a kid, I had always been a natural at driving at high speeds, whether it be boxcars or BMXs. As I got older, it had evolved to trucks, dragsters, and motorcycles, as well as to more novelty items, like dune buggies or off-road vehicles. With more time suddenly on my hands, I figured I could probably get a little more devoted to the sport, and have plenty of fun in the process.

With practice, I managed to gain some competence. I played around doing things like Figure 8 endurance racing, where you whipped around on the same track until you were dizzy, crossing in the middle; but what I loved most and found I was most talented at was stock car racing. It was so incredibly fast. It satisfied the part of me that lived for speed.

"Damn," I laughed exultantly, after finishing one of my practice sessions, "why'd I even bother playing ball? This is so much cooler."

In a matter of months, I'd managed to place myself into the Winston West series, a preliminary stock car race that took place at the Irwindale Speedway. Sandy, ever supportive, came out to cheer me on.

"Aren't you nervous?" she asked. "*I'm* a little nervous."

"No chance," I said, patting my helmet. "This is going to be great."

I started out sensationally, ripping out of the gate, in contention to place. But minutes into the race, my rear axle broke. My car careened out of control, and I crashed head-on into the wall at 140 miles an hour.

It was an awful, gory wreck. The dash collapsed into my face and broke my helmet, nose, and cheek. I shattered my ankle, spiral-fractured my tibia, cracked my sternum. The car was completely destroyed, and when I woke up, I found myself in an ambulance, covered with blood.

"Where I am?" I managed to mumble.

"Oh my God, you're alive!" Sandy cried. "He's alive!"

Though I hadn't realized it at the time, I'd been unconscious for more than six minutes. It had been the chaplain who had gone and fetched Sandy—they hadn't thought I was going to wake up.

As I lay there on the gurney in the ambulance, my vision distorted, my face covered in blood, Sandy reached out and gently touched my hand. She was trembling, just super shaky. I still remember the look that was on her face. She looked like she'd already been told I was going to die.

"It's going to be okay," she whispered, finally. "You're going to be . . . fine."

My whole life, I'd always lived full throttle, placing myself in positions of danger over and over, as if that was my right. If I lived, if I died, that was my business. But there was something different about what I'd created with Sandy. To see her so shaken there, it really made me evaluate things on a different level—it made me realize that I had a responsibility to the woman I loved to stay alive, and live sanely.

"Look, I'm done," I told her, a few weeks later. "That NASCAR racing is for suckers."

Sandy didn't try to hide her happiness. "Thank goodness," she sighed. "I don't want you in a wheelchair."

"Yeah, me neither, I guess," I said. "Not unless you're in the one next to me."

"Ooh, a cute wheelchair duo," she said, laughing. "Tempting. Pink, perhaps?"

"They'd make a romantic comedy out of it," I said. "You could star in it. Keanu would play me."

"Oh, be quiet!" Sandy laughed. "I'm just happy you're going to be around for a while. You really had us worried for a second." Her face grew more serious. "I mean . . . I love you. I don't know what I'd do without you."

—

That night, I couldn't fall asleep. I lay in bed next to Sandy, feeling her warm, innocent body next to me.

Why had I really crashed? I wondered. *Was it really the car's fault? Or had it been a mistake I'd made?*

I was getting older. When I stared into the mirror in the morning, a thirty-seven-year-old face stared back at me. I didn't exactly mind aging, but damn, it sure felt like a harsh surprise some days. It seemed like only yesterday that I'd been laughing about girls with Bobby, getting drunk in the middle of the day, stealing cars and cutting them up for cash. Life had been so exciting, with no consequences to speak of.

Silently, I rose from the bed and limped my way out of the bedroom. Heading out into the hallway, I began a slow survey of the rest of the house. I checked in on my kids. They were asleep. As I gazed down at my son, I wondered rather guiltily how he and Chandler would have gotten along if my crash had been fatal. They would have survived, of course. But they would have gone through terrible grief and hardship.

Life just got a lot *harder* as you got older, that's what I was learning. It got more complicated, more difficult to understand. I cherished Sandy, I really did. She felt like the love of my life, and she was quickly becoming a mom to my kids. The idea of finding a woman I thought more highly of was laughable. I wanted to honor her by retreading my life in a way that she approved of, and in a way that made her feel proud.

But at that moment, alone in the house at night all by myself, I couldn't help but feel overwhelmed by the responsibility of having somehow transformed into a grown-up, a father to three kids, the husband to one of the most famous, impossibly perfect women in the world. It was a weakness welling up inside of me, no doubt about it. But sometimes I just wished I could find a way to make it all disappear.

16

We received the news in the summer of 2008: Janine was headed to jail.

"They got her on tax evasion," I told Sandy. "I knew right from the start that she was going to get knocked one day."

My ex-wife owed the IRS several hundred thousand dollars in back taxes. I'd been sending Janine fifteen grand a month ever since we'd divorced, but apparently, she'd never made much effort to pay back the government the considerable debt she owed them. Instead, she'd purchased two new cars and put a down payment on a $647,000 home. Janine wasn't going to turn it around until someone made her. She was just going to continue to fuel her self-destructive habits and lifestyle.

"That's pretty frightening," Sandy said.

"I know," I said. "I can't believe she's been raising my daughter all this time. I don't even want to think about it. But there's a silver lining."

"Really? And what's that?"

"If she really does goes to prison, I'm going to get custody for sure."

To this point, my attempts to win custody of my daughter Sunny, now a toddler, had been ineffectual. The courts were for the most part still really traditional. They tried their hardest to keep a child with her mother, no matter how obvious it seemed, at least to me, that I was the more stable party by a long shot.

But no judge in the world could refuse me now. Janine pled guilty to the charges of tax evasion, and she received her sentencing. In late October, we learned that she was going to be spending half of the next year in a Victorville prison.

"They're going to grant me custody. It's really happening," I told Sandy. "I'm going to pick Sunny up next week in Oregon."

"Can I come with you?"

"Of course," I said. "I want you to."

We drove up to Oregon quietly. I was nervous: I hadn't seen my daughter much throughout her life. Now I wondered if I hadn't fought quite hard enough to be with her. Janine had been allowed to parent her for a long time, because I hadn't figured out a way to prevent her. I just hoped that in the long run, her better instincts would have taken hold, that her influence hadn't been too damaging.

"Sunny's going to be fine," Sandy said, reading my mind.

"Yeah," I said. "I know."

She reached over and put her hand softly on my thigh. "This is the first step. We'll go on from here."

We reached the house and got out of our car. I caught sight of Sunny on the porch of her house, with the court-appointed guardian. She looked small and short and pale. My heart rose into my throat when I stooped down to hug her.

"You remember Sandy, don't you, sweetie?" I asked her.

Sunny nodded.

"We're both real excited, because you're going to come live with us," I explained. "You're going to have a big brother and sister. They can't wait to meet you."

Sunny looked down, not saying anything.

"We live right on the beach, Sunny," Sandy said gently. "Have you ever been in the ocean before?"

Sunny looked up, interested. "Yes," she said, after a second. "It was *cold*."

Sandy laughed. "Well, the water will be warmer in California. I think you'll like it."

I looked uncertainly at my two girls.

"Well?" I said. "It's a long drive back. Should we get on it?"

"Yes," Sandy said, extending her hand down to Sunny. After a moment's hesitation, Sunny clasped on, and they began to move forward. "Let's do it."

I felt hopeful.

—

And so, our family expanded once more. It was an exciting time for all of us: for Sandy, to be a mother for the first time; for Chandler and Jesse Jr., to be siblings to someone who really needed it; for Sunny, to slowly unfold into an environment filled with warmth and support; and for me, to feel like a dad who finally got his game right.

I'd become a parent so young. It had taken me a long time to grow fully into the role. But I felt like I'd finally arrived at my destination. I'd identified the people about whom I cared most deeply. I'd committed the rest of my life to making sure they were happy and safe.

"I'm turning into a regular family man," I remarked to Sandy, as we prepared to spend Friday and Saturday nights at home with the clan, fitting together puzzles with Sunny, watching movies with the older kids.

"Would you ever have predicted it?"

"What, me being this *boring*?" I laughed. "I guess not. But weirdly enough, I kind of like it."

It was a good thing that I did, too, because recently, I had started to feel like my family was the *only* thing that I was running right.

West Coast Choppers, according to the plan that I'd set up in my mind, was supposed to have focused me during what I saw as a transitional time. It was supposed to take my mind off the fact that my main project for more than half a decade, *Monster Garage,* was over and done with. But instead, the shop was just getting on my nerves. Without intending to, I had let it grow into a kind of unruly monster over the years. I had more than 145 employees on my payroll, and even keeping their names straight was a challenge at times.

"Who's *that*?" I frowned.

"Her name's Susan. She's been here six months, man. She's one of the accountants. Don't you remember?"

Things had just gotten way too big for me. And unfortunately, I had never learned to delegate very well. I wasn't one of these crafty CEOs with ten underlings running his arms and legs for him. Instead, every single goddamn tiny decision seemed to run directly across my desk. Every sale, every customer complaint, every bit of shop drama: it all came to me.

But the real killers were the lawsuits.

"I can't believe it," I exploded, one day. "*Another* one?"

They had been coming in, like biblical plagues, over the course of the last several years. Ever since I had married Sandy, my legal luck had turned to shit. The leeches had come out of the swamp, suing me more than half a dozen times. In 2007, the California Air Resources Board accused me of churning out bikes in violation of their clean-air standards, and they stuck their hands deep in my pockets, even though I offered to recall each of my bikes and make them smog compliant. Later that same year, a customer going through a messy divorce wanted to renege on his deal to buy a custom chopper, but

I'd already spent his down payment on labor, so I refused; he sued me, too. In 2008, even my freaking *lawyer* sued me.

I don't know if I had a sign on me, saying "Take my money!" Maybe I'd kicked around in the spotlight too long, let my brand get too well known, because things had sure been simpler when I was selling fenders out of my garage. I think people thought that because I was married to Sandy, I had access to her money, which wasn't true. She and I kept our finances separate. Both of us understood it was the path of least drama.

But if the intention was to wear me down, my various litigants were succeeding. My legal bills were enormous, and I went from feeling like West Coast Choppers was my retreat, the one place where things made sense, to not even really wanting to be there that much anymore. I couldn't help but feel like I was milking the cash cow for everything it was worth. And that had never been my style.

"It just doesn't make me happy anymore," I told Sandy. "There's so much stress associated with being there."

"Oh, honey, I'm sorry," Sandy sympathized. "Is there anything I can do?"

"Unless you can make me excited about doing something I've done a million times before, over and over again," I said, "I think the answer might be no."

I hated to act ungrateful. I knew that I'd achieved every blue-collar guy's fantasy, having created what was probably the biggest and most prestigious custom motorcycle shop in the world. I'd built it up from the ground, from absolutely nothing, just by my own sweat. But now I couldn't help but wish to be rid of it. I couldn't help but want to be free to do something, anything, else with my life.

"I think we need to go out to a nice dinner," Sandy suggested. "Just you and me. I'd like some alone time with my amazing husband."

"Yeah, all right," I agreed. "Maybe that'll help."

"Make the reservations," Sandy said, flashing me her famous smile. "I'll get dressed."

But even that didn't seem to work out for us.

"Jesse! Sandra! Can you give us a shot? Can you give us a second?"

"Sandra, when's the football movie starting? You guys start filming yet?"

The paparazzi battled with one another to get a photograph of Sandy and me entering the restaurant. It was just kind of lame, to have to battle through this horde of photographers just to get into a space of borrowed peace for about three hours.

"I wish just once we could go out and be totally left *alone*," I grumbled.

"Let's try wearing disguises," Sandy suggested, smiling.

"Nah, these guys have radar," I sulked.

"Don't let it ruin your dinner," she said. "There's no point."

"I won't," I said. But inside, I had already kind of let it spoil my mood.

It just felt like my chances to ever be normal again had completely faded away, and forever. To ninety-nine percent of the people out there, I was Sandra Bullock's husband, the owner of West Coast Choppers, some reality TV star. But that's not how I really felt as a human. I was a regular old dude from Southern California. Not a sophisticate, not a hero, just an average dad who liked football and racing. But I'd allowed the media to construct an identity for me, because it seemed like the right thing to do from a business and personal perspective. And now I was trapped inside of it.

Against all odds, I'd become a *personality*. That truly baffled me. In a shoe box at home, I had an old black-and-white photograph of myself on *Romper Room* when I was a kid—we'd lived half an hour away from where they filmed. Who in the hell would have predicted that someday I'd be stumbling around, playing an adult version of myself on so-called reality TV? It was just so unlikely, a one-in-a-million occurrence. And yet as much as I found it odd, and not really in accordance with my own vision of myself, I couldn't exactly bring myself to give it up, either. Fame annoyed me, but at least that massive block of attention showed that people cared. If I quit TV, what exactly would I have *left*?

So I ventured forward, not really knowing what the hell else to do. The producers for the *Apprentice* had been on me for years, trying to convince me to do the show. To this point, I'd never really been interested, but now, I forced myself to listen to their pitch.

"Look, Jesse, it'll be fantastic! I promise. We got Andrew Dice Clay!"

"You're going to have to do better than that," I said drily.

"We've got Dennis Rodman!"

"Incredible." I yawned.

"We've got Scott Hamilton lined up, too," the producer pleaded.

"Scott Hamilton's doing the show?" I perked up. "Seriously?"

"Sure," she said. "Interested?"

"*Yes,*" I said decisively. "Sign me up."

I'd been on the fence: like a lot of America, I considered the *Apprentice* a little hokey. But the mention of Scott Hamilton tipped the scales. I'd been trying to find a way to hook up with him for more than twenty years, ever since I'd stolen his Porsche from outside the San Diego Sports Arena in 1986.

The story was a strange one: I was seventeen years old, and in the prime of my car thieving days. I'd already stolen another Porsche the month before, ripped it down to the bare essentials, sold what I could. Now I was looking for parts I could transplant into the shell I already had. I was cruising downtown San Diego and found myself at the Sports Arena, where Stars on Ice! were having their big day. Right outside the arena, a green Porsche 911, with a vanity plate reading "ISKATE," just pleaded to be stolen.

So I burglarized it and drove it away.

I knew it was Scott's car, and later, when I got more well known,

Scott had found out that I'd been the guy who'd ripped it off. I'd never really managed to make a good apology, though, and I'd always felt kind of like an ass about that, particularly because Scott Hamilton was known to everyone as a really sweet guy. I figured doing the *Apprentice* would give me the opportunity to work alongside him, and make my amends.

And in fact, it did. We hit it off immediately, and gradually we became real friends as the filming wore on. It took me a couple of weeks, but finally, I screwed up the courage to say to his face, "Hey, Scott, I just wanted to tell you how sorry I am for what I did."

"Jesse," he said, "I forgave you for that a long time ago. You'll always be my favorite thief."

It was amazing, just how good that made me feel.

As for the rest of the show? I kind of surprised myself by how much I enjoyed it. They gave you the opportunity to work pretty hard if you wanted to, which I respected, and when it came down to it, how well you did was contingent on how well you functioned with your team. I worked with some awesome guys: Herschel Walker, Clint Black, and of course Rodman. He and I got into a little on-screen drama, when I suggested that he might have a drinking problem, but I never regretted saying it.

"I can kick anybody's ass at *any* task," I remember Dennis saying, when he was defending himself in front of Trump.

"What would you say to that, Jesse?" Trump asked me.

I thought about it for a second and replied, "I'd say, Dennis, why don't you kick our asses at being a good person?"

I don't know. Maybe he thought I was being a dick, especially since I'd had a drinking problem myself. But I didn't want to come off like I was better than him; I really believed what I said. Rodman was such an awesome athlete, and he had this unique jokester personality. He didn't want people remembering him as the guy who started pounding vodka at ten in the morning.

Being on the *Apprentice* kept me entertained. The way they cut the show together was a little cornball—that fake-drama music is the worst—but the actual experience of doing the show was great. I dug the challenge of being a bellman, or baking cupcakes, or designing a costume for a comic book character; whatever they threw at me, I tried my best to succeed at it. I got fired toward the end of the show for not bringing any real donors to the table for my charity—maybe Trump expected me to ask Sandy for a whole bunch of money or something, but I had no interest in doing that.

And then it was over, and I was back to twiddling my thumbs professionally. Bikes were my bread and butter—I'd built this whole empire in Long Beach. Still, for my whole life, I had always prided myself on being ready to move on to the next big thing. Now was no exception: I was waiting for the next big inspiration to hit my brain, to give me a new direction and inject my life with some much-needed excitement. But it wasn't happening.

During this time, Sandy was often working. Occasionally, she'd be gone for weeks, or even months, on end.

"I don't want you to go," I remember telling her.

"Got to," she said, smiling. "This is my job, remember?"

"Well, how about I stow away with you?" I joked. "Live in your trailer?"

"That would only be, like, the best thing in the world," Sandy said. "But I'll be back before you know it. I love you."

It was an odd time for me. I felt fatigued with the reality I'd created for myself, but there was no one to complain to about it. Everyone on the outside looking in at my life probably would have said, *What the hell are you complaining about? I got a mortgage, a nagging wife, a clock-punching job I hate. You married America's sweetheart! You have money, and freedom, and fame. So shut the fuck up.*

And that's precisely how I would have thought, too. When I was younger, the absolute last dude in the world who would have gotten my sympathy would be some famous guy, lamenting the glamorous problems of the elite. It just wouldn't have sat right with me. But now that I was inside that situation myself, things felt a little bit more complicated.

There was pressure stacking up from every direction, particularly on a business level. I'd spread myself increasingly thin with the various operations I'd developed over the years: my Walmart clothing line; my restaurant, Cisco Burger; my production company, Pay Up Sucker Productions; as well as a whole merchandising operation and the manufacturing facility that we'd connected to the bike shop. All told, the Jesse James conglomerate I'd built up spanned an entire city block. If I wanted to step away from that, it would have to be one hell of a step.

I'd love to just fucking blow it all up, I found myself fantasizing, as I sat behind my desk at West Coast, blinking my reddened eyes. *How sweet would that be?*

It was a great image. All this responsibility gone: no more staring down at yet another payroll sheet, calculating just how much money I'd have to bring in this month to make all the labor worth it. No more hordes of people outside, craning their necks, desperate to catch a glimpse of the action. My life could shift back into a more manageable gear. I could return to the average workingman grind, just me in a small garage somewhere.

But if I closed West Coast down, it would hurt Sandy. That was the catch. In the eyes of the public, my fate was directly tied to hers. So just like I couldn't punch somebody's teeth out on the red carpet, I couldn't really fuck up businesswise, either, because it would reflect badly upon her, and probably affect her successful image.

You're trapped, I thought suddenly. *It came out of nowhere, but you're trapped pretty good, aren't you?*

Before I met Sandy, I'd romanticized the stable, calm married life: the idea of me finally growing up. But now I missed leaning up against the fence at the dragster races in Pomona, laughing, talking shit, cracking jokes with my no-good friends. Too many people knew me now. I couldn't escape. Not even for an instant.

Hell, I didn't even have most of those old friends anymore. They all thought I'd pissed on them, gone Hollywood.

Mentally at a loss, desperate for something to make me feel like I had some sense of freedom, I ran through the list of things I *could* do to assert my independence over my life. Infidelity, unfortunately, was at the top of the list.

—

Sex is strange. For men, it's on our minds every minute of the day. It's what gets us out of bed in the morning; it's the gold at the end of our rainbow. Sex is part of what makes us fall in love with a woman. It's also part of what keeps us perpetually alone.

Ever since I had gained even a moderate amount of fame, I'd had women offering themselves to me—online, in person, and over the phone. I say that not to brag, but to tell you the truth about what fame does. I'm not special, by any means: the same thing happens to every man who makes his living in professional sports, music, television, movies, or politics. It's part of what motivates men to strive to be famous in the first place. After all, when you take money out of the equation, what's the point of being famous *besides* having your pick of attractive partners?

Throughout my life, I'd always had opportunities to hop on the train. But from the groupies at the concerts to the biker chicks who crowded our booth in Daytona, I'd mostly said thanks, but no thanks. It's not because I was a great person; it's just my nature to get emotionally caught up with the women I'm involved with. I'm into sex, but contrary to whatever biker stereotype got built up around me, sex is mostly a cerebral experience for me. If there's no personal connection there, then it's sort of pointless.

But with that said: I still did it. I screwed around behind Sandy's back, and the whole world came to know about it.

I can't go back, and I can't save my marriage. What I can do is try to understand why I did it.

When Sandy and I first fell in love, I was so overjoyed to be with a woman who was obviously a superb person. And on the flip side of that same coin, I think part of what got her excited about being with me was my "bad boy" image. Opposites really do attract. During the initial period of our romance, we were carried along on the wave of the good we so clearly saw in each other: kindness, a willingness to give affection, our physical attraction, and a strong feeling of safeness we got from each other. But as we got to know each other better, I think we both came to realize that we really *were* a bit oddly matched. Sandy wasn't rich, but she came from a stable, middle-class family—she'd grown up singing in a choir with her mom. I'd grown up with a dad who sent me a hooker in the middle of the day.

After Janine and I had split for good, a whole bunch of my friends had commented on how rash my decision to marry her had been. "Man, you thought you and *Janine* could make it work? You must have been *high*." But weren't Sandy and I almost an odder combination? I mean, I knew I could count on Sandy not to punch me in the face for snaking her parking space. But that didn't mean we liked to do any of the same activities, or that the things that motivated me would do the same for her.

The more important factor, though, was the fact that I'd grown up in an environment where love hadn't been shown to me on a regular basis. My dad had torn me down every time he could, and my mom had been pretty absent. Now I had a *great* woman who was telling me she loved me, but that didn't mean I was in any shape to believe her. Sandy was an actress, after all. I think in the back of my mind, I always told myself she was pretending.

I never really trusted Sandy. It's shameful to admit it, especially considering how hard she tried to let me know that I was accepted, and that she saw the good in me. But no matter how many times she told me, it just didn't take. I nodded when she said she loved me. Inside, I was always thinking to myself, *Sure. We'll see.*

I guess I always felt like sooner or later, she was going to see the real me. And then she'd leave me. Well, I figured, if I was going to be left, then I wanted to make the first break. I'd reject Sandy before she could reject me. I'd expose myself as broken and incapable of love before someone else could beat me to the punch.

I have no problem admitting that I fucked up. I cheated on a woman I cared deeply about and I am so regretful. If there was any possible way to undo my actions, to communicate instead of cheating, to be able to say to her, "Hey, I think we need to change some things about our marriage, because I'm losing my mind in this world we've created for ourselves," then I would. But I can't. I transgressed against the vows of my marriage, and it doesn't really matter whether I did that ten thousand times or just once. Once you've lied, there's no taking it back. There's no way to erase the deceit that you've created.

Instead, you have to live with it.

———

I probably almost blurted out the truth to Sandy more than a hundred times.

"How's the steak taste to you, Jesse?"

I fucked someone. I didn't mean to, but somehow it happened and I can't take it back.

"Jesse? Anybody home?"

"Yeah," I said, shaking my head. "Sorry. I'm just tired."

"Well?" Sandy said. "Everything taste okay?"

"It's great," I said, stiffly. "Just like always." *And also, do you have a moment while I admit something that will end all happiness as you know it?*

Being around my kids was almost as bad as being around Sandy. I'd always prided myself on being straight with them. I wanted to *earn* my kids' respect, not demand it, and I knew that the only way to do that was through honesty and by being a decent person. Now

I was caught up in this big lie that followed me around from room to room like a dark cloud.

I'd never lived as a liar before. It was something to get used to.

I couldn't look in the mirror for too long. I didn't want to examine myself too closely.

I couldn't listen to the lies I told Sandy, my weak cover-ups. I pretended that my voice was coming from someone else.

All the self-respect I'd accumulated over the years, through seasons of hard work, through refusal to quit even in the face of hardship, it was all gone, because I was full of shit and I knew it. My confidence was at an all-time low. And ironically, the sex that I'd sold my soul for wasn't even good. There was no relationship and no personal connection. I was just there coldly, for myself, and even though I figured that detachment would make me feel less guilty about being unfaithful, *that* made me feel like a heel, too.

Months went by like this, the guilt mounting and my loathsome behavior making me feel like the lowest rat in the world. Then, one morning, I stepped out of the shower, and caught a good look at myself. I was a fully-grown man, complete with graying temples and a few wrinkles across the forehead. I wasn't a child any longer. I had the power to stop what I was doing. I'd acted mindlessly. If I continued down this road, I'd lose everything, starting with my self-respect.

And so I stopped. The decision, arrived at in a moment, was final, and my execution of it was cold and definite. It was just like turning off a switch. *Bam.* It was all over. Several weeks after the fact, I realized that I'd quit drinking in precisely the same way.

It took a good long while before I began to feel better about myself—not to mention secure enough around Sandy to act like a normal human being.

"Want to go take a walk on the beach? It's so beautiful out tonight."

"All right," I answered carefully. "That'd be great."

We strolled along the beach in the evening air, arm in arm. Sandy was a trusting woman at heart, and that made me feel even more guilty. She'd never suspected a thing. Sometimes, I awoke sensing I loved her even more now, having gone outside of our marriage and finding no happiness there. I wished I could tell her. There was a story inside of me now—maybe if I phrased it right, I could share it with her.

I strayed, but realized that no one could replace you.

"Look up at all these *stars*," Sandy exclaimed. "They're so incredibly perfect. I mean, are we the luckiest people on earth, or what?"

No, I realized. I couldn't tell her the truth.

"We are," I agreed, gazing up at the black, quiet sky that loomed over our private stretch of beach. "We're very, very lucky."

That evening, as I walked along the beach with Sandy, I knew that I'd have to swallow what I'd done. I had no choice. It was the only plan that made any sense to me.

As time passed, strangely, our marriage began to gel again. I felt satisfied with my wife, and far less constrained by the specter of being known as Mr. Sandra Bullock. So what if I had to act in a certain way? So what if I couldn't go to the racetrack anymore? Wasn't being with a remarkable woman worth that much? In the grand scheme of things, was that really much to ask?

My creative lull also seemed to be on its way out, and that helped a lot. We'd developed a new reality show called *Jesse James Is a Dead Man,* where I performed challenging stunts. The show premiered on Spike TV, a new network for me, where it enjoyed moderate success. We didn't break the world in two, exactly, but then, audiences were a little harder to overwhelm these days. More important was the fact that I'd created a show again, and I'd expanded my horizons for what I could do creatively. It opened the doors for future projects and gave me ideas about what more I'd like to do.

The bigger event for our family, though, turned out to be Sandy's participation in a movie about, of all things, football.

"I think this film is going to do *really* well," Sandy announced the day she returned from filming. "I don't know, it's just a feeling I have."

"Pretty much every movie you do does well," I reminded her.

"Oh, hush," Sandy said, smiling. It was obvious she was finding it impossible to contain her excitement about the difficult role she'd mastered. "I'm *telling* you, this story is really special. People are going to relate to it."

The film was *The Blind Side*. Based on a true story, it centered around a conservative Christian family in Tennessee who'd decided to adopt an exceptionally gifted, young black football player from an impoverished background. Initially, Sandy had turned down the role of Leigh Anne Tuhoy, the mother, feeling uncomfortable with the idea of enacting a woman whose philosophy in some ways ran counter to her core beliefs. But in the end she'd taken it on, and from the way she was acting now, she'd emerged gratified and energized by the challenge.

"I got the chance to stretch a little bit," she explained. "I can't tell you how good that feels for an actor."

I just nodded, staying quiet.

Sandy's instinct turned out to be right: *The Blind Side* opened in mid-November of 2009 to great interest. It had a huge opening weekend, taking in more than $35 million at the box office. Through all of Sandy's success across the years, she'd never been part of a movie that had grossed that high in initial sales.

The Blind Side kept rising. Incredibly, it made even more its second weekend, taking in sales of upward of $40 million. On its third weekend, it ousted the new *Twilight* movie, to become the number-one box office draw in the United States.

"This is wild," Sandy breathed. "I knew it was going to be good, but *this* good?"

But the film hadn't stopped yet. By January, it had grossed over $200 million, making it one of the most profitable sports movies of all time. And Sandy had earned strong reviews from critics across the board for her portrayal of Leigh Anne Tuhoy, the adoptive mother of Michael Oher. It appeared as if the award season might be a busy one for her.

"This really might finally be your year," I said.

Sandy waved me off. "People like to make fun of my movies," she said. "I'm just not the kind of actress who takes home statuettes. Which is fine! I don't need them."

"You're so great in whatever you do," I said.

"I do a certain thing," she said, reasonably. "Either you like it or you don't."

"People *love* you."

"But the critics never have," Sandy said, with a wink.

This time, though, they did. Nominations poured in for Sandy: the People's Choice, the Screen Actors Guild, the Golden Globes, the Critics' Choice, and then, the most prestigious of them all, the Academy Awards. They all lauded her performance, and presented her with the opportunity to join the ranks of the best and most celebrated actresses of the last century.

Needless to say, our house was a whirlwind of activity that winter. Sandy was constantly doing press junkets for her movie, taking interviews, and planning for the next award show. On January 6, 2010, we attended the People's Choice Awards, where she took home the award for Favorite Actress. But that was just a warm-up. Nine days later, Sandy emerged victorious as Best Actress at the Critics' Choice Awards, and then, just forty-eight hours afterward, she took home the same honor at the Golden Globes. The Screen Actors Guild Awards were on January 23. She cleaned house again.

"I'm going to have to buy you a storage unit," I joked. "I'm not sure we have room for all this hardware."

"Quiet, you." Sandy laughed. She embraced me. I hadn't seen her this happy in a long time. "Thank you so much for supporting me through all of this. I know you don't exactly adore the red carpet."

"I don't mind it," I said truthfully. "It's good to be there next to you. I'm so proud of you."

When the day for the Academy Awards ceremony came, March 7, 2010, she was nervous as anything.

"Those other women are *so* incredible," she said, as we dressed in the afternoon, readying ourselves for the long day ahead of us.

"You're going to win it," I said. "This is your year."

Sandy looked at me. "Meryl *Streep* is nominated."

"Yeah?" I said, frowning. "I guess she's supposed to be a pretty good actress or something, huh?"

Sandy gave me an incredulous smile. "Yes, she's okay." She struggled with her dress. "Can you help me with this, please?"

I walked up behind Sandy and helped her struggle into her white Marchesa gown. "Man, you look amazing."

"It's not me. It's the gown."

"Sorry, but it's you," I told her. "You're breathtaking."

"Come on," Sandy said. "Stop complimenting me. It's bad luck. I'm nervous enough already."

"Don't be so nervous," I said. "This is going to be a cinch. Just remember, when you go up there to get that little statue, don't trip, okay? It could be embarrassing."

We rode to the Oscars in style, in the backseat of a chauffeured Town Car. "I never got to do this in high school," I remarked. "Aren't you supposed to get all liquored up before prom?"

"You must have been quite an adorable little football player in high school," Sandy said, looking out the window distractedly.

"I had a lot of acne, actually," I said. "Man, maybe it was in the helmets we wore. Pretty much all of us had acne. Of course, if you *really* want to talk acne, we gotta bring up my best friend, Bobby. He had a *ton* of zits. Not just on his face. His neck, too."

"Okay," Sandy said. "Very nervous. Don't want to discuss neck pimples just this minute."

I squeezed her hand. "Sorry. It's going to be good. I promise."

Though I wasn't much for award shows, even I had to admit that the Oscars was special. Just to be inside that room, packed to the gills with people I'd seen on big screens for my entire life, sort of blew me away. Even though I wasn't part of their clan, and probably didn't see the world the way they did, I recognized the magic of the occasion.

We waited for hours, patiently smiling and applauding through the endless awards: Best Sound Mixing, Best Original Score, Best Adapted Screenplay.

"You deserve an Oscar just for looking interested this whole time," I whispered. "Couldn't we have showed up a couple hours late?"

"Don't be bad," Sandy said, laughing.

Finally, the time arrived for Best Actress category. Sean Penn sauntered up on stage, and announced the nominees: Sandy, Meryl Streep, Carey Mulligan, Helen Mirren, and Gabourey Sidibe, from *Precious*. Then he ripped open the envelope.

"And the winner for Best Actress is . . ." he announced, "Sandra Bullock."

Around me, the entire arena exploded with applause.

"What did I tell you?" I said to her. "Congratulations. You deserve it."

She gave me a look that said, thank you. For just a split second, we shared that privacy, before she gave herself up to the rest of the room.

Sandy began to make her way down the aisle, and I rose to my feet, clapping loudly. The whole room followed suit. We watched as my beautiful wife boarded the stage in her elegant gown, her long hair dark, shimmering, and perfect.

I felt a knot rise up in my throat as I watched her clutch her trophy for the first time, knowing what it meant to her.

"Did I really earn this?" Sandy asked. "Or did I just wear you all down?"

We all laughed, and the tension was broken. *How foolish I was to have ever risked hurting this woman,* I thought.

"I have so many people to thank for my good fortune in this lifetime," she continued. "And this is a once-in-a-lifetime experience, I know."

She's everything that any man in the world could want. Beautiful, talented, but somehow humble.

Sandy complimented each of the other actresses, then thanked the real-life Leigh Anne Tuhoy, after whom her character had been molded. Then she proceeded to thank her own mother, who had been gone for ten years:

". . . for reminding her daughters that there's no race, no religion, no class system, no color, nothing, no sexual orientation that makes us better than anyone else. We are *all* deserving of love."

Then she pointed tearfully into the audience at me. "And thank you for allowing me to have . . . that."

It took everything I had not to cry. It was almost like a fairy tale. My heart felt close to bursting.

As Sandy held her Oscar in the air, the applause rose to a deafening peak. I clapped until my hands hurt. I suppose, at that moment, I was lost in my own fairy tale, the one in which my actions would never catch up to me.

17

You really never know what you have until it's gone.

Tuesday, March 16, 2010, was the day I understood exactly how much I'd been given. It was also the day I learned what it was like to lose everything.

The morning started off like any other: I rose early, kissed my sleeping wife good-bye, ate a quick breakfast, then headed into the shop. But at around ten o'clock, Sandy's publicist called me with news she had to share.

"Jesse? I have to run something by you."

"Sure, what's up?"

Sandy's publicist related to me that a woman had come forward saying that she and I had been carrying on an affair together. She had gone to a gossip magazine with the story. They would be publishing the news within the next forty-eight hours.

My insides curled inside of me.

Sandy's publicist continued. Sandy herself would soon be hearing the news; thus, it might be a good idea to speak to her as soon as possible, to put to rest any concerns she might have.

Shortly thereafter, we ended the conversation, and I hung up the phone. I stumbled into the bathroom, shut the door behind me. I tried to breathe, but my heart was hammering in my chest.

I could try to deny it. Play dumb. But Sandy would know, anyway. She would see it on my face.

I had been lying for long enough by this point. So after about an hour of waiting for something to happen—a nuclear warhead to hit the shop, perhaps, saving me from my fate—I called her.

"Hey," I said.

"Hi," Sandy said. She sounded worried. She and her publicist were very close. I guessed that they had probably talked already.

"Can you come to the shop?" I said. "I think we need to talk."

"Okay," Sandy whispered. "I'll come over right now."

Waiting for her to arrive, I paced back and forth, wishing for some way out.

Give me a do-over . . . I pleaded. *I really didn't mean this one.*

But that was just the frightened kid in me talking. I'd done the crime; now it was the time for me to step up and do my time like a man.

"Hi," Sandy said, when she came in the door. She gave me a hesitant, forced smile. "So, what's up?"

I looked at her, searching for the words to tell her. Nothing came out of my mouth.

"This woman's full of it, right?" Sandy asked. "Do you want to get your lawyer on her?"

I didn't say anything at all for a long second.

"Come into my office," I said, finally.

Sandy came in and sat down on a chair. I closed the door after her and sat down myself. We stared at each other. And then, finally, I told her the truth.

I admitted the affair. I told her the hard details. I let her know that I had never loved this woman, that I had never cared for her at all.

Then Sandy asked me why had I done it. But I had no answer for her.

The feeling of shame and sadness that washed over me as Sandy began to cry was almost beyond measure. I'd never felt that in my body before. I watched her, and for a moment, I wanted to be dead.

I didn't touch her. I sat frozen in my chair, watching, as Sandy's small body shook with sobs.

There is nothing I can say right now to make this better, I thought. *There is nothing I can do.*

Instead of feeling freed from the guilt of having lied to my wife for months on end, all I felt inside was stunned and horrified.

Sandy rose to her feet. She unfolded her sunglasses and put them on her face.

She walked steadily and purposefully to the front of the shop, opened the heavy, metal door. For a moment, the sunlight enveloped her. The door closed behind her, and she was gone.

—

I sat, rooted behind my desk, for the better part of an hour, unsure of what to do.

Things were about to get really ugly. For a moment, I remembered being in Iraq, when we saw those dark, ominous dust clouds on the horizon. An awful storm was brewing. I could feel it.

For the remainder of the day, I stayed at the shop, sleepwalking like a zombie through my work, incapable of erasing the image of a weeping Sandy from my head.

At around seven in the evening, I threw on my coat and prepared to leave.

"See you tomorrow, Jesse!"

None of them got it. None of them understood that by tomorrow, everything would be changed. They would never see me the same way.

At home, I found the kids in the kitchen, hanging out and laughing with each other.

"Hey, Dad, can we order pizza tonight?" Jesse Jr. asked.

"Dad, if we do, this time can we *not* get sausage?" Chandler said. "It like, *pollutes* the other pizzas . . ."

"How does that even make sense?" Jesse Jr. said. "If you want to be a retarded vegetarian, fine, but it doesn't mean we can't have ONE pizza that has meat on it . . ."

"Guys, hold it for a second," I said. "Where's Sunny?"

"She's in the living room, watching cartoons."

"All right. Good," I said. "Listen up. I have to talk to you two about something." I think they saw from my tone that I was serious. "It's . . . it's about Sandy."

"What is it, Dad?" Chandler said, coming nearer to me.

"She's gone," I said after a second. "She's gone, and she's not going to live here with us anymore."

Both of my kids stared at me, uncomprehendingly. "What are you talking about?"

"Did something happen to her, Dad?" Jesse Jr. asked.

I cleared my throat. "Sandy is okay. I mean . . . she's *safe*. That is, I think she's safe, at least . . ." I let my voice trail off, confused.

A long moment of silence in the kitchen.

"Look," I said, finally. "I grew up not knowing anything that went on between my parents. I never want to do that with you guys. So I'm going to tell you something private and difficult. And it's going to hurt. But just listen to me."

Both of them nodded. I stared at the refrigerator for a moment, finding it hard to look directly at them.

"I was . . . unfaithful to Sandy," I said. Every word sounded strange in my mouth as I spoke. Like it was a speech I'd seen on TV that now had found its way into my mouth by chance. "I went outside our marriage. And now, well, she found out about it."

"What did she say?" Chandler asked.

"She ran out of the shop this morning, crying," I said. "I don't see her coming back here any time soon."

"Will we . . . see her again?"

"I don't know," I said. "Maybe eventually. But the thing is, well, even if you do, it'll never be the same around here."

"What do you mean?" Chandler asked.

"When you're as famous as Sandy," I said, "something like this can become a real story."

"You mean, like, it's going to be in the papers?"

"Whatever happens, it's not going to be good," I said. "She's going to be hurt. In front of a lot of people. Which means I probably won't ever be able to make it up to her." I looked them straight in the eyes, to see if they understood. "It's over."

Now it was my kids who couldn't meet my eye.

"I screwed up real bad," I said. "But it doesn't mean I don't love you. I care about you guys. More than anything else in my entire life."

I must have looked pretty beat up. Chandler came over to me and gave me a hug.

"It's all right, Daddy."

"Dad, things will be okay," Jesse Jr. said. "Just give it a couple of days."

Slowly, I walked up the stairs to the master bedroom. Our bedroom looked like it had been ransacked. Sandy had removed all of her clothes and books and small possessions. Her bedside table was swept clean.

I sat on the side of the unmade bed, unable to move, dimly aware there was worse to come.

———

The following morning, the news broke.

". . . in emerging news, the husband of megastar Sandra Bullock, recent recipient of Best Actress honors, has been hit with allegations of infidelity . . ."

I'd known it would be coming, but I was unprepared for the force of the blow. My guilty face was on every channel. I sat in my living room alone in front of the TV as reports continued to file in. Filling the screen was an image of me and Sandy on the red carpet only days before. We looked proud, on top of the world.

I switched the channel. But the same story was running on a different station. Even the same picture was up on the screen. Me wearing that black tie against a black suit. Sandy in her Marchesa gown, clutching her statuette.

Masochistically, I switched from channel to channel. It was all the same. The bad news rolled in over and over again, like waves of toxic radiation.

"Bullock moved out of the couple's Sunset Beach home yesterday, fleeing to an undisclosed location . . ."

Click.

"The actress has canceled her trip abroad to promote The Blind Side *. . ."*

Click.

"A source close to the couple reports that James, once abnormally protective of his wife, had grown sullen and discontented in recent years . . ."

After several more minutes of watching the news of my disgrace unravel, I finally got it. The news media weren't going to drop this. They'd been handed their dream story. Now it was time to run with it.

"Gosh, Dad, they're killing you," Jesse Jr. said to me sympathetically.

"Hey," I said, turning around guiltily, seeing my son witness my public execution. "Look, bud, let's just turn it off. Let's do something else."

But the news was so widespread, it couldn't be turned on and off like a valve. I could ask my kids not to watch TV, but their friends were watching. So were their friends' parents. People who had never met me could follow the trail of my public disgrace. The news was splashed on every gossip website. It was the top story on Google news.

TV had always been an avenue of escape for me, a way to zone out when I didn't want to deal with my own internal monologue. But now some nightmare version of my guilty conscience was being broadcast on four hundred channels, all day and night. The title of my most recent show came to me in a flash: *Jesse James Is a Dead Man.*

The shop was the only place I could hide. But even there, no one would look at me. I felt like a pariah.

I built this place, I thought bitterly, *and now they've turned on me, too.*

Fuming and fumbling, I retreated behind my desk, but I lacked the strength to turn on my computer. I just stared at the black screen. My own reflection stared back at me. Dark, hopeless circles ringed my puffy eyes.

Mustering the last vestiges of strength I had left, I tried to lose myself in work.

"All right," I announced, emerging from behind my desk. "We got shit to weld. Business as usual. Let's get everyone organized and on deck."

Bill approached me. "Hey man, a whole bunch of the guys, well, we just wanted to let you know that we're all behind you, no matter what."

"Thanks," I managed.

"I don't envy you right now, man."

"I don't know anyone who would. Come on. Let's get to work."

It was a cosmic beatdown, the perfect retribution for all the fame I'd enjoyed over the past ten years. The media had never really liked me anyway. I was always that "heavily tattooed biker dude" to them. At best, a bizarre fit for Sandy; at worst, a menace to her reputation and safety. During the last few years, they'd begun to warm up to me, but now this scandal confirmed the worst opinions the public had harbored all along.

"*Where has Sandra Bullock* gone?" major television network anchorwomen wondered around the clock, as if the absence of my wife and partner of five years was equally troubling to them as it was to me.

The worst thing about it, though, was that they had as good an idea of where Sandy was as I did. I had no idea how to get in touch with her. That was the strangest aspect of this whole surreal journey. In a normal marriage, if something like this happened, she would have holed up with her parents for two weeks, or I would have gone to sleep at a motel down the street until I'd worked myself out of the doghouse enough to plead my case. Eventually, we would have had a chance to speak.

This wasn't a normal marriage, though. Sandy was a powerful woman with the means to escape into a sealed, insular environment. And even if I could get the chance to contact her, there was no way in hell she could risk taking me back, not even if she had wanted to. It would soil her professionally.

And that was a problem. When you got up to Sandy's level of fame, the personal *became* the professional. News of our scandal was impossible to separate from news of her career, so she and her publicity team had to perform emergency surgery. She had to remove the tumor immediately: me.

"Pass me that frame," I said, sick to death of my own thoughts. "Let's get down to it."

I welded. The flame obscured my vision, incandescent blue white light hypnotizing me, and gratefully, I sank into the rhythm of the work.

—

I might have been able to weather the storm. Eventually, the networks would have found another disaster, and they'd have moved on. But then the paparazzi closed in.

Hordes of photographers began to stake out my house. They were poised to make between $15,000 and $35,000 for a snapshot of something "newsworthy," so from the moment I stepped out of my doors with my kids in the morning to drive them to school, they rolled incredible amounts of film on us. The clicking sound never stopped, from the moment I opened the door of our house until the second I managed to herd my kids into our truck.

I was being flayed in public. The pain and the embarrassment stung. But the truth was, I hadn't been happy or comfortable in my own skin for years. I'd never really believed that any of my wives had loved me. Deep in my heart, I'd never believed that I was worthy of their love. I'd always adhered to that same old plan I'd grown up with: push them away before they do it first.

"Don't come around here anymore," I snapped at the leering horde of men with cameras as I walked by them swiftly, my head down. "That's just low, man."

I slammed the door of my truck behind me, taking a huge breath. Back when my dad had brought me to school in his junk truck, loaded down with used mattresses, I had felt so embarrassed and mortified. Dully, I wondered if that's how my kids felt about me now.

—

With each stage of vilification came greater understanding. I had always thought of my wife as "just Sandy." But I don't think I had ever really absorbed just how famous she was, and just how much the American public loved her. Her fans and sympathizers were probably nearly as outraged and hurt by my infidelity as she was. Now, clearly, the gloves were off.

"You can't believe all of that crap that you're seeing on television, Chandler," I told my daughter. "You know that, right?"

My daughter looked down at the floor. "Yeah, Dad, sure. I know."

During this time, I came to see how true a friend Karla was to me. She was my salvation and partner throughout the ordeal. She knew I'd screwed up bad, but never once, not for a single instant, did she waver in her loyalty to me.

Together, we figured out how to get the kids to school, how to keep them sane amid the hell of the scandal. Being able to talk to her was the one thing that kept me stable.

"It'll be all right, Jesse."

"Yeah," I said. "Sure it will."

"Jesse," Karla said. "You have always been the toughest guy in the room. Always. Now it's time to prove it."

Karla wasn't just a loyal friend, though. She was also a comrade against the paparazzi.

"Hey! YO, KARLA! Isn't it true that he cheated on you, too?"

"Fuck you!" Karla snapped, furious.

She was a menace to them. If anyone was going to go Sean Penn on someone, I think it would have been her. No one yelled at Karla after the first day.

I kept waiting for things to cool off, but incredibly, like in a bad dream, new sludge just kept seeping to the surface. On Monday morning, after one of the loneliest weekends of my life, when all I could think of was Sandy and how she was holding up under this craziness, *Us* magazine published a photo of me in an SS cap, doing a Nazi salute.

"Oh my fucking lord," I sighed. "They are going to absolutely kill me for this one."

The photo had been taken at a party at my house ten years before: I'd been given the cap by a buddy of my dad's, Barry Weiss. Barry rented a building in Gardena to a guy whose job it was to make costumes and uniforms for films like *Schindler's List* and *Band of Brothers*. The cap was a reproduction, something he'd given to me as a joke. In a moment of stupidity, I'd put a couple of fingers over my top lip to form a Hitler mustache, and had thrown up a Sieg Heil. You could tell by the goofy expression on my face that I was anything but serious.

But of course, no one was in the mood to believe *that*. The perfect storm had formed around me: first, I'd betrayed America's Sweetheart, and then a decade-old picture of me doing a Hitler salute had made the cover of *Us* magazine. Yep, I was ready for the shit bin.

"I might as well have stuck my dick in the pope's mouth," I said to Bill wearily.

"That would have gone over better," he said.

I had a lot of explaining to do. But how do you explain that you're not a racist? That in fact, you were *kidding* when you threw up the Nazi salute, while wearing an SS cap? At that point, everything just sounds like a lie.

"Barry," I pleaded. "You have to come out and support me. You're my one phone call."

"Can't do it," he said, regretfully. "I got a show on A&E this fall—I can't afford to get mixed up in all this crap. Sorry, Jess. You're on your own, kiddo."

So I just chose to clam up. I hoped my record would stand for itself. I had been the first person to feature a black dude in an ad in *Easyriders* magazine. I'd traveled to Israel and lived on a kibbutz for a month just the previous year with my son, for Pete's sake, while I was apprenticing under a blacksmith. I wasn't a Nazi, or anything like that.

What really got me was the fact that it had been a former assistant of mine who had sold the photo to *Us Weekly*, for $200,000. It wasn't even a revenge thing; she and I had parted on good terms. I was learning all kinds of things about human nature, it seemed. Friendship could be sold. Money trumped all.

Smelling blood, the gossip magazines dove for the kill. They spread their talons out in a five-mile radius, their wings overshadowing the entire Long Beach area, pupils dilating on anyone who might have ever known me, even incidentally. They knocked on doors, offering my friends and acquaintances serious money to attest to all kinds of bullshit, like that I was an animal abuser or a skinhead. Women I'd never met were offered $50,000 to swear that they'd had an affair with me. "Just give us a statement we can use! It doesn't matter if it's true."

My life was falling apart, and there was nothing to do but watch it happen. I got a text from Robert Downey Jr., who I'd developed a friendship with. The text read, simply: "What a glorious shitstorm." I laughed for a full minute.

I needed diversion, so I tried to have some fun with the paparazzi. I developed a routine: I'd drive sanely to school when I was dropping my kids off. But as soon as the kids were out of the car, it was go time, and we were on a racetrack. I barreled down back alleys and one-way streets at 130 miles an hour, threatening my own life and limb on a pointless, high-speed chase to nowhere. Testament to their incredible, leechlike hold, the paparazzi never gave up: if I lost them, they'd always show up for the next leg of the race.

Infidelity wasn't a new story to Hollywood, but we were in the Internet age now. There was no getting away from constant twenty-four-hour news, gossip sites, the endless supermarket tabloids. News was nonstop now. And my story was just trashy enough to interest the average American. I was just big enough, just famous enough, and just tattooed enough, that you didn't feel a need to sympathize with what I might be going through personally.

The punishing days wore on. I worked all day in the shop, pushing myself relentlessly, clocking in fifteen-hour days. But at night, I wasn't sleeping. I twisted and turned, little snippets from the voices on TV pushing themselves in behind my eyes.

. . . serial philanderer . . .

. . . Nazi . . .

. . . mistresses emerging on a daily basis . . .

My kids saw how beat down I was. I couldn't help it. They even tried to cheer me up.

"Dad," Chandler consoled me, "it'll be all right."

But I wasn't actually sure if that was true. There was nowhere to hide. Every day, it seemed more and more photographers would show up, increasing the numbers of their little tailgate party. Three of the four sides of my house were visible from the road. They had me cornered, all right.

On the fourteenth day of my siege, I drove the kids to school, ignoring the insults thrown at me from the leering mob. I made my way over to the shop, too disheartened to take anyone on a chase. I arrived at West Coast and shut off the truck. Predictably, six of the most stalwart photographers hopped out to torment me with their cameras.

I stood there like a dumb animal as they loaded and unloaded on me. I closed my eyes, hoping that somehow, when I opened them, I would be alone. That I would have woken up to discover this was all some kind of horrible dream.

"All right," I said finally, humiliated and starting to feel angry. "You guys done for today? Got what you needed?"

"Whatever, Jesse," said this Mexican cat with a shaved head. He edged closer to me, continued to shoot directly at me.

"Get the fuck out of my face," I said, dangerously quiet.

"Ha. Yeah, sure, man," he said, chuckling. He wore a beat-up suit jacket over a white button-down dress shirt.

"I'm not kidding," I warned him.

"Dude, why are you freaking out on me?" he sneered. "I'm just doing my job."

"You have to leave," I whispered, seething. *"Now."*

"Why are you tripping?" he asked. "Fuck, dude. Chill out, already." He shook his head, as if he was annoyed, then continued to snap off shot after shot, determinedly.

I could feel the anger rising in me. All of a sudden, I felt just like the messed-up, angry teenager I used to be, when if I was mad enough at someone, I'd do anything to fuck them up, and if they locked their door, I'd smash their window, yank them out of their car, and beat the shit out of them.

There were no consequences back then, I had nothing to lose. And what scared me very badly at this moment was the fact that, my pulse quickening dangerously, I was starting to feel precisely the same way. A sick feeling rose in my throat. I saw red, and somehow I knew that if I didn't leave that very instant, I was in real danger of doing something terribly violent.

Trembling, I shuffled away from the photographer. I walked back to my truck, where I opened the heavy front door and climbed behind the wheel. I sat there for a long moment, frightened, gripping the steering wheel, my hands like claws, knowing I had to somehow escape from this hell.

I turned the key in the ignition, and tore away from the lot.

"Yo man!" called out the paparazzo after me, puzzled. "Why you *tripping?*"

———

I drove endlessly in circles around Long Beach, and for once, no cars followed me. But I still felt completely defeated and undone.

As I orbited the blocks so familiar to me from my childhood and youth, I passed high schools, gas stations, strip joints, taco stands, and auto parts stores. None of them were open to me now. Everyone knew about me. Everyone hated me.

I drove on, faster now, drumming on the dash with my fingertips, feeling light-headed, like I was ready to take a chance, do something rash. By coincidence, I passed the black church that I'd found years before. Immediately, I pulled into the parking lot.

Maybe this spot is the answer, I thought. *Maybe I can talk to someone—that preacher. Maybe he'll listen to my story.*

I made my way up the walk and pounded on the front door.

"Hey," I called out desperately. "Is anybody there? Hello?"

But the door was locked. Panicked, I knocked louder and louder, again and again, slamming the flat of my hand heavily against the wooden frame of the door.

"Hey!" I said. "*Come on! Open up!*"

"Yo," a homeless guy passing by said to me. "Nobody home."

"I can see that," I muttered.

"No, they *moved*. They went to Compton about a year ago," he said. "Not enough black folks in Long Beach for a congregation anymore."

I said nothing for a moment. Then, dejected, I began to walk back to my truck. There would be no salvation for Jesse James. Not today.

I sat behind the wheel of my truck, my head spinning. There had to be a solution, a place I could go to get away. But no clear answers came.

If only I could escape, I thought frantically. *If only I could go somewhere and leave this fucking horrible mess behind.*

Nothing came to me, so I drove home. I had no other place else to go. But I felt like a trapped animal in a cage there, too.

I couldn't turn on the TV. I couldn't read the newspaper. I couldn't go to work.

And then somewhere, amid my panic and distress, I remembered a friend of mine telling me, years before, about a rehab facility he'd gone to in Arizona called Sierra Tucson.

"It's an amazing place," he'd said. "It turned me right around."

With trembling fingers, I turned on my computer and found the website of the facility. I scrawled the address down on a piece of paper. It would be a five-hundred-mile drive from Long Beach to Tucson—a grueling, narrow journey down the I-10. But I knew I had to go there.

Because if I don't, I thought, *something terrible is going to happen. And soon.*

18

Blue-black light hung on the horizon as I throttled down the I-10, the vibrations of the tires and the frame tranquilizing my wrecked mind.

I'm finally going somewhere, I thought. *I'm finally getting out of this hell-zone.*

It was four o'clock in the morning.

I pressed harder on the accelerator, watching my speed increase to 120 miles an hour, then 130, then higher. The industrial shitscape of Los Angeles gave way to something even bleaker as I passed out of lonely Riverside into the wide-open range of horse stables and twisted trees and spinning giant wind turbines outside of Indio. In the back of my mind, I remembered a carefree, drunken trip I'd taken once many years before on the same route . . . heading to a spring break party at Lake Havasu . . . the car full of delirious teens, everyone smoking and yelling

. . . Hey, don't you know what all those wind turbines are for, man? someone said, coughing, *they suck all the smog out of Los Angeles*—and then the trusting expression of one of the girls we'd brought along—*Really?*

Onward I drove, scenery melting, now dust, now desert, now mountains, and I ripped along the empty roadway through the breaking light of dawn, the blues and blacks rising into something brighter now. I rumbled by cowboy towns like Blythe and Brenda, swallowing hard, wishing I had water to drink, past Quartzsite and Tonopah, *never even heard of them, who lives there, and why,* the windows shaking from the speed and my head pleading, *just let me get there, just let me go . . .*

With morning breaking, I pulled off the highway, stopping at a gas station, my shirt soaked through with sweat. I dipped my head low, tucking my chin nearly into my chest, as I filled up the tank. *Nobody better come up to me,* I thought, *nobody even come near me, because now is not the time.*

I filled the tank without incident and settled back behind the steering wheel and gunned the engine. I ripped out of the gas station, flying off the mark, cutting against the wind, heading east toward Phoenix, racing against my own pulse *calm down calm down.* Then I laughed, at nothing, and the vulnerable, awkward sound I made frightened me.

Sweat beaded on my forehead, and I lowered the window and let the wind whip in at me. The coldness of the early April morning buffeted my face and neck and chest, giving me a meager sense of clarity that was gone as soon as it appeared.

I snapped on the radio, fumbling between stations. A snatch of Top 40 pop filled the front seat, somebody singing over and over *imma be, imma be, imma be . . .* The chorus tore at my brain, like some infant's simple demands.

"No," I mumbled, and pressed my thumb onto the dial, switching over to the next station, but it was even worse, something swoony and pseudo-soulful, *wherever you are, whenever it's right, you'll come out of nowhere, and into my life . . .*

"I'd rather crash into the wall again at Irwindale," I muttered. I jabbed my thumb at the stereo again: give me something better.

"Okay, we got a *great* show today," came the familiar, confident, nasal New York voice. "Listen, we got Jesse James with us today . . ."

"What the fuck?" I whispered.

"He's a guy who first became successful when he started building *motorcycles.* I've been *reading* about this guy. I guess he used to be a real badass. Listen, you talk to him, Robin. Hey, Jesse, Robin wore extra cleavage for you . . ."

I sat bolt upright in my seat, unable to believe the coincidence. I'd done the Howard Stern show one year ago; and now, today, as I sped through the desert, driving myself either toward rehab or the great beyond, they were airing it again.

As the morning heated up around me, the mountains growing brighter, sharper in their cut against the sky, I listened to my voice. It was as if the show was being broadcast solely for me.

I traveled all around the world, ten times in five years . . .

. . . that whole time, all I was doing was going to motorcycle shops . . .

. . . Yup, when I was off the road, I'd just work on my bike in my mom's garage . . .

. . . She contacted my office, and wanted to bring her godson on a tour of the shop . . .

. . . I contacted her assistant, and said I wanted to ask her out . . .

It was just almost too much to believe.

"You were married to the beautiful, *stunning*—who I wished *I* coulda had sex with—Janine Lindemulder for a while, weren't you?" came Howard's voice. "Boy, she must have been a *monster* in bed . . ."

. . . Sometimes, things aren't what they seem . . .

"She's one of the sexiest broads on the *planet,* though!"

It was surreal. I listened to myself break down the dissolution of my marriage to Janine, then go on happily to tell the story of how Sandy and I met: how she'd refused me at first; how I hadn't stopped trying, and eventually, I'd won her over. I spoke about our relationship, about how completely different it was from any other thing I'd ever experienced.

The words sounded hollow and false. Suddenly, behind me, I saw the flashing lights of a cop car.

"Dammit, what *now*?"

I pulled to the side of the highway. A police officer pulled his squad car behind me and leisurely sauntered out onto the blacktop.

"License and registration."

I handed it to him. Squinting down at the paperwork, the officer frowned, then glanced back up at me.

"What's up?" I said.

"Are you that Jesse James guy everybody's talking about in the news?" he said. "You *are*, aren't you?"

"Yep," I said, forcing a tight, small smile. "Hey."

"Well, whatcha going so fast for, Jesse James?" The police officer looked pleased with his catch.

"Heading to Tucson."

"Well, what the heck's in Tucson?" the officer asked. He waved to his partner, who was sitting in the front passenger seat of the cop car, motioning him to come up to my car. "I thought you were a Hollywood guy."

"I'm . . ." I shrugged, too exhausted to lie. "Look, I'm going to rehab."

The cop frowned. "You got a drug problem? Let's see your eyes."

"I'm not high," I muttered. I widened my eyes for him to inspect. "I'm just . . . trying to get better."

The second cop joined us. "Hey, shit. Hey, you know who this is? It's *Jesse James*!"

"I've already ascertained that information," the arresting officer said. "Okay, listen up, Jesse. Here's a deal for you. You were going over a hundred twenty miles an hour, so we can write you a big fat ticket. Or, you can take a picture with us."

"You won't give me a ticket?" I asked. "All I have to do is take a picture with you, that's it?"

"No ticket."

"Well, all right," I said, almost cracking up at the absurdity of the situation. I climbed gingerly out of the car. "Just don't sell it to TMZ or something."

"Would we do that?" the second cop said. "Come on."

The first police officer pulled an iPhone out of his pocket. He shoved it toward his partner, then threw his uniformed arm around me, grinning widely.

"Go ahead. Take a picture of me and Jesse."

We stood on the edge of the blacktop, our arms around each other, as the other cop fumbled with the phone. The morning traffic whizzed by me. Sweating, I tried to swallow.

———

At around eight o'clock in the morning, I arrived in the visitor parking lot at Sierra Tucson. I'd covered over 450 miles in little more than four hours. My hands were shaking.

From the backseat, I grabbed the small bag of clothes I'd hastily thrown together the previous evening, and slammed the door closed behind me.

The air around me was crisp and cool. I looked at the main building: it appeared to have been constructed out of some sort of adobelike material. The whole thing had this Southwestern feel about it, with cacti and brush trees all around. We were in the foothills of a mountain range.

Hesitantly, clutching my bag and my keys tightly in my hands, I walked up the path to the building.

Fuck, I thought. *Maybe I should turn around and head back. There's still time. Back into the car. Maybe drive to Mexico . . .*

"Hey, there," came a rasping voice. I turned to look toward a silver-haired woman, about fifty years of age who was smiling at me with a twinkle in her eye. "I'm Fay."

"Hey," I said. "Jesse."

"Jesse?" Fay said warmly, putting her arm around me. "You came to the right place."

I said nothing, just felt the way her arm hung on me.

"Come on," she said, taking in the scared look on my face. "Let's get you inside."

Suddenly I realized that in my haste to leave home, I hadn't bothered to let anyone at Sierra Tucson know that I was coming. I had made calls making sure my kids would be cared for, but I'd neglected to phone this center and ask if there was room for me.

"I don't have a reservation," I told her. "No one's expecting me."

"Shouldn't be any problem," Fay said. "I'll take you to reception and we'll figure it out."

We walked down the quiet hallways, passing only a few people, who gave us interested looks then returned to their own business. "Do you work here?" I asked.

"Sure do," Fay said. "I'm on the kitchen crew."

"Oh," I said. "I thought you might be . . . well . . ."

"One of you?" Fay laughed heartily, the skin around her eyes coming together in friendly crow's-feet. "I *have* been, you can believe that. Come on, Jesse, I'm going to take you to the folks in charge. We'll get everything all squared away for you."

Fay handed me off to the woman at the reception desk, who took me in pleasantly. If either of them had recognized who I was, they didn't let on.

"Jesse," she said, "now that you're here, we ask that you make a commitment to stay with us for thirty days. Can you do that?"

I nodded. "Yes. I want to be here."

As I said it, I realized it was the truth. I had only been inside the building for fifteen minutes, but already, my pulse had slowed.

It was quiet here. Slowly, the realization that no paparazzi were allowed inside these doors came to me. I smiled, tentatively, feeling the importance of the victory.

"Here's your bedding, and some towels," another staff member said. "There's already soap in your bathroom." I was shown to a room of my own. It was nothing special at all: bare white walls and a bunk bed. It reminded me of a college dorm more than anything else.

"If you need anything else, just come up to the front desk. You'll have a meeting with Dr. Thomas at one o'clock. She'll acquaint you further with our program. Lunch is at noon. Until then, feel free to relax and enjoy yourself."

She waved good-bye, closing the door behind her. I dropped my bag on the floor, tossing my bedding onto the desk in the corner of the room. I lay back on top of the bare mattress, my feet still on the floor, and studied the ceiling of my room, as if there were some answer there. Soon my eyelids grew heavy, and then closed. Minutes later, I was asleep.

———

"I don't know why I'm here."

"Well, you made it," said Dr. Thomas, a friendly, middle-aged woman. She smiled at me, as we conducted my intake interview, a clipboard with my paperwork in her hand. "That's the first step."

"But, I mean . . . aren't I supposed to know, like, what's wrong with me?"

"You'll figure that out," she said. "Over time. Everything takes time. We have people here who are dealing with chemical addiction, eating disorders, anxiety, depression . . ."

"But I don't *have* any of that," I said. "I've been sober for almost ten years. I eat just fine. I'm not a depressed person."

Dr. Thomas smiled at me patiently. "But still, you felt the need to be here."

"Yeah," I admitted.

"Be patient," she advised. "Do our program. It's pretty rigorous, that much I can tell you. You'll have individual therapy, group therapy, EMDR, if you want it, not to mention all sorts of meetings. You'll find yourself pretty busy, I guarantee that much."

I gritted my teeth. "So, there's lots of talking here, huh?"

"Yes, that's true. You can gain a lot, in fact, just by listening to what other people are going through. Think you're up for it?"

"I guess so," I said. "I don't really know if I'll be any good at it, but I can try."

"That's all we ask of you, Jesse," she said, patting me on the hand. "So come on. You've got your first group session this afternoon. Step lively."

Half an hour later, I walked downstairs to a large meeting room, where about fifteen residents gathered.

"How's everyone doing?" asked a male therapist, a young man named Ben. "We have a new member of our group joining us today. Everyone, this is Jesse."

Most of the members of the group waved to me. "Hi, Jesse."

I waved back tentatively. "Hi."

"Does anyone want to start us off today?" Ben asked. "What's on everyone's mind?"

After a few seconds, an older woman raised her hand.

"Hi. I'm Jill. Most of you know me already. For those who don't, I've been battling with addiction to alcohol and drugs for more than ten years. I've been here for a couple of weeks, and each day, it seems like I'm getting a little bit better. I mean, it's still hard . . ."

Her voice broke off.

"What's the hard part, Jill?"

"I just don't know if things will change when I leave here . . . I mean, it's pretty easy to be sober here, but I'm scared that when I leave, I'll just go back to my old ways."

Jeez, I thought. *How about just trying to be tougher? I mean, if you don't want to drink, then just don't drink.*

A young girl, not much older than Chandler, raised her hand.

"I'd like to share."

"Go right ahead."

"I'm Catherina. The reason I'm here is, I've been struggling with an eating disorder. I'm anorexic, and it makes me so unhappy . . . every day, I wake up with this feeling like I can't do it, I can't get better. I don't want to be like this, you know, but I feel trapped."

Holy shit, I thought. *These people really have issues.*

"How's everyone else doing? Can we hear from our new member, maybe? Jesse, would you like to share?"

"I don't know," I said uneasily. "I mean, sure, I'm open to sharing, but I don't exactly know why I'm here."

"Well, that's fine, Jesse. Tell you what, how are you feeling right now?"

"I'm feeling okay, I guess. I'm glad that I'm here . . . I think I just need some time to figure some things out. I need some time to be alone, I think."

"That's a good start," Ben said. "There's no hurry. Ease into it."

I sat in my seat, fidgeting, but at the same time trying to listen as the other members of the group listed a staggering catalog of psychological conditions: anxiety, PTSD, cocaine addictions, and abusive relationships.

Hell, I thought wearily. *Compared to these folks, I'm practically normal.*

My first private session came later that afternoon, with Dr. Thomas. I sat on a chair directly across from her in a small, cozy little office.

"I thought people had to lie down when they did this sort of thing," I joked.

"No room for a couch in here," Dr. Thomas said, smiling.

"Although, if you want to lie on the floor, we can probably accommodate you."

"That's okay." I laughed. "I'm good just like this."

"So, Jesse," she said. "What brings you to my office? What do you want to discuss? This is your time."

"Well," I said. "I guess . . . my marriage ended. I'd kind of like to figure out if I can save it."

"All right," she said. "Tell me about it."

"Oh, man," I said. I paused for a while, letting the silence fill the room. "I just . . . don't know if I'm ready to go into all of that. It's been pretty painful."

"Is it recent?"

"Real recent," I admitted.

"Do you need some time to settle in here, first?"

"Yeah, I think so," I said. "I mean, I don't want to be a dick. I mean . . . sorry." I blushed.

"That's okay. You can say whatever you want to here, Jesse. Everything's allowed."

"Well," I said, haltingly. "I just . . . I've never done anything like this before. Like, talk about my feelings. Any of that. I'm more of a take-action type of person. I never saw the point in therapy, to be honest."

"You might be surprised what happens when you open up," Dr. Thomas said patiently. "Tell you what, let's just meet again, tomorrow, and go from there—how does that sound?"

"Good," I said gratefully. "Thanks. I'll do better next time. I promise."

"It's all at your speed," Dr. Thomas said. "There's no need to rush it."

I wandered around the grounds, outside of the building, killing time before dinner. A guy with a receding hairline, a few years younger than me, approached me carefully.

"Hey, man," he said. "How are you doing? I'm Tim."

"What's up, Tim. I'm Jesse."

"Dude! I figured that was you. You're the guy from *Monster Garage*."

"Yup," I said.

"Well, welcome. This is a pretty cool place."

"What are you here for?" I asked.

"Oh, depression, you know, anxiety . . . my whole life being kind of fucked up . . . that kind of thing." He laughed. "It's not so bad, I guess. I swear, some days, I actually feel like I'm getting better. What about you?"

"What do you mean?" I said.

"I just mean . . . why are you here?" he said. "That is, if you want to talk about it. No pressure."

"You mean, you don't know?" I said.

"How would I know?" Tim asked, confused.

"I thought you knew who I was."

"I do," he said. "You're that *Monster Garage* guy. But that's all I got, man." He grinned. "Look, we'll talk about it in group. I just wanted to say what's up and welcome you."

"Well, thank you, Tim," I said, after a second. "I appreciate it. See you around."

We separated, and I continued to wander around on the grounds, in the shadow of the mountains.

Of course, I thought. *Most everyone's been here longer than me; they weren't on the outside when the story broke.*

There were no newspapers, magazines, TV, or Internet at Sierra Tucson. I realized, with incredible relief, that this place really was an escape for me. No one knew about me and Sandy. And, I decided, I was going to keep it that way.

That evening, all of the residents gathered together after dinner for a large group meeting, about two hundred people in all. It felt more laid-back than the smaller group session, almost like a social gathering, and the room buzzed with discussion as a few patients halfheartedly tried to read the minutes from previous meetings, amid the conversations going on in every corner of the room. I kept mostly to myself, but couldn't help observe the friendship and camaraderie evident in the room.

The next morning, we had another group session.

"This is pretty embarrassing for me to admit," said one young man. He looked like he was in his mid-twenties. "I . . . hadn't left my apartment more than a handful of times in the past few years."

"Really?" I asked. It just slipped out. This was a normal-looking kid. I couldn't imagine what could have kept him so alone.

"Yeah," he said, looking at the ground. "Pretty fucking loony-sounding, I know . . ."

Ben, the therapist in charge of the group, talked with the young man for a few minutes, teasing out the details of his story: he had been enrolled in the armed forces, then had been discharged for an anxiety disorder. I listened to him with real sympathy.

"Anyone else? Who'd like to share?"

Slowly, I raised my hand.

"Hey," I said. "I'm Jesse. I just came in yesterday, so I'm sort of new to this. But sitting here listening to you guys, I'm really impressed by how honest and open everyone is. I wanted to try to open up a little bit."

"That's great, Jesse. What's on your mind?"

"Well, I think . . . I came from a pretty violent family. That's my . . . I think that's my issue."

"Is there anything in particular that stands out to you?"

"Man." I laughed. "There's so much to choose from." The other residents laughed, and I felt a bit more comfortable talking.

"One of my first memories," I continued, "is of this girl with freckles and red hair. She used to live around the corner from me when I was a kid."

"What do you remember?" Ben asked.

"She was a Jehovah's Witness," I said, laughing. "But I don't know why I remember *that*. Anyway, I always used to ride my bicycle by her house. One day, she was lying down on the sidewalk, with her little skirt on, just staring up at the sky without blinking, like she was dead. And I remember it made me cry. I was like four or five years old."

"Go on," Ben encouraged me.

"So I went and told my dad," I said. "He was in the backyard, refinishing some furniture, and I went up to him, crying, all, 'Dad, Laurie's lying on the sidewalk! I can't ride my bike!' And my dad, he looked up and yelled, 'Well, then fuckin' run her over!' Well now I know he was kidding, but I was just a kid so I did what he said. I went and got my bike and ran her over with it. I remember my front wheel hitting her square in the ribs, and I fucked her up really bad."

I looked at the group, a little apprehensively. "He was a pretty gnarly dad," I added. "I have all kinds of stories."

"How did it make you feel to grow up in that kind of household?"

"Not too good," I said, remembering. It felt kind of odd to be talking about my family; I had only ever done it with a very few people in my life. Sandy and Karla, that was about it. But for some reason, this felt right. "My folks split when I was about six. I didn't see my mom much when I was growing up. I just had a whole bunch of stepmoms—and my dad."

"It sounds like you have a lot of unresolved feelings toward your father, does that sound right?"

"No, I think they're pretty much resolved." I laughed, kind of bitterly. "He hit me. He doesn't know his grandkids, and I haven't spoken to him in about ten years. That's how I feel."

Soon we moved on to other residents, but a curious feeling of release and tentative happiness stayed with me for the rest of the hour. It felt like I'd dislodged something.

After the meeting broke up, I kind of mingled around the room a little bit, feeling more open than I had been previously. Meeting the eyes of the other people in the room, part of me wondered if they'd judge me, now that they knew I'd grown up in a weird, violent type of life. But oddly enough, no one seemed to bat an eyelash.

They're all dealing with their own shit, I realized. *I have problems, but so do they.*

"How are things developing for you, Jesse?" Dr. Thomas asked, during our private session later that day.

"Not that bad," I said. "I'm starting to feel a little bit more at home here, I think."

"And what do you think of the group meetings?"

"I was a little resistant at first," I admitted. "But today, I kind of opened up and talked."

"How'd that feel?"

"Not too bad. In fact, it was sort of amazing." I laughed. "So that's what therapy is, huh? You unload all your baggage, get it out into the air?"

"I think that's probably part of it," Dr. Thomas said, smiling. "Actually, it's a big part. Our theory is that it's helpful for you to tell your story. Your job is to put it all together into some kind of narrative that makes sense to you and the people around you."

I nodded, absorbing that. "I talked about my dad today," I said, after a moment.

"What'd you get into?"

"Oh, I just talked about what a loser he was."

"Tell me about him."

"Oh, hell," I said, exhaling. "He was a beatnik, I think. But not the fun kind. My dad bought unclaimed storage units at auction and then tried to sell all the shit inside them. He got his kicks fucking people over for a living. That's my dad."

My therapist laughed gently. "Well, was there anything that you liked about him?"

"Well, sure, I guess," I said, considering. "He knew how to work hard. He taught me that, at least. My function on this planet was to be a worker for his business. If he had a bunch of trucks to load, he had no problem with keeping me out of school. I don't care if it was a test day or anything: I was going with him to work."

"Did you ever feel taken advantage of?" Dr. Thomas asked.

"I think I was too young to really know how it worked," I said, after considering for a second. "I wanted his approval, and work was the way to get it. So I got real good at it. After a few years, it even got to the point where my dad would sit on his ass in the truck and watch me do all the work, and I was thrilled. Like, 'Dad! Check me out! I did it!'"

"And did you get his approval, then?"

"Sometimes," I said. "But there was always more work to do. I didn't care. I was a strong kid. I was like six feet tall by the time I was thirteen. Sometimes I worked twenty hours in a weekend for him."

"It sounds to me," Dr. Thomas said, "like you had to grow up pretty quickly."

I sat there, looking at her, thinking, *yes, I guess I had.*

—

As those first days passed, I settled into a routine. Group in the morning, private sessions in the afternoon, then the large communal meeting after dinner. In between, there was strange hippie bullshit I never thought I'd do in my entire life, like yoga and meditation. But I tried everything, and the peace that I'd felt at moments here and there over my first days began to come a little more often.

I was safe here. That was the big realization for me in the first week: once I understood that I was actually freed from the media vultures outside, who had pecked at me until I thought I'd go crazy, the relief was impossibly sweet. Essentially, I felt like I was among people who, for once, actually sympathized with me. The other residents were ordinary folks who had gone through some pretty hard problems, and they had undertaken the same challenging unwinding process that I had. In a way, we were all in this together.

"Yo, Jesse," Tim said, nodding at me. "What's up, man?"

I smiled at him. "Hey, Tim, what's happening."

He shrugged. "Just another day in paradise. You?"

"Same here," I replied.

It wasn't like everyone was my best friend right away. But somehow, it totally gave me strength to know that other people were fighting some sort of battle to make themselves better, too.

It was probably on the fourth or fifth day that I decided I was going to work as hard at Sierra Tucson as I'd worked at everything else in my life: football, bodyguarding, building my own business. I would put in the hours and do whatever they asked me to. Some of the stuff was kind of corny, no doubt about it: they had this small outdoor walking maze that you were encouraged to wander around in—I guess the idea was you could sort out your feelings alone, after a hard day of talking trauma or something. But I'll be damned if wandering around that little maze didn't hold some answers for me. Some afternoons, watching my feet as I stumbled across the small stones, I remembered things there I'd been trying to forget for thirty years.

My mom never remarried. She had only one boyfriend after my dad left.

I pivoted, trying to keep my balance in the narrow pathways of the circular maze.

He was a typical 1970s East L.A. Cholo . . . drank a lot . . . worked as a truck driver . . . I remember seeing him drunk and yelling at my mom, threatening to kick the shit out of her.

I turned again, putting one foot directly in front of the other, treading as slowly and as deliberately as possible.

Once, I told him to leave my mom alone and he directed his alcohol-fueled rage toward me . . . "What's that?" he yelled. "You got something to say to me? Huh, you fuckin' crybaby?" I think I was about eight years old . . .

It was hard stuff, all of it. And I had always been unwilling to dwell for too long on it. I guess it hurt too bad. I'd bury myself in my work, or in getting fucked up, or wrenching on big, imposing machines. But all that had done was put me where I was now. The only way out was through the hard memories.

Joanna, my stepmom, came to pick me up from football practice in sixth grade, and I was late getting out of the locker room . . . "Where were you?" she snapped. I didn't say anything.

"I SAID, where were you?"

I didn't respond.

"Did you hear me??" She backhanded me, and her fake nail caught on my mouth and cut my lip and then I was bleeding onto my shirt . . .

The memory hit me full force. I swayed for a second, then continued forward, breathing with each footfall, just looking at the ground, letting my body lead me.

So I punched her in the side of the head. She shut right up. It was the worst feeling I'd ever had.

Slowly, I felt something expanding inside of me. Just having the courage to investigate the way I'd grown up gave me this sense of maturing, of advancing past this limit I'd always set on myself. Instead of constantly pretending that I'd grown up normally, just like everyone else, now I was allowing for the possibility that I'd been hurt. And pretty bad.

"I came here thinking that if I followed the directions, and did what you guys told me to do, I'd maybe be given a second chance with Sandy," I told Dr. Thomas. "But lately I've been thinking, maybe that's not the point."

Dr. Thomas smiled at me. "So tell me, what's the point, Jesse?"

"Well, it feels like . . . I've stumbled into this amazing opportunity to work on myself. I think I better make sure I focus on that."

"That's good," she said. "I think that's an excellent idea."

Gradually, I fell back into a regular sleeping schedule. Each night, I fell asleep around ten. Then I would rise the next morning at five, take a quick shower, throw on a pair of jeans, and step quietly out the front doors.

A seven-mile horse trail led off the property. I wasn't supposed to go on it, because it was off the grounds, but nonetheless, I did each day. The path wound itself through the mountains, and as I followed it, the nature around me filled me with a sense of freedom and wonder. It was just so incredibly quiet out there. There wasn't a single soul around to bother me. Back in L.A., I'd taken early-morning walks on the beach a few times, but there'd always been company: I'd usually see between fifteen and twenty folks, running over the same stretch of ground as I was. Here? My only company were deer and javelinas and jackrabbits. Just me and cold desert morning air.

And yet it was still surprisingly tough, some days. One morning in group therapy, I had been telling the other residents a little about my teenaged years, when it seemed like all I'd done was steal cars and get into fights—and, as usual, my attitude was one of mild pride, at what a badass I'd been.

"I was probably a little out of control." I laughed. "I remember this one time, my buddy, he stole a vintage Schwinn from outside of my house. I caught up to him the next night at a party and confronted him, like, 'Hey, man, give my bike back!' but he wouldn't do it, so I called him out into the street."

The other residents smiled, and prepared for one of those "my life was so crazy way back when" stories that all AA meetings specialize in.

I was just about to indulge them, just about to conclude my story with *and then I jumped on his back like a fucking monkey, and rode him into the ground. BAM, just beat the living shit out of him, there was blood flying everywhere . . .*

But instead, I just burst into tears.

I sobbed, right there in front of everyone, for a long minute.

"Whoa," I said finally, taking a huge, crazy breath. I was trembling. "Man. I'm sorry. Where the fuck did that come from?"

"It's okay, Jesse. Take a second to tune into what's going on inside you."

I took in another big inhalation. I was actually really spooked; I'd never just started crying for no reason before.

"I'm . . . I was just thinking about how many times I've used my fists to settle things in my life," I said. "I guess the truth is, I feel kind of bummed about it."

"Why do you think you were in so many fights?"

"Why do you *think*?" I snapped. "I was a messed-up kid! That's the only thing I knew."

"All right, Jesse," said Ben, our lead therapist. "Take note of what you're feeling now. This is important."

"I'm fucking angry," I said. "All right? That's how I feel."

I stared at the faces around me in the circle. Quietly, they gazed back at me.

"You all want me to break down or something," I complained. "Well, I'm not doing it."

"No one wants you to do anything," Ben assured me. "We're here to listen. The important part is for you to . . ."

"Yeah, yeah, I remember, concoct my own narrative, or whatever. Well, I got news for you. My narrative fucking *sucks*."

"Listen," he said. "We do a role-playing exercise here, where we have members of our group act out a pivotal scene from one person's life. I'm wondering if that might be helpful to you today, Jesse."

I stared at him balefully. That was about the last thing I wanted to do at this moment. All I wanted to do was run, get off the grounds, do anything but be here.

But you said you'd work as hard here as you did everywhere, a little voice inside my head reminded me.

"Aw, fuck, I guess so," I grumbled.

"Great," Ben said. "So first of all, you have to pick out a memory. Something that stirs up emotions in you, makes you feel sad, or outraged, when you recall it . . ."

"No problem," I said flatly. "Got mine."

"Okay," Ben said. "Now, how many characters are there going to be?"

"Just me and my dad," I said.

"How old are you?"

"I'm seven. My dad is, I don't know, in his thirties."

"Who wants to play seven-year-old Jesse?" asked Ben. A balding guy named Phil raised his hand. "Great. And can I have a volunteer to play his father?"

Tim raised his hand.

"Okay, great. So set the scene for us, Jesse. What are we looking at?"

I grimaced. "You really want to do this?" I breathed in deep, then began to tell my story. "Fine. Me and my dad are tossing around the football. It's late at night, and we're in the yard behind my house."

Phil and Tim pantomimed passing around a football.

"We throw it around for a while, then he tosses the ball over my head. It goes into this open field right next to our house. And I'm scared of the dark, so I don't want to go in there."

No way, Dad. I'm not going over there.

"And my dad, he says to me, you better get your ass out there and get it. His face clenches up real bad. I can see the cords in his neck, and I get real scared. Then he starts to chase after me . . ."

The memory was coming back to me, even more vividly than when I had told Sandy. My voice had started to shake, but I continued.

"So I take off running into the darkness, my heart racing, scared out of my mind of the dark, afraid that my dad's going to beat the shit out of me . . . I run, but there's a low fence, and I trip and land on my arm."

Tim and Phil enacted the scenario, and I watched them, remembering.

"My arm's broken for sure, but I still limp over and go find the football. I throw it back to my dad with the arm I didn't land on," I said. "Then I come back to the house, and I'm crying bad. But my dad just stands over me and laughs at me."

You dummy.

"How are you doing, Jesse?" Ben asked. "Is it okay to continue?"

I didn't say anything. I was lost in remembering.

I remember, it was a greenstick fracture, the kind that happens to kids' bones. I was so young they gave me only a local anesthetic . . . so they strapped me down to the table and gave me a racquetball to bite down on . . . they bent my hand all the way back, until it touched flesh. Then bam, *they set it . . . the pain was so intense, it squeezed tears out of my eyes. But I didn't cry.*

"Jesse? Everything okay?"

I looked up at the group. "Yeah," I said. My eyes were wet. "Thanks. That was pretty intense. Man, to watch it . . ."

"Is there anything else you want to share?"

I thought for a second. "I was always scared of hospitals after that. I told everyone I hated them. But the truth is, I was totally frightened of being in them. They always reminded me of that night."

I laughed softly, relieved to speak the truth to a group of people. So many emotions were running over me, from grief to giddiness to this strange sense of solace. They merged and mixed, and somehow, they all felt like something I wanted to let in.

———

As the days wore on, things got better—a little easier. I kept going to my therapy sessions, and even tried some new ones just for the hell of it. EMDR spooked me, but I did it. Equine therapy was a blast—those horses are wise, there's no way to hide from them. Hell, I even went to AA meetings, even though I had never been into them before. At the end of the day, I felt exhausted and wrung out. But my insides were becoming more spacious. Instead of a bunch of rage and pushed-down feelings, it was like there was suddenly more room for things to circulate.

One day Fay, the older woman who'd greeted me on my first morning at Sierra Tucson, motioned for me to come over to her.

"Jesse," she whispered. "Let me talk to you for a second."

"What's up, Fay?" I asked, smiling. I liked nearly everybody at Sierra Tucson, but she was definitely one of my favorites, partly because I'd met her first, and partly because, looking at her, you could tell that she'd been a real crazy chick when she was younger. She kind of had that strut to her.

"Every morning I listen to Howard Stern on the way to work," she said softly, looking over her shoulder to make sure no one was listening in on us. "They're talking about you, every single day!"

I grinned. "Hey, it's news, I guess. What all does Howard have to say?"

"Oh, they just say that you're in rehab, I guess for sex addiction."

"Sounds like Howard," I said, laughing. For some reason, being safe inside these walls, the idea of my name being batted around on a national scale didn't bother me at all. It had a tinge of unreality to it even. "We'll set 'em straight when I get out, I guess."

"I'll keep you informed on all breaking news," Fay said, winking at me. "Hang in there, Jesse, I can tell you're doing real good."

Fay wasn't my only cheerleader. I guess the word had gotten out where I was: maybe those cops really *had* sold their story, the fuckers. As a result, I started to get mail on an almost daily basis. Receiving letters from friends who pledged their support meant a lot to me, but it was the letters from the random chicks in jail that made me laugh the most.

Hey there, soldier, what's good with you?

I know you don't know me but my name is Callie and as you can see I am in penitentiary right now . . . I am 31 years old and I have black hair, brown eyes, I am covered in tattoos. I have big titties. I am obsessed with choppers, especially yours. I have your name tattooed on my lips, and when I stroke it I am always stroking "Jesse James." As you can see, I got mad love and respect for you. Please respond.

I heard from Sandy, too. But it wasn't good news. She would be divorcing me. I was devastated, of course, especially since I felt that I was making so much progress. But in spite of it hurting, I stayed focused on getting better. I had to persevere and fix what was broken.

Somewhere around the midpoint of my time at Sierra Tucson, I assumed a kind of informal leadership role. It wasn't anything that I'd planned on doing, but as I grew more comfortable, I just naturally started to step up. Our general lodge meetings after dinner were often pretty chaotic and disorganized, so I decided to take control of them, reading the minutes, organizing the agenda, telling funny stories to get the ball rolling.

"Okay, you guys, I don't have the crazy drug stories that most of you do, but damn, I want to tell you about something even worse: it's called working for Donald Trump . . ."

My whole life, I'd been a leader, from captaining football teams to running a business with more than a hundred employees. I just couldn't *not* step up and take charge.

It was great, too. People really appreciated my go-to attitude, and the more I saw I could help people out a little bit by cheering them up, the more I *wanted* to do that. There were people there who were so wadded up, it looked like they hadn't smiled in about five years. My heart went out to them. I considered it a personal challenge and responsibility to get them out of their shell a little bit.

"Hey, how's it going?" That was all it took, sometimes. "Hey, can I give you a hug?" There was one woman there who'd seen all her kids die in a car accident. She'd done every kind of self-medicating known to man, and she just looked crushed, wrinkled.

The day I got her to grin, to finally engage in a real conversation with me, that felt as good to me as winning a race. Better.

I was figuring out that I had the power to *help* people. Not just to hire them, or sell bikes to them, but to really be part of their healing. And on the other side of that coin, I was seeing that I needed people, too. It might sound kind of contrived or whatever, but for the first time in my life, I was beginning to see that, sometimes, I needed to *ask* for what I wanted.

"With Sandy, or Janine, or Karla," I told Dr. Thomas, "I'd want to be touched, or taken care of sometimes, but I'd never say it out loud."

"And? What would happen?"

"I'd get all pissed," I said. "I'd resent them for not being able to read my mind, and that'd lead me to go off and do whatever."

Finally, I was starting to get it: fuck, if you want affection, you gotta *tell* her. I vowed that the next time I had a relationship, I'd do better at asking for what I needed.

I didn't feel fixed. I don't think letting go of your past can really happen in a month. I'd gained valuable insight, that was for sure. But none of it was going to alter the fact that I had run my life like an abused kid for so long. My entire adult life, my attitude had been, hey, if you've wronged me, then I'm gonna break your jaw. You can sue me, but you're going to do it with a broken jaw . . .

Everything was going to have to change when I got out. I knew that. And the fact was, I was going to have to deal with the paparazzi circus all over again. On my morning walks, I gradually began to see more and more cars parked on the road outside the gates. They had found me, and they would be waiting for me when I got out.

And as my release date loomed closer and closer, I started to get a little frightened of the future.

"I feel *safe* here," I said. "I like everyone. They like me. I feel valued."

"Well, your real challenge, Jesse," Dr. Thomas said, "is to take that feeling out into the world. You're going to have to keep in mind just why the people here seem to like you so much."

"I'm . . . scared to do that," I admitted. "I've always kind of pushed everyone away from me. Letting them in seems like the hardest thing in the world."

She smiled at me. "You've done so well. I have faith in you."

Right toward the end of the month, I had a dual celebration: my forty-first birthday and my ten years of sobriety. The residents got together and threw a big party for me, with cake and coffee and everything.

"We're going to miss you, Jesse!"

"Don't go!" Phil laughed. "Stay here, man!"

"I would, if I could," I said, grinning. "This place is the most fun I've had since juvie. But I gotta see my kids, man. I'm starting to miss them pretty bad."

It was true. Celebrating my birthday without my family around me felt lonely. I wanted to be with Chandler and Jesse and Sunny again. They gave my life purpose and joy. They made it make sense.

The following morning, I rose early to take my last walk on the horse trail. As I strode along through the cold desert morning, I scrolled through all the emotions that had been heaping down on me ever since I'd come here: guilt and shame for ending my marriage. Anger and sadness, courtesy of my rough childhood. Guarded optimism, for the hope of a new beginning.

I was scared to leave, for sure. But I'd gained so much understanding here. I felt like I had the tools I needed to get through the rest of my life—or at the very least, the next couple of months, which were gonna be trying.

I hadn't always been the best guy, or the best husband. That much was obvious. But now that I knew more about what made me happy, that meant I knew more about how to make others happy, too.

I walked faster, my feet pounding the hardpack, my hands stuffed into the pockets of my jeans.

When I make a gas tank out of aluminum, when I weld, I thought, *I make sure my hands are spotless. I make sure the table's clean. I scrub all my tools, make sure the metal is immaculate, so no grease or moisture sucks into my weld and leaves a blemish. It takes a lot of work, a half day's worth of work, just to prepare.*

In the end, my goal is to make a tank that doesn't leak. I've gotten really good at it over the years. I've had bikes that have rolled end over end, smashed the tank up like a wad of foil. Not a drop leaks.

I gazed up at the mountains above me. A red sun was starting to rise on the far horizon. Day was coming in.

I'm going to figure out a way, I thought, *to put that kind of dedication and detail into building a life.*

If I do that, I don't think it'll ever leak.

AFTERWORD

I press down on the gas pedal, feeding the engine. I am leaving Sierra Tucson, gunning up 77 North. Wind flies in the lowered windows of the car, cold and clean.

I fumble for the radio, watching the road, searching for the dial with my hand. I turn on the power: static.

I merge onto Highway 79 and open her up. The needle on the speedometer climbs to seventy miles an hour. Then eighty. Then ninety.

My speed keeps climbing. I see it in the dust that hangs in the air above me. One hundred. One hundred five. One ten.

The desert sun is getting low in the sky as I head west.

I slide the sunroof open, and I think about Jesse and Chandler and Sunny. How excited I am to see them. To be with them, as the new person I've discovered after the pain and triumph of this last month.

Entering rehab had been like committing suicide. I'd been at the end of my rope in life—pushed to a limit, no end in sight. Some mornings at Sierra Tucson, I experienced a quiet euphoria that I would imagine the suicide jumper feels when he steps off that fateful ledge. Turmoil put him up there, willing to end it all, but when falling through the cool air to his demise? He has to feel some peace and quiet. I wonder if that feeling lasts forever. I hope so.

One twenty, one thirty. My speed keeps going up until the scenery blurs. Cacti streak by my window.

So much has happened in such a short amount of time. It makes you realize just how much of a razor's edge we walk in life. In the blink of an eye, everything we have can be gone. If I've learned anything from the life I've lived, it's that through adversity, something good always comes.

My foot presses down on the gas pedal a little more. I blast through the desert, wind whipping at my face, toward home.

I would like to thank Judge Diesler from the Riverside Juvenile Court. I am sure that if he wasn't as hard on me as he was, I wouldn't be around today to write these words. He just gave me the maximum sentence every time without bothering to look up at me. I never actually saw his face all of those times I was in front of him. I wish he were still around, so I could shake his hand.

Would also like to thank the following football coaches:

Gil Lake
Dave Perkins
Coach Bradshaw
Coach Reed

These guys were not afraid to spit in my face and tell me I was wrong. They filled a huge gap in my life and gave me the discipline I needed to make it.

I would also like to thank Jennifer Bergstrom for letting me do things my way.

Also a heartfelt thanks to Jeremie Ruby-Strauss, because he told me, "Thank your editor, fucker!" And to Jen Robinson, for getting the word out.

Last, would like to thank Sam Benjamin, for taking my lifetime of stories and making them into an actual book.

Page 1 *(clockwise from top left)*: the author; the author; Carol James; the author

Page 2 *(clockwise from top left)*: Carol James; the author; Scott Patterson; Melody Groom

Page 3 *(clockwise from top left)*: the author; Carol James; the author; the author

Page 4 *(clockwise from top left)*: the author; Karla James; Karla James; Carol James

Page 5 *(from top to bottom)*: Karla James; Alain Saquet

Page 6 *(from top to bottom)*: Karla James; the author

Page 7: the author

Page 8 *(clockwise from top left)*: the author; the author; Tyson Beckford

Page 9 *(from top to bottom)*: Rob Fortier; the author

Page 10: the author

Page 11: Hildie Katibah

Page 12: the author

Page 13: the author

Page 14: the author

Page 15: the author

Page 16: Hildie Katibah